D0864390

Selenium Simplified
A Tutorial Guide to Selenium RC with Java and JUnit

Alan Richardson

Second Edition

Copyright ©2012 by Alan Richardson

The right of Alan Richardson to be identified as the author of this work has been asserted by him in accordance with the Copyright, Design and Patents Act 1988.

The views expressed in this book are those of the author.

Second Edition First published in Great Britain in 2012 by:

Compendium Developments

http://www.compendiumdev.co.uk/selenium

contact details:

alan@compendiumdev.co.uk

Author's Software Testing Blog: http://www.eviltester.com

Compendium Developments: http://www.compendiumdev.co.uk

Official Book Website: http://www.seleniumsimplified.com

Every effort has been made to ensure that the information contained in this book is accurate at the time of going to press, and the publishers and author cannot accept any responsibility for any errors or omissions, however caused. No responsibility for loss or damage occasioned by any person acting, or refraining from action, as a result of the material in this publication can be accepted by the editor, the publisher or the author.

Apart from any fair dealing for the purposes of research or private study, or criticism or review, as permitted under the Copyright, Design and Patents Act 1988; this publication may only be reproduced, stored or transmitted, in any form or by any means, with the prior permission of the publishers, or in the case of reprographic reproduction in accordance with the terms and licenses issued by the Copyright Licensing Agency, 90 Tottenham Court Road, London, W1T 4LP. Enquiries concerning reproduction outside these terms should be sent to the publishers.

e-book ISBN : 978-0-9567332-2-1

paperback book ISBN : 978-0-9567332-3-8

Contents

4

20 Using JavaScript with Selenium   221

21 Starting Selenium From Code   227

22 Running Tests Outside Eclipse   233

Introduction

Welcome

For some people, seeing some Java code for Selenium RC on the web, does not help as they don't know how to use it. They don't know:

- where to put the code,

- what a package is,

- how to run the code,

- how to install an IDE

In this guide I present, in simple steps and supported by screenshots, the fundamental knowledge required to program Selenium tests in Java.

Once you have the basics, we move on to exploring common Selenium API commands and how to automate HTML pages, Forms and JavaScript enabled web applications.

I assume no previous knowledge of Java, or Automated Testing.

This book uses Selenium 2 the new version of Selenium which supports the Selenium API, and the WebDriver API. Mention is periodically made of version 1.0.3 and occasionally 0.9.2 to illustrate the differences between the versions in case you have a need to use earlier versions of Selenium as part of your automation toolkit.

At the time of publication, the version of Selenium 2 available to download is 2.19.0. The source code in this book has been tested with Selenium 2.0.0 through to 2.19.0. The examples specifically refer to 2.0.0 and 2.1.0 simply because those were the versions available when the initial text was written, you should be able to replace the 2.0.0 or 2.1.0 with the version of Selenium 2 that you are using and still follow all the instructions.

NOTE:
Version 0.9.2 is not a suitable version for this book because it misses some functionality that we cover: screen capture, addScript, RemoteControlConfiguration, Cookie functionality.

Since this book targets beginners with programming and automation we use the Selenium API, and not the WebDriver API. Be assured that the Selenium API is perfectly capable of automating your web applications and you do not need to move straight to the WebDriver

API. I think the Selenium API is more suited to beginners and when you have a better grasp of automation and Java you can move on to the WebDriver API.

I have chosen Java as the programming language because it is the language that the Selenium Server is written in (so by understanding Java you can understand Selenium more readily). It is also mature and very well supported by IDEs (Integrated Development Environments) which make coding simple for a beginner.

Getting the Source-code

This book takes a tutorial approach. So we present a lot of source-code. To save you having to type it all out - although there are benefits in doing this. You can download the source-code from:

- http://unow.be/rc/initialSource[1]

- http://unow.be/rc/finalSource[2]

Follow the instructions in the later section ''Playing along at home'' to install the source-code.

This way, if you are following the explanations and typing in the code, should you get stuck, you can compare your source-code to that in the archive.

The later section ''Structuring the tests and code'', where we make our testing production quality, uses the code provided in finalChapterSource_2ndEdition.zip listed above.

If you understand subversion and have it installed then you can checkout the same source-code from the public subversion repository in the trunk folder.

- http://unow.be/rc/xpdevcode[3]

This is hosted on a free subversion server provided by xp-dev (http://unow.be/rc/xpdev[4]).

Windows, Linux or Mac

This text takes a Windows centric view of the world. So the main text assumes you are working on a Windows system and all screen shots have been taken on a Windows system.

This was purely to limit the install explanations for software. All the tools listed are available for Linux and Mac systems: Eclipse, Firefox, the various Firefox plug-ins, and Selenium.

If you visit the various tool websites and follow the install instructions for your particular platform then you should still be able to follow along with the text and instructions.

---

[1] http://www.compendiumdev.co.uk/selenium/InitialSeleniumTests_JUNIT_2ndEdition.zip

[2] http://www.compendiumdev.co.uk/selenium/finalChapterSource_2ndEdition.zip

[3] http://svn2.xp-dev.com/svn/seleniumsimplified

[4] http://www.xp-dev.com/

Typographical Conventions

In the print and pdf versions of this book you may see some URLs shortened e.g. http://unow.be/rc/selsimp[5] These will be shortened using a URL shortening service. I have done this to make them easier to type in, to improve the book formatting, and to allow me to keep those URLs up to date without amending the book text. In the print and PDF versions, when a short URL is used then you will also see a footnote with the URL that the short form redirects to (at the time of writing). Sometimes the shortened form is actually longer but I decided to value the ability to amend the redirection if the site moved, above the concise form.

Keeping Up To Date

Selenium is not a tool that stands still. This book represents a snapshot of time for the version of Selenium mentioned and the browsers and associated tools described. As such, some of the instructions in the book may fall out of date.

For this reason, the author maintains the following book related web sites and pages:

- a blog at www.eviltester.com,

- an associated site called www.seleniumsimplified.com

- the publishers web page www.compendiumdev.co.uk/selenium

If you discover anything out of date, or instructions that you can not follow. Please have a look at the sites above. If we know about the inconsistency then we will have written something up as post on those sites, with links from the main book page.

Also if you have any questions, please email the author of the book directly.

- alan@compendiumdev.co.uk

From time to time we also release tutorial videos on youtube under the user id ''Evil Tester Videos'', again these will be listed on the blogs or the main publisher page for the book.

- http://unow.be/rc/EviltesterVideos[6]

---

[5] http://www.compendiumdev.co.uk/selenium
[6] http://www.youtube.com/user/EviltesterVideos

Acknowledgements

No book has the exclusive influence of the author. Normally in this section the author would give thanks to the editors, publishers and technical reviewers.

No technical reviewers were involved in this book. This book was forged through the usage of real readers. Readers like yourself that started with little knowledge of how to write program at all. Readers who can now use both Java and Selenium to include automation in their testing process.

In this case I give thanks to my early readers and guinea pigs.

This book grew from a 2 year period of working on an almost daily basis with Selenium on production test automation. So I need to thank the Channel 4 test team that worked with me during that time as we experimented with different ways of automating. Extra special thanks go to Tony Bruce and Michael Kiely, who participated in my Selenium training sessions based on this book. Their feedback led to immediate improvements and scope changes.

And a big thank you to the people who bought the beta e-book version. The early feedback and questions as they learned Selenium working through the book helped me tremendously. I was amazed at the speed of progress they made learning Selenium and found it hard to work through the later, more advanced, sections of the book fast enough to satisfy their learning needs. From this group I need to specifically thank those readers who submitted questions and comments that directly impacted the structure and content of this book: Jack Carden, Alex Crookes, William Dutton, Gopi Ganesasundaram, Jay Gehlot, Ard-Jan Glas, Sunny Jain, Anthony Kearns, Felipe Knorr Kuhn, Richard Li, Darren Louie, Mary Ann May-Pumphrey, Michael McCollum, Krishnan Mahadevan, Kaushik Mahata, Nga Nguyen, Dennis Pham, Mahmoud Passikhani, Adrian Rapan, Doug Seward, Rajat Sud, Manupriya Vijay.

And most importantly... love and special thanks to my family: Billie and Keeran

Chapter 1

Getting Started With The Tools

This chapter will introduce you to the tools we are about to install and use:

- Selenium IDE

- Java

- Eclipse

- Selenium Remote Control (RC)

Each tool has links to the official documentation so that you can learn more from the most authoritative sources.

1.1   Selenium IDE

The Selenium IDE is an add-on to Firefox.

At a basic level it allows us to:

- Record user actions when browsing in Firefox

- Replay recorded scripts

- Convert recorded scripts into programming languages such as Java, Ruby, and more

- Add verification and synchronisation steps to the script during the recording process

The IDE provides excellent support for writing automated test scripts in Selenium and gets better with every release. In this text we will focus on its use as an aid to writing automated test scripts in Java, rather than as a test tool in its own right.

For more information on Selenium IDE visit:

- Official documentation

    - http://unow.be/rc/officialdocs[1]
    - http://unow.be/rc/sidedocs[2]

- Official Selenium IDE site

    - http://unow.be/rc/ide[3]

---

[1] http://seleniumhq.org/docs
[2] http://seleniumhq.org/docs/02_selenium_ide.html
[3] http://seleniumhq.org/projects/ide/

1.2 Java

Java is a programming language. The Java that we will be using in this text is very simple. If your work environment uses a different language e.g. Ruby, .Net, Python. Chances are that you will be able to use Selenium RC in that language.

For more information on Java visit:

- Official Java Home page
    - http://unow.be/rc/java[4]
- Official developers page
    - http://unow.be/rc/javahome[5]
- Java Community page
    - http://unow.be/rc/sside[6]

1.3 Eclipse

Eclipse is a free and open-source IDE which supports many programming languages.

Out of the box it provides many useful support aids for beginning java programmers:

- wizards for code creation
- code completion
- automatically fix common coding errors

It is also simple to install, incredibly popular among developers, and has a lot of additional plugins that you can use to increase your productivity.

For more information on Eclipse visit:

- Official Home Page
    - http://unow.be/rc/eclipse[7]
- Free Video Tutorials
    - http://unow.be/rc/etutorial[8]

---

[4]http://java.com
[5]http://java.sun.com/
[6]http://theserverside.com/
[7]http://www.eclipse.org/
[8]http://eclipsetutorial.sourceforge.net

1.4 Selenium RC

Selenium Remote Control is the server version of Selenium. You write your tests using a programming language and client library. Your tests issue commands which the client library sends to the server. The server then performs your actions for you in the browser and reports the results back to your client.

Using Selenium RC allows you to write Automated tests in any supported programming language.

Tests written in this way allow you to use standard programming practices to make them easy to maintain, robust and easy to collaborate on as a team.

For more information on Selenium RC visit:

- Official Home Page

    - http://unow.be/rc/rc[9]

- Official Documentation

    - http://unow.be/rc/rcdocs[10]
    - http://unow.be/rc/officialdocs[11]

1.5 Summary

All of the tools we will use in this book are open source or free.

All of the tools used are used on commercial projects so the skills you learn here will transfer into the working environment directly.

The tools have strong communities behind them with development work continuing on all the tools. This may have the side-effect of making some of the step by step instruction in this book redundant over time. For this reason I have added links to official sites, also remember that the author amends the blog and websites listed in the About The Author section with hints and tips to help you follow this book if the tool updates impinge upon the instructions.

---

[9]http://seleniumhq.org/projects/remote-control/
[10]http://seleniumhq.org/docs/05_selenium_rc.html
[11]http://seleniumhq.org/docs

Chapter 2

Selenium IDE Basics

2.1 How To Download and Install Firefox

Firefox is a major help when working with Selenium:

- Selenium IDE runs as a Firefox add-on,

- Firefox has a lot of plugins that we will find indispensable. And we will cover these in later sections e.g.

    - http://unow.be/rc/firebug[1]

    - http://unow.be/rc/firepath[2]

- Runs cross-platform so you retain your tool knowledge regardless of the operating system you are using.

Because the Selenium IDE is a Firefox add-on we first have to download and install Firefox.

The instructions in this book have been run against Firefox v5 to v9. If you encounter any issues using Selenium RC or Selenium IDE with your version of Firefox then check on the Selenium site which versions of Firefox are supported by the version of Selenium RC that you plan to use, and the version of Selenium IDE. Sometimes the browsers advance faster than the plug in tools or Selenium can cope with. To download and install the most recent version of Firefox, visit:

- http://unow.be/rc/firefox[3]

The official site should make it easy to install Firefox. By redirecting you to the correct download page.

---

[1]https://addons.mozilla.org/en-us/firefox/addon/firebug/
[2]https://addons.mozilla.org/en-US/firefox/addon/firepath/
[3]http://www.mozilla.com/firefox

Figure 2.1: Download Firefox

2.2 How To Install The Selenium IDE

Download and install the Selenium IDE from within Firefox itself.

Start the Firefox browser.

Visit Selenium HQ Downloads and click on the Download link for the Selenium IDE.

http://unow.be/rc/getSelenium[4]

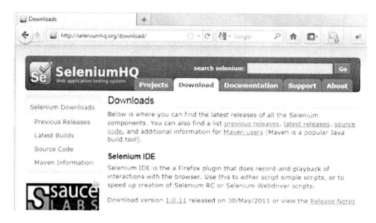

Figure 2.2: Download Page And Link For Selenium IDE

Follow the series of dialogs that walk you through the install process, as illustrated below. First you have to acknowledge that the add-on is safe to install.

Figure 2.3: Trust The Install of the Selenium IDE

You also have to accept the install of the Selenium IDE formatting plugins. These are used when exporting the Selenium IDE script to the various programming languages that

---

[4]http://seleniumhq.org/download/

the IDE supports.

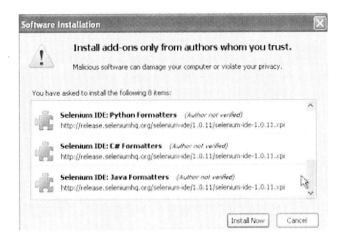

Figure 2.4: Trust The Install of the Selenium IDE Formatters

After it has installed you will be prompted to restart Firefox.

Figure 2.5: Accept Restart Firefox

When Firefox restarts, you should now have a new entry in your Tools Menu for the Selenium IDE.

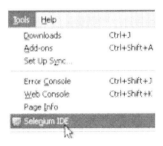

Figure 2.6: Start the Selenium IDE

If you have hidden the menus in Firefox then you can find the Selenium IDE entry under the Web Developer menu on the Firefox Menu Tab.

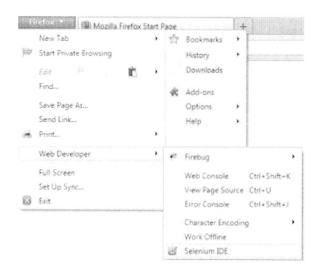

Figure 2.7: Start Selenium IDE from Firefox Web Developer Menu

2.3 Capture Playback - Recording a Script With Selenium IDE

The Selenium IDE supports capture playback of test scripts by recording the actions you take when browsing web sites, and then replaying these in the browser.

Start the IDE by clicking on the `Selenium IDE` entry in the Tools Menu, or, if you have hidden the Menu Bar it will be in the Web Developer Menu.

Hover the mouse over the recording button to check the recording status. If it is not recording then press the button to start recording your actions in Firefox.

Now perform the following actions in Firefox:

1. Type http://www.compendiumdev.co.uk/selenium/search.php in the browser URL field to visit the "Selenium Simplified Search Engine".

2. Perform a search for `Selenium-RC`

You should see that the IDE has tracked your actions, set the `Base URL` field, and created the necessary commands to repeat that script in Firefox.

Press the red recording button to stop the IDE recording any more actions. Then press the `Play Current Test Case` button to have the IDE replay your actions in the browser.

You should have seen your actions repeated very quickly in Firefox. If so, then congratulations, you just recorded your first automated test script through the IDE.

Figure 2.8: Blank Selenium IDE Dialog

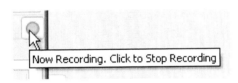

Figure 2.9: Now Recording Message

2.3.1 Command, Target and Value

You can edit any of the recorded commands in the IDE.

Click on any of the commands in the table and you will see that the Command, Target and Value fields fill with the values on the table.

You can then use the `Command` drop down to choose any of the commands available.

When you use select a command, you will see documentation describing the command in the Reference pane.

2.3.2 Save The Test

Save this test to the disk for future use.

Figure 2.10: A Recorded Selenium IDE Script

Figure 2.11: Play Test Case Button

Figure 2.12: Edit any of the commands by selecting them in the table

Use the `File \ Save Test Case As` ... menu and save it somewhere you can find it again. I named mine `search_Selenium_RC.htm` and saved it in `c:\selenium_ide`

2.3.3 Further reading

If you want more information on the Selenium IDE you should read the following links:

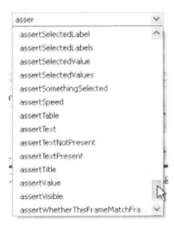

Figure 2.13: Select any of the commands from the command drop down list

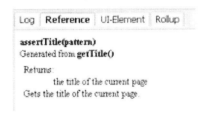

Figure 2.14: Learn about the commands in the reference pane

- Start with the official documentation as this explains the Selenium IDE in detail

http://unow.be/rc/sidedocs[5]

- Adam Goucher's posts on Selenium IDE:

http://unow.be/rc/adamg[6]

- Particularly Adam's plugin posts:

http://unow.be/rc/adamide[7]

- Selenium IDE Extensions:

http://unow.be/rc/sideExt[8]

---

[5]http://seleniumhq.org/docs/02_selenium_ide.html

[6]http://adam.goucher.ca

[7]http://adam.goucher.ca/?s=The+Selenium-IDE+1.x+plugin+API

[8]http://wiki.openqa.org/display/SIDE/Contributed+Extensions+and+Formats

- The Firefox plugins search may reveal some plugins for Selenium IDE

http://unow.be/rc/splugins[9]

- Video tutorials for Selenium IDE are available on YouTube:

http://unow.be/rc/sidevids[10]

[9]https://addons.mozilla.org/en-US/firefox/search/?q=selenium
[10]http://www.youtube.com/results?search_query=selenium+ide

Chapter 3

How To Install Java

3.1 Is Java already installed?

You can check if you have Java installed by:

- visiting http://unow.be/rc/java[1] and using the ''Do I have Java?'' check, available at the url http://unow.be/rc/installed[2] or,

- running the command `java -version` from the command line

When you enter the following code into your command line:

```
java -version
```

If you receive a message stating that `'java' is not recognized...` then you do not have Java installed.

```
'java' is not recognized as an internal or external command, operable program
    or batch file.
```

If you have Java installed then running the command `java -version` will show the version number of the Java installation.

```
java version "1.6.0_25"
Java(TM) SE Runtime Environment (build 1.6.0_25-b06)Java HotSpot(TM) 64-Bit
    Server VM (build 20.0-b11, mixed mode)
```

3.2 Install Java

If you don't have Java installed then visit http://unow.be/rc/java[3] and follow the Download links and instructions to install it on your machine.

Java comes in 2 main flavours, an end-user focused Java Runtime Edition (JRE), and the various Software Development Kits (SDK).

At this point you are installing the Java Runtime Edition, which contains the basic tools we need to start working with Java and Selenium.

In a later section we will install the SDK.

---

[1] http://java.com
[2] http://java.com/en/download/installed.jsp
[3] http://java.com

I have kept this section deliberately short as the Java site and installation instructions change frequently. But they are easy to follow so visit the home page and follow the instructions there.

Chapter 4

Install and run Selenium RC

4.1 How To Download and Install Selenium RC

Before we can actually automate any web applications, we need to install Selenium RC. ''Install'' is really the wrong word when all we will do is download and extract the Selenium RC archives to a directory.

4.1.1 What to Download?

At the time of writing there are three versions you can download

- 2.x (refers to 2.x.x versions e.g. 2.0.0, 2.1.0, 2.15.0, etc.)

- 1.0.3

- 0.9.2

All versions of Selenium allow creating a Selenium RC server and connecting to it with a client, and programming it using the Selenium RC API. This is the basic approach covered by Selenium Simplified.

Each version has nuances all of its own.

- 2.x has the best better browser compatibility and incorporates the WebDriver API. You should use the most recent 2.x version available from the web site when working through this book.

- 1.0.3 had better browser compatibility than 0.9.2 but has issues with running Selenium suites from the command line. It has all the features you need to follow this book, but preference should be given to 2.x versions.

- 0.9.2 was a solid performer, but since it was released in 2007, it is incompatible with some more recent browser versions. This is still used by companies for their automation.

We will explain downloading all of them, and how to chop and change between them if you need to. The most recent incarnation of Version 2.0 should meet your needs and I recommend it as the preferred choice, it is the version that will be updated going forward.

4.1.2 Download from Selenium HQ

The main Selenium site http://unow.be/rc/hq[1] undergoes periodic re-organisation. But by visiting the main site we should be able to find the Download page.

At the time of writing the download page is located at:

- http://unow.be/rc/getSelenium[2]

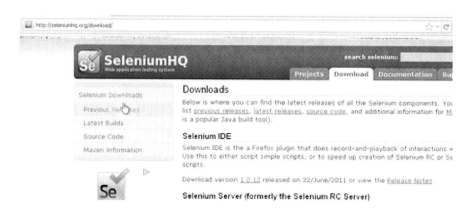

Figure 4.1: Downloads Page on SeleniumHQ.org

Create a folder on your hard drive to save the files to. For simplicity I created a folder on the `c:\` root called `selenium`.

- `c:\selenium`

4.1.3 Downloading Selenium 2

The downloads page can seem cluttered. The current version is usually near the top of the page. From version 2.0.0, the Selenium RC server is now known as the ''Selenium Server''

Clicking on the Selenium 2 Download link will take you to a download page for the ''standalone server .jar'' file.

This is what we want to download.

You will also want to download the Java Selenium Client Driver. You should find this in the ''Selenium Client Drivers'' Section, and you want to download the same version as the ''Selenium Server''

When I did this I downloaded two files:

---

[1] http://seleniumhq.org

[2] http://seleniumhq.org/download/

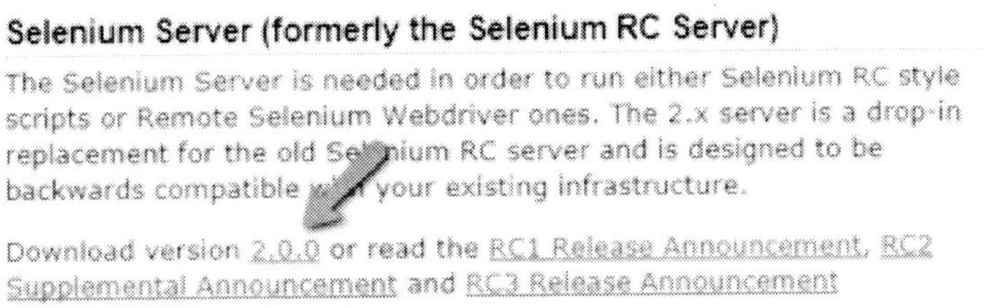

Selenium Server (formerly the Selenium RC Server)

The Selenium Server is needed in order to run either Selenium RC style scripts or Remote Selenium Webdriver ones. The 2.x server is a drop-in replacement for the old Selenium RC server and is designed to be backwards compatible with your existing infrastructure.

Download version 2.0.0 or read the RC1 Release Announcement, RC2 Supplemental Announcement and RC3 Release Announcement

Figure 4.2: Download Selenium 2.0.0

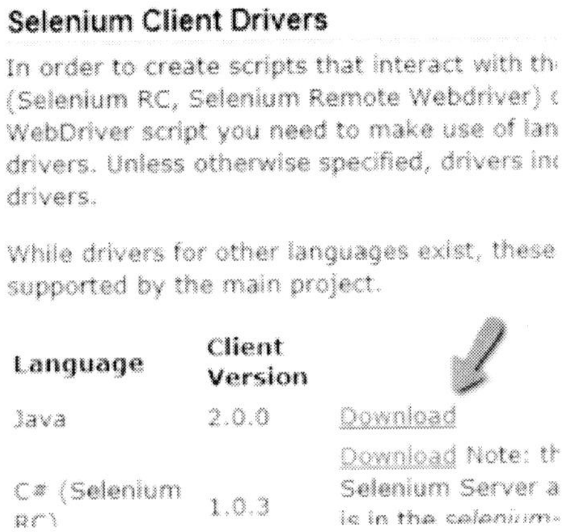

Selenium Client Drivers

In order to create scripts that interact with th· (Selenium RC, Selenium Remote Webdriver) · WebDriver script you need to make use of lan· drivers. Unless otherwise specified, drivers inc· drivers.

While drivers for other languages exist, these supported by the main project.

Language	Client Version	
Java	2.0.0	Download
C# (Selenium RC)	1.0.3	Download Note: th· Selenium Server a· is in the selenium·

Figure 4.3: Download Selenium 2.0 Client Driver

- The client: `selenium-java-2.0.0.zip`

- The server: `selenium-server-standalone-2.0.0.jar`

The version you download will be numbered based on the version e.g. for version 2.15.0 it would be selenium-java-2.15.0.zip and selenium-server-standalone-2.15.0.jar

Create a subfolder for selenium 2 e.g.

- `c:\selenium\selenium_2`

Move the server file to this folder and unarchive the contents of the client `.zip` file to this folder.

4.1.4 Downloading Selenium 1.0.3

At the time of writing, Selenium 1.0.3 is not available for download on the official web site.

Selenium 1.0.3 can be downloaded from the Google Code Web Site:

- http://unow.be/rc/gcode[3]

Follow the Downloads link and Search ''All downloads'' for ''1.0.3''
When I did this I downloaded the file:

- The client and server: `selenium-remote-control-1.0.3.zip`

Create a subfolder for selenium 1.0.3 e.g.

- `c:\selenium\selenium_1_0_3`

Unarchive the contents of the downloaded `.zip` file to this folder.

4.1.5   Downloading Selenium 0.9.2

The Selenium 0.9.2 download is currently listed on the previous releases section.

Figure 4.4: Link to Previous Releases

Then it is listed in the ''Selenium RC'' section.

Figure 4.5: 0.9.2 Listed in Selenium RC

Download this file to your computer.

When I did this I downloaded the file:

- The client and server: `selenium-remote-control-0.9.2-dist.zip`

---

[3]http://code.google.com/p/selenium

Create a subfolder for selenium 0.9.2 e.g.

- `c:\selenium\selenium_0_9_2`

Unarchive the contents of the downloaded .zip file to this folder.

4.1.6   Downloading Troubleshooting

The SeleniumHQ site may have had a re-organisation since these instructions were written. The following list represents the basic process we went through. If the site does not exactly map the instructions use this guide, read the pages carefully and you should still be able to install Selenium.

- Find the main Selenium site.

- Find the downloads section.

- The current release is usually obvious on the downloads page.

- Download the client and the server.

- For previous versions look at the previous releases section, and scan the main download page.

4.2   Overview of the Contents of the Selenium Archive

4.2.1   Archive Contents for 2.0

The unarchived `selenium-java-2.0.0.zip` and the `selenium-server-standalone-2.0.0.jar` file moved into a folder `c:\selenium\selenium-2.0` are shown below:

Figure 4.6: Archive Contents for 2.0

The `selenium-server-standalone-2.0.0.jar` contains everything you need to add to your build path. This keeps everything simple and you don't have to worry about including all the relevant dependencies from the libs folder.

If you were only using the client connection then you would not need to add the server .jar file `selenium-server-standalone-2.0.0.jar` to your build path, and would have to use the `selenium-java-2.0.0.jar` and the associated dependencies in the libs folder.

`selenium-java-2.0.0-srcs.jar` contains most of the Java source code for Selenium and is useful for attaching to the project to improve the information provided by code completion in the IDE.

4.2.2   Archive Contents for 1.0.3 and 0.9.2

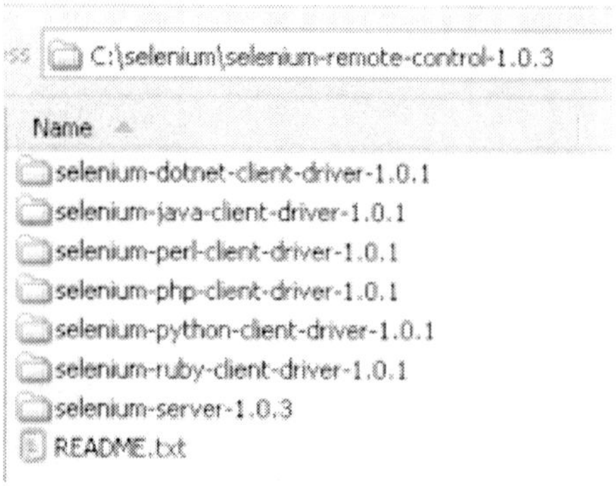

Figure 4.7: Archive Contents for 1.0.3

There are two main folder types in the 1.0.3 and 0.9.2 distributions:

- specific language client drivers

- selenium server

Each of the supported languages has a client driver. You can see from the list of folders that the Selenium distribution supports:

- Microsoft .Net

- Java

- Perl

- PHP

- Python

- Ruby

40

The client drivers are what we use in our tests to communicate with Selenium RC. We use the client drivers because our tests act as clients, which communicate with the server, in order to execute commands through the browser.

The client drivers contain the source code, tests, documentation and libraries that we need to work with the Selenium tests.

The selenium server directory has the documentation, source code, tests and executables for working with the Selenium server.

4.3   How to Work With Windows Command Line

On Windows XP, open a command window by clicking on the `Start` button, selecting `Run....` and typing `cmd`

On Windows 7, open a command window by clicking on `Start` typing `cmd` into the search field. Then choosing the cmd application from the returned list.

With a command window open. The command to change directory is `cd`. To change to the directory where I installed the selenium versions I have to type:

- `cd c:\selenium`

I can go up a level in the directory hierarchy by issuing the command `cd ..`

When in a directory I can go to a child directory by `cd directoryname` e.g. if I am at the root directory, having issued the command `cd c:\`, I can change to the selenium directory by typing `cd selenium`

Hint: Try pressing the `tab` key as you do this to automatically complete folder details. Pressing the `tab` key multiple times will iterate through all matching filenames in the directory.

4.3.1   Give Your Command Window a Title

I give the command window a new title so I can find it easily by issuing the DOS command `title`.

```
title SELENIUM SERVER
```

This makes it much easier to find when I `Alt-Tab` or look for it on the taskbar.

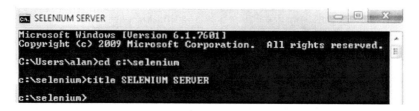

Figure 4.8: An easy to identify Selenium Server command window

4.3.2 An Alternative Command Line Tool

I also use the open-source `Console` application.

http://unow.be/rc/console2[4]

This allows me to have multiple console windows open in a single application.

There is a very good write up of this application on Scott Hanselman's ComputerZen.com blog.

http://unow.be/rc/c2review[5]

4.4 How to Open Command Windows At A Specific Folder

When using the Windows operating system we tend not to have command prompts open all the time. So having some software to boost our productivity makes a real difference.

4.4.1 On Windows 7 and Vista

In Vista and Windows 7 you can browse to a folder in Windows Explorer, hold down the `Shift` key, right-click on the folder and choose `Open Command Window Here`.

4.4.2 On Windows XP

Windows XP may be getting older but I still use it as an automation operating system. It has low memory footprint, most of the browsers work on it. Plus it runs really well in a virtual machine.

I just need to install the `Open Command Window Here` Microsoft Powertoy for XP. I recommend you install this very helpful tool, if you use XP.

- http://unow.be/rc/cmdhere[6]

---

[4]http://sourceforge.net/projects/console/
[5]http://www.hanselman.com/blog/Console2ABetterWindowsCommandPrompt.aspx
[6]http://download.microsoft.com/download/whistler/Install/2/WXP/EN-US/CmdHerePowertoySetup.exe

- http://unow.be/rc/xppowertoys[7]

4.5   How to start Selenium Server From Command Line

4.5.1   Generic Instructions

The Selenium server is written in Java, and so we run the `.jar` file using the generic format.

```
java -jar selenium-server-filename.jar
```

Where `selenium-server-filename.jar` is the name of the `.jar` file that you want to run. This filename changes depending on the version of the Selenium server you are trying to run.

- for version 2.0.0

    - `java -jar selenium-server-standalone-2.0.0.jar`

- for versions prior to 2

    - `java -jar selenium-server.jar`

NOTE:

For generic sections or sections without screen shots, I may refer to the Selenium server `.jar` as `selenium-server.jar`. If you type these commands into a command line, make sure you use the filename for the `.jar` you have downloaded e.g. instead of `selenium-server.jar` use `selenium-server-standalone-2.0.0.jar` (or whatever version you are using). I have done this to try and make the book less dependent on the version of Selenium you have installed because it updates so frequently.

If you have a number of candidate `.jar` files that you could run in your directory, but have difficulty with the first one you try. Then try the other ones and see which works.

Some of the `.jar` files you could download require setting up your runtime class path to locate the dependency .jar files. For this reason I recommend you download the standalone version as it has all the dependencies packaged into the jar file.

When you run the java command you will see a set of messages describing the Selenium startup sequence and versions in use.

If you don't see a set of diagnostic messages then you should check

---

[7]http://windows.microsoft.com/en-US/windows/downloads/windows-xp

```
07/07/2011  20:14          526,648 selenium-java-2.0.0-srcs.jar
07/07/2011  20:14        2,070,029 selenium-java-2.0.0.jar
12/07/2011  09:45       24,451,271 selenium-server-standalone-2.0.0.jar
              3 File(s)     27,055,948 bytes
              3 Dir(s)  82,842,234,880 bytes free

C:\selenium\selenium-2.0.0>java -jar selenium-server-standalone-2.0.0.jar
12-Jul-2011 14:34:00 org.openqa.grid.selenium.GridLauncher main
INFO: Launching a standalone server
14:34:00.953 INFO - Java: Sun Microsystems Inc. 20.0-b11
14:34:00.954 INFO - OS: Windows 7 6.1 amd64
14:34:00.967 INFO - v2.0.0, with Core v2.0.0. Built from revision 12817
14:34:09.099 INFO - RemoteWebDriver instances should connect to: http://127.0.0.
1:4444/wd/hub
14:34:09.100 INFO - Version Jetty/5.1.x
14:34:09.101 INFO - Started HttpContext[/selenium-server/driver,/selenium-server
/driver]
14:34:09.103 INFO - Started HttpContext[/selenium-server,/selenium-server]
14:34:09.103 INFO - Started HttpContext[/,/]
14:34:09.163 INFO - Started org.openqa.jetty.jetty.servlet.ServletHandler@434628
51
14:34:09.163 INFO - Started HttpContext[/wd,/wd]
14:34:09.168 INFO - Started SocketListener on 0.0.0.0:4444
14:34:09.168 INFO - Started org.openqa.jetty.jetty.Server@4277158a
```

Figure 4.9: Start up messages from Selenium Server 2.0

- Is Java installed?

- Are you in the correct directory?

- Is the .jar file in the directory? You can use dir to see the contents of the directory.

- Have you typed the filename correctly? Using tab to auto-complete filenames can help ensure long filenames type correctly.

If you saw messages like the above then you have just started the Selenium RC server and it is listening on port 4444 for commands.

4.5.2   Selenium 2.0

For Selenium 2.0 we want to run the selenium-server-standalone .jar

This filename will have the version of Selenium we want to use so for 2.0.0 we want to run: selenium-server-standalone-2.0.0.jar

Later versions of selenium are likely to have different names with 2.0.0 being replaced by the version number of the Selenium release.

I right click on the selenium-2.0.0 folder and choose Open Command Window Here from the context menu.

Now run the selenium server by typing the command:

```
java -jar selenium-server-standalone-2.0.0.jar
```

4.5.3   Selenium 1.0.3

I right click on the `Selenium-server-1.0.3` folder and choose `Open Command Window Here` from the context menu.

Now run the selenium server by typing the command `java -jar selenium-server.jar`

```
C:\selenium\selenium-remote-control-1.0.3\selenium-server-1.0.3>title SELENIUM S
ERVER

C:\selenium\selenium-remote-control-1.0.3\selenium-server-1.0.3>java -jar seleni
um-server.jar
12:59:55.828 INFO - Java: Sun Microsystems Inc. 16.0-b13
12:59:55.828 INFO - OS: Windows XP 5.1 x86
12:59:55.843 INFO - v2.0 [a2], with Core v2.0 [a2]
12:59:56.484 INFO - RemoteWebDriver instances should connect to: http://127.0.0.
1:4444/wd/hub
12:59:56.484 INFO - Version Jetty/5.1.x
12:59:56.484 INFO - Started HttpContext[/selenium-server/driver,/selenium-server
/driver]
12:59:56.500 INFO - Started HttpContext[/selenium-server,/selenium-server]
12:59:56.500 INFO - Started HttpContext[/,/]
13:00:00.531 INFO - Started org.openqa.jetty.jetty.servlet.ServletHandler@2bbd86
13:00:00.531 INFO - Started HttpContext[/wd,/wd]
13:00:00.562 INFO - Started SocketListener on 0.0.0.0:4444
13:00:00.562 INFO - Started org.openqa.jetty.jetty.Server@b6ece5
```

Figure 4.10: Start up messages from Selenium Server 1.0.3

The same filename is used for Selenium Server 0.9.2

4.6   How to Stop the Selenium Server

4.6.1   From the command line

Since you have started the Selenium server in a DOS window you can simply use `ctrl+c` to stop it.

4.6.2   From a browser URL

Since selenium server operates a web server under Jetty it can receive commands via http through browsers. Issue the following to shutdown the server:

- http://localhost:4444/selenium-server/driver/?cmd=shutDownSeleniumServer

If you wanted to leave the server running and just close down the current Selenium session, you could issue the following command in a browser:

- http://localhost:4444/selenium-server/driver/?cmd=shutDown

```
C:\selenium\selenium-2.0.0>title SELENIUM SERVER

C:\selenium\selenium-2.0.0>java -jar selenium-server-standalone-2.0.0.jar
12-Jul-2011 14:39:30 org.openqa.grid.selenium.GridLauncher main
INFO: Launching a standalone server
14:39:30.891 INFO - Java: Sun Microsystems Inc. 20.0-b11
14:39:30.892 INFO - OS: Windows 7 6.1 amd64
14:39:30.904 INFO - v2.0.0, with Core v2.0.0. Built from revision 12817
14:39:31.031 INFO - RemoteWebDriver instances should connect to: http://127.0.0.
1:4444/wd/hub
14:39:31.033 INFO - Version Jetty/5.1.x
14:39:31.034 INFO - Started HttpContext[/selenium-server/driver,/selenium-server
/driver]
14:39:31.035 INFO - Started HttpContext[/selenium-server,/selenium-server]
14:39:31.036 INFO - Started HttpContext[/,/]
14:39:31.095 INFO - Started org.openqa.jetty.jetty.servlet.ServletHandler@6bdab9
1
14:39:31.095 INFO - Started HttpContext[/wd,/wd]
14:39:31.100 INFO - Started SocketListener on 0.0.0.0:4444
14:39:31.100 INFO - Started org.openqa.jetty.jetty.Server@3716ab4e
14:39:34.057 INFO - Shutting down...

C:\selenium\selenium-2.0.0>
```

Figure 4.11: After Ctrl+c the server shuts down

4.7   How to Run IDE Tests In Different Browsers

Although only Firefox has the IDE, we can run IDE recorded scripts in other browsers. This requires the use of Suites, and Selenium RC.

NOTE:

I do not recommend this approach to using Selenium for long term automation. I mainly include it for completeness, although it can prove useful for constructing a quick set of tests that you intend to run a few times. Selenium IDE tests are hard to maintain and very often require re-recording.

There were issues getting this to work with Internet Explorer on Selenium 1.0.3 using *iexplore, *iehta, or *piiexplore. No such issues appear to occur with Selenium 2.0 versions.

With earlier versions of the Selenium IDE you had to construct the suite files by hand. Now the Selenium IDE has the ability to create new Suites, and Add Test Cases to those suites, from within the GUI itself.

For the purposes of this particular section I have created a folder `c:\selenium_ide` and I have two tests:

- `search_Selenium_RC.htm`

    - opens `compendiumdev.co.uk/selenium/search.php` and performs a search

        * You created this script in the previous section.

46

- `submit_form.htm`

  – opens `compendiumdev.co.uk/selenium/basic_html_form.html` and submits the form

  * You have not created this script, if you want to create it now then use the steps from the previous section, or create a suite with a single test.

I can use the Selenium IDE to create a test suite, by selecting `New Test Suite` from the File menu.

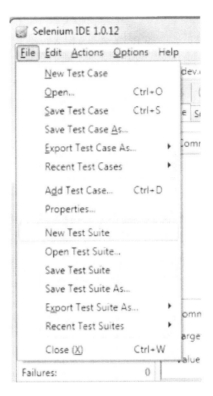

Figure 4.12: Selenium IDE File Menu

This will blank the Test Case panel and show a test called "Untitled".

I can add the Selenium IDE scripts that I already saved by selecting the `Add Test Case` menu item from the File menu, or from the right click context menu from the Test Case panel.

Selecting `Add Test Case` will show a file dialog and I can select and add the Selenium IDE scripts from here.

I can then delete the "Untitled" test case. And save the suite as `test_suite.htm` using the `Save Test Suite As...` menu item from the File menu. I save it into the same folder as the previous test .htm files.

Figure 4.13: Selenium IDE Context Menu

With Selenium RC installed I can use the following command line syntax to run a suite of Selenium IDE scripts in other browsers.

```
java -jar
    "<insert-selenium-server-filename-here.jar>"
    -htmlSuite
    "<insert_browser_name_here>"
    "<insert_root_domain_here>"
    "<insert_full_path_to_suite_here>"
    "<insert_a_full_path_to_store_reports_here>"
```

e.g. To run it in Google Chrome using Selenium 2.0.0

```
java -jar selenium-server-standalone-2.0.0.jar -htmlSuite "*googlechrome" "
    http://www.compendiumdev.co.uk" "c:\selenium_ide\test_suite.htm" "c:\
    selenium_ide\results.htm"
```

To execute the above command you would need to run the command from the directory where the appropriate selenium server `.jar` is located, and your suite would need to be stored in `c:\selenium_ide`

I have found that on windows I need to store the suite in the same folder as the test scripts and that I have to pass the full path for the suite file.

When you run the above command you will see the Selenese suite runner with the suite of tests in the right and it will run through and report the results.

Running the tests will result in the generation of an HTML file with the results using the path that you used in the command line.

Try this after following the instructions on installing Java and Selenium RC.

If you want to try with other browsers then here are a selection of browser codes:

- `*firefox` - Mozilla Firefox

- `*iexplore` - Internet Explorer

- `*googlechrome` - Google Chrome

- `*safari` - Apple Safari

- `*opera` - Opera

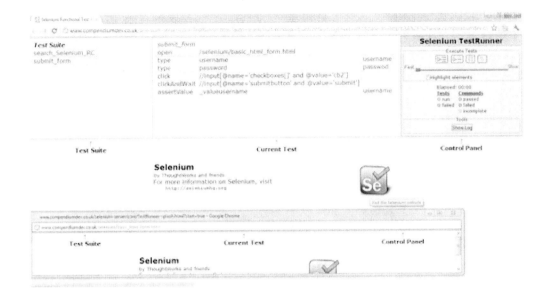

Figure 4.14: Running a suite of tests

Test suite results

result:	passed
totalTime:	0
numTestTotal:	2
numTestPasses:	2
numTestFailures:	0
numCommandPasses:	0
numCommandFailures:	0
numCommandErrors:	0
Selenium Version:	2.0
Selenium Revision:	.0

Test Suite

search_Selenium_RC

submit_form

search_Selenium_RC.htm

submit_form

open	/selenium/basic_html_form.html	
type	username	username
type	password	passwod
click	//input[@name='checkboxes[]' and @value='cb2']	
clickAndWait	//input[@name='submitbutton' and @value='submit']	

submit_form.htm

submit_form

open	/selenium/basic_html_form.html	
type	username	username
type	password	passwod
click	//input[@name='checkboxes[]' and @value='cb2']	
clickAndWait	//input[@name='submitbutton' and @value='submit']	

```
info: Starting test /selenium-server/tests/search_Selenium_RC.htm
info: Executing: |open | /selenium/basic_html_form.html | |
info: Executing: |type | username | username |
```

Figure 4.15: Results of running a suite

49

4.7.1　End Notes

There are many more functions available in the IDE and you could use it as a tool to manage an entire suite of test cases. However we are aiming to manage our test cases as code. In later sections we use the IDE to create our basic test cases and as a support tool for our automation. But never more than a supporting tool.

Chapter 5

The Eclipse IDE

5.1 How to Install and Run The Eclipse IDE

5.1.1 Install Eclipse

Visit http://unow.be/rc/eclipse[1] and click on the big download button.

Figure 5.1: Download Eclipse

Then download the "Eclipse IDE for Java Developers"

Figure 5.2: Download the appropriate IDE

Select a mirror from the list.

Figure 5.3: Choose the location to download from

Download the zip file and save it to a folder.

---

[1]http://www.eclipse.org/

Extract the contents of the archive into a folder using your favourite zip archive manager. I right click on the file and choose the unarchive option from the context menu to extract the contents of the archive to a folder. I chose `c:\selenium_eclipse_galileo` (at the time of writing the current version of Eclipse was named "Galileo"). If the version you installed has a different name then don't worry. Eclipse versions are backwardly compatible and improve with each release, so use the most up to date version of Eclipse.

5.1.2   Run Eclipse

Run Eclipse by double clicking on `eclipse.exe` in `c:\selenium_eclipse_galileo\eclipse`.

You will see the splash screen for Eclipse.

Choose a "workspace" - where your project files will be saved. You can easily change this at a later date so choose a location that seems sensible for you. I have put it on the `c:\` drive for clarity in the explanatory text and screen shots.

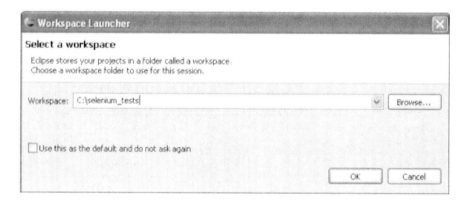

Figure 5.4: Choose a location where Eclipse will save your source code

And then you will see the Eclipse "Welcome" screen, which I always find a bit confusing.

You want to click on the curved arrow to the right which displays the text "Workbench" "Goto the Workbench" when you hover the mouse over it.

And then you will see the Eclipse workbench screen that will become very familiar and you will grow to know and love.

5.2   How to Create a New Java project

We are going to create tests in Java so to do that we need a Java project to store them in.

Start by using the file menu in Eclipse to create a new Java project.

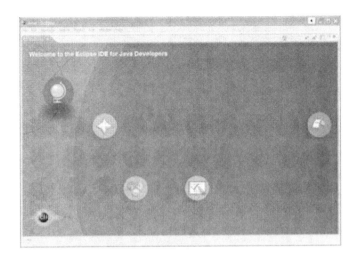

Figure 5.5: Eclipse Welcome Screen

Figure 5.6: Goto Workbench

Figure 5.7: The Eclipse Workbench Screen

Type in the name of your new project - I called mine `InitialSeleniumTests`, just leave everything else on the dialog with the default entries and click the `[finish]` button.

Figure 5.8: Create a New Java Project from the File Menu

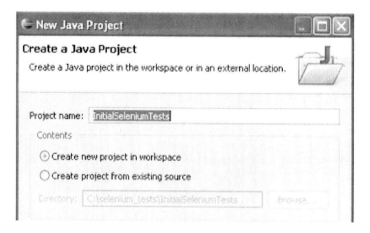

Figure 5.9: Project Named Initial Selenium Tests

This will create a folder in your workspace directory called `InitialSeleniumTests` which has the basic folders that you need when working with Java in Eclipse.

Figure 5.10: Automatically Created Files

In Eclipse, in the Package Explorer tab on the left, you will see a tree with a root node named `InitialSeleniumTests`, this is your project.

Now you are ready to start creating Selenium tests in Eclipse. We still have a few changes to make in the Eclipse configuration, but we will make those changes in the context of writing tests so that you will see and understand why we make them.

Chapter 6

Create a JUnit Test Using Selenium IDE

6.1   Overview of Exporting Section

In this section we are going to:

- export an IDE script as a Java JUnit test

- get the exported test running in Eclipse

6.2   Export an IDE script as a JUnit test

We have already done this in the preceding section. So in the IDE, load the test that you saved `search_Selenium_RC.htm` or create a new test script.

6.2.1   Load an existing script into the IDE

Start up the Firefox browser. Then start the `Selenium IDE` from the `Tools` menu, or the `Web Developer` menu.

In the IDE select `File \ Open...`

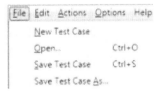

Figure 6.1: select ''File\Open...''

Then navigate to the test case and Open it in the IDE. You should see the test loaded into the IDE in the table view.

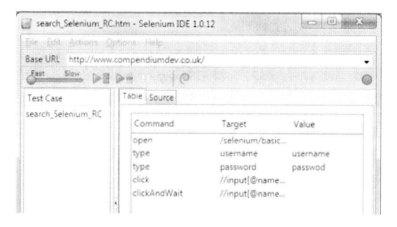

Figure 6.2: Test in table view

6.2.2 Formatting and Exporting using the IDE

Versions of the IDE prior to 1.0.10, had the facility to to show the test in the source tab in different source languages.

Consequently at the time of writing in version 1.0.12 a legacy `Options \ Format` menu exists, but in disabled form.

The source tab displays the test in HTML Selenese format.

The menu option `Options \ Clipboard Format` controls the format of the items when copy and pasting specific lines of the test from the Table view. This can be useful if you want to take snippets of tests into your code.

To convert tests to Java or other languages, we use the `File \ Export Test Case As...` menu items.

We need to convert this test into a Java test and we do this by changing the format of the test from the options menu. In this text we are using Java, JUnit and Selenium RC so we export the tests as `JUnit 4 (Remote Control)`.

I exported my test to a file called `exportedTest` and this is also the name that the test will be exported with.

When you export the tests from the IDE they are written to the disk with Unix new line characters. This means that if you want to view the test in a text editor on windows, you need one which supports different new line characters, otherwise your entire test is shown on one line in the text editor.

I use Notepad++ as my alternative text editor on Windows. Exported tests are displayed well in Notepad++, but you could also view the files in WordPad if you didn't want to install anything else on your machine.

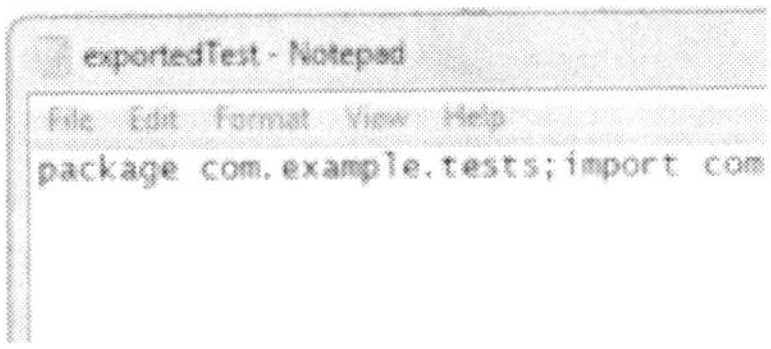

Figure 6.3: Exported Java JUnit Code in Notepad

- http://unow.be/rc/nplusplus[1]

You don't need to understand the exported test code yet. We will explain it as we go through this section. But rest assure it will make sense.

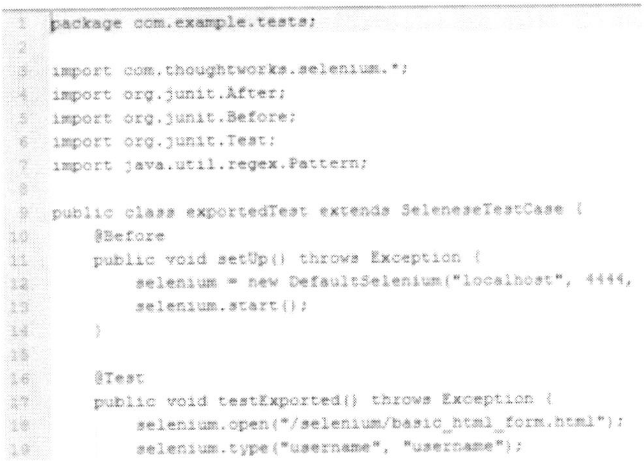

```
package com.example.tests;

import com.thoughtworks.selenium.*;
import org.junit.After;
import org.junit.Before;
import org.junit.Test;
import java.util.regex.Pattern;

public class exportedTest extends SeleneseTestCase {
    @Before
    public void setUp() throws Exception {
        selenium = new DefaultSelenium("localhost", 4444,
        selenium.start();
    }

    @Test
    public void testExported() throws Exception {
        selenium.open("/selenium/basic_html_form.html");
        selenium.type("username", "username");
```

Figure 6.4: Exported Java JUnit Code in Notepad++

6.2.3 Create a New Class in Eclipse

The first thing we are going to do is create a new class to store our tests in.

In Java all of our ''tests'' are going to be ''methods'' of a Java Class.

Java is an Object Oriented programming language so all of the code is built from classes. And the only way to have the program do something is to execute a method of one of the classes.

You don't need to understand this yet and we will revisit this in a later section to explain the basics of classes, methods, objects, packages and other terminology you will encounter.

So, start Eclipse (If you haven't already got it running), and use the Menu system: `File \ New \ Class`

[1] http://notepad-plus-plus.org/

NOTE:

Depending on the order that you did actions in the Selenium IDE you might find that the base URL in the exported sourcecode is not www.compendiumdev.co.uk, but is instead change-this-to-the-site-you-are-testing.

```
selenium = new DefaultSelenium("localhost", 4444, "*chrome",
                "http://change-this-to-the-site-you-are-testing/");
```

If this happens, then all you have to do is edit the code after you have pasted it into the Eclipse IDE so that it has the base URL that you are working with. e.g.

```
selenium = new DefaultSelenium("localhost", 4444, "*chrome",
                "http://www.compendiumdev.co.uk/");
```

Figure 6.5: Start creating a New Class

The Eclipse `New Java Class` wizard will appear and we can use this to create our basic class - don't worry if you don't understand all the items in the dialog, just follow the instructions, you will understand everything there eventually as you become more experienced with Java. Right now, we just want to create a simple class called `MyFirstSeleniumTests`.

Figure 6.6: Name the class

In the name field type `MyFirstSeleniumTests` - if you choose a different name then you should start the class name with an uppercase letter.

After typing in the name, did you notice that Eclipse showed you a warning message about default package usage? Saying:

```
The use of the default package is discouraged
```

Packages are how we organise our Java code so that we can reuse it and manage it effectively on a large project.

Eclipse provides plenty of warnings to help you code. This warning means that we should really type in a package name - and we will.

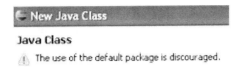

Figure 6.7: Warning to choose a package

I type my package name into the `Package` field.

```
com.eviltester.seleniumtutorials
```

Links to some guidance on package names:

- http://unow.be/rc/wikipacknames[2]

- http://unow.be/rc/packages[3]

Figure 6.8: Enter a package name

The rest of the dialog can be left with the default values provided by the wizard.

And then press the `[finish]` button.

Eclipse will have created an empty class and a package for you.

Now we just have to add the code generated by the IDE.

6.2.4 Copy and Paste the code generated by Selenium IDE into Eclipse

Open the file generated by the IDE into an editor and copy the code from the editor into the clipboard.

Either by using the right click context menu, or Edit menu to do a `select all` followed by a `copy`, or by clicking on the source code and using the keyboard and pressing `Ctrl+a` followed by `Ctrl+c`.

We can't just paste the Selenium IDE code into Eclipse because we need some of the code that the New Class Wizard created for us.

Paste the Selenium IDE code at the end of the MyFirstSeleniumTests.java code so you end up with a code listing like the one below.

---

[2]http://en.wikipedia.org/wiki/Java_package#Package_naming_conventions
[3]http://java.sun.com/docs/books/jls/third_edition/html/packages.html#7.7

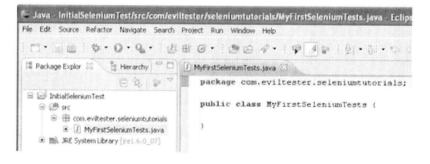

Figure 6.9: New Java Class Wizard

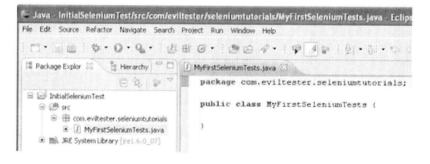

Figure 6.10: Created Class in Eclipse

As you can see there are a lot of Eclipse error symbols on the left hand side of the screen. This is because we have written invalid Java with two package declarations and two class declarations. So we will tidy that up:

We can only have one package declaration in each class, and we want the one at the top of the file: .

```
com.eviltester.seleniumtutorials
```

Figure 6.11: Copy and Pasted Class with errors

- To fix this error, remove the following line:

```
package com.example.tests;
```

We only want one class declaration per file, and the name of the class must match the name of the file.

- copy MyFirstSeleniumTests and overwrite exportedTest

- then remove the declaration of MyFirstSeleniumTests that the wizard generated ie.

```
public class MyFirstSeleniumTests { }
```

This should give you a listing like the following, which although valid Java is not yet correct because we need to make a few more changes to make it work in Eclipse:

```
package com.eviltester.seleniumtutorials;

import com.thoughtworks.selenium.*;
import org.junit.After;
import org.junit.Before;
import org.junit.Test;
import java.util.regex.Pattern;

public class MyFirstSeleniumTests extends SeleneseTestCase {
  public void setUp() throws Exception {
```

```
     selenium = new DefaultSelenium("localhost", 4444, "*chrome", "http://www.
         compendiumdev.co.uk/");
     selenium.start();
  }
  public void testGoogle_for_selenium_rc() throws Exception {
     selenium.open("/");
     selenium.type("q", "Selenium-RC");
     selenium.click("btnG");
  }
}
```

6.2.5 Resolve Import Errors

The first thing we need to resolve is the error on the first import statement.

```
import com.thoughtworks.selenium.*;
```

Import statements are how we tell Java about the methods and classes we are using from external packages.

If we hover over the red cross at the side of this line then Eclipse will tell us what the problem is.

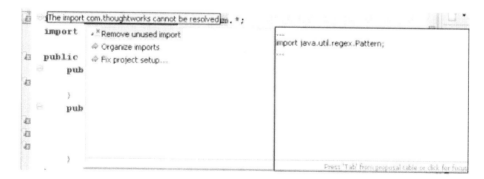

Figure 6.12: Eclipse Explains the Error

In this case it is:

```
The import com.thoughtworks cannot be resolved
```

A failure to resolve means that Eclipse does not know where to find this package. In this case because we haven't told Eclipse where to find the Selenium library yet.

We can fix this error automatically by clicking on the red cross to the left of the source code line.

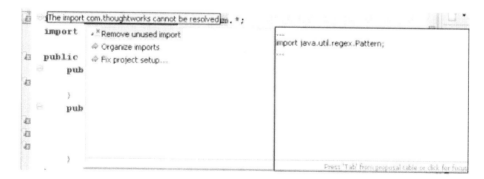

Figure 6.13: Try to Automatically fix the error

Double click on the `Fix project setup...` option and Eclipse will tell us that it doesn't know how to do that automatically.

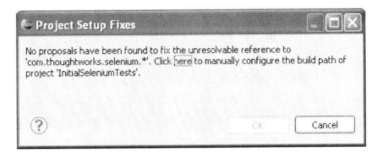

Figure 6.14: Manually fix the error

So we accept Eclipse's offer to allow us to manually configure the build path for the project. By clicking on the `here` in the dialog text:

```
click here to manually configure the build path
of project "InitialSeleniumTests".
```

The build path is how java knows what external libraries are used in this project. Java searches through those libraries looking at the different packages to find the classes and methods that we want to re-use from those libraries.

When we click `here`, we will see a subset of the properties of the project we are working on. We want to add a new library so click on the `Libraries` tab.

Figure 6.15: Basic properties for the default project

We want to amend the Java Build Path by pressing the `[Add External JARs...]` button.

Navigate to your Selenium directory, then into the Selenium 2 directory where you have the Selenium `.jar` files.

```
C:\selenium\selenium-2.0.0
```

And select the Selenium server standalone `.jar`:

- `selenium-server-standalone-2.0.0.jar`

Upon clicking [open] from the file dialog, that file should be displayed in the Libraries list.

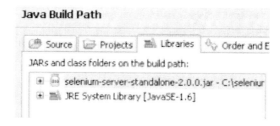

Figure 6.16: Client driver added to libraries

Click [OK] to exit the dialog.

The display of the test should now look better, with either one or no error symbols displayed by Eclipse.

6.2.6   Add JUnit to the build path if necessary

Skip this step if you had no errors in the preceding section. As before, hover over the symbol to see the error Eclipse reports.

Figure 6.17: JUnit TestCase not defined

In the first error Eclipse reports that we haven't added JUnit to the build path.

Click on the error symbol and choose `Configure build path...` from the list of options.

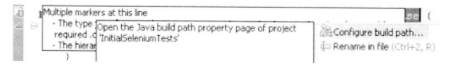

Figure 6.18: Select Configure build path for JUnit

This time we are going to choose the [Add Library...] button because Eclipse is distributed with JUnit. From the list of libraries presented, choose JUnit and click [Next >].

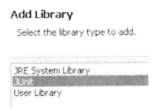

Add Library

Select the library type to add.

JRE System Library
JUnit
User Library

Figure 6.19: JUnit distributed as a standard library with Eclipse

From the list of JUnit library versions, choose JUnit 4 and click [Finish].

JUnit Library

Select the JUnit version to use in this project.

JUnit library version: JUnit 4

Figure 6.20: Choose JUnit 4 from the drop down

Click [OK] on the properties dialog and you should see your test with warning symbols.

6.2.7 Fix the Warning Messages

The exported test from the IDE has code that we do not need, and generates code using a class which has been deprecated in Selenium 2.0, the seleneseTestCase class. We cover seleneseTestCase class in an Appendix, just in case you are curious about it. But we will be removing it from our code in this section.

Remove the unused import

We have a warning symbol next to the import java.util.regex.Pattern; line.

If we hover over this warning then we will see Eclipse report that the imported classes are never used.

Figure 6.21: IDE creates unnecessary code

We can safely use the option provided when we click on the warning symbol to remove the unused import.

65

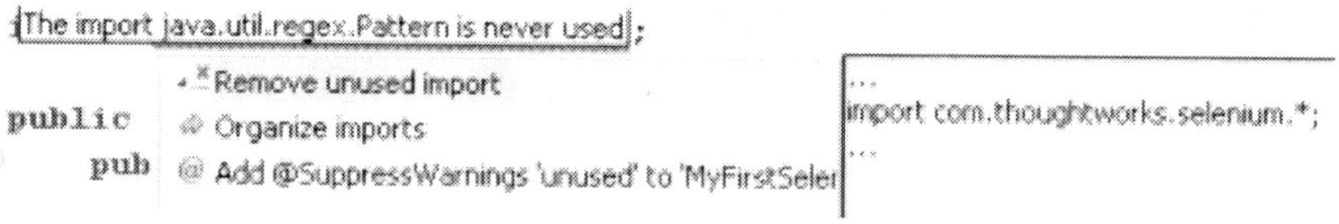

Figure 6.22: Remove the line throwing a warning

Remove deprecated seleneseTestCase

Remove the `extends SeleneseTestCase` code.

More error symbols will be displayed. This is because the `selenium` object was created in the `SeleneseTestCase` object.

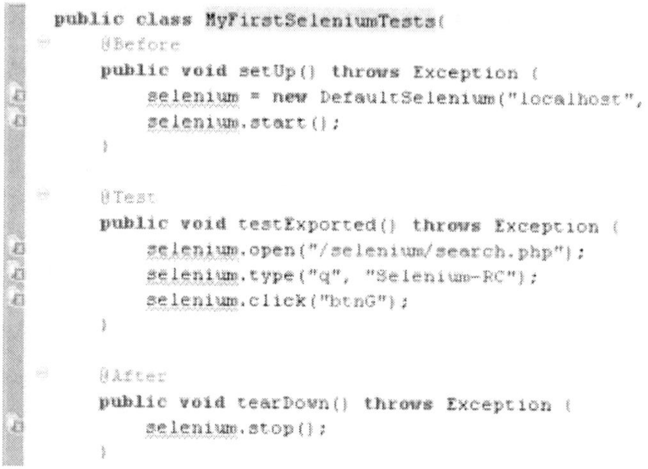

Figure 6.23: Errors after removing SeleneseTestCase

We will fix that error by adding `Selenium selenium=null;` as a new line above the `@Before` annotation.

And having done all this, our code should be clean and ready to run:

```
package com.eviltester.seleniumtutorials;

import com.thoughtworks.selenium.*;
import org.junit.After;
import org.junit.Before;
import org.junit.Test;

public class MyFirstSeleniumTests{

  Selenium selenium=null;

  @Before
  public void setUp() throws Exception {
    selenium = new DefaultSelenium("localhost", 4444, "*chrome", "http://
        compendiumdev.co.uk/");
```

```
    selenium.start();
  }

  @Test
  public void testExported() throws Exception {
    selenium.open("/selenium/search.php");
    selenium.type("q", "Selenium-RC");
    selenium.click("btnG");
  }

  @After
  public void tearDown() throws Exception {
    selenium.stop();
  }
}
```

6.3   Run the JUnit test

We run this by right clicking on the `MyFirstSeleniumTests.java` in the Package Explorer.

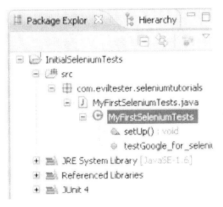

Figure 6.24: The Test in the Package Explorer

And selecting `Run as \ JUnit test`.

Try running it, remember first of all to start the Selenium RC server as explained in earlier sections.

If you don't then Selenium client will display an error in the Eclipse console, asking if you have started the server.

6.3.1   Allow it through the Firewall

If you encounter any Firewall prompts when you run Eclipse or Java then you should allow it access through your Firewall.

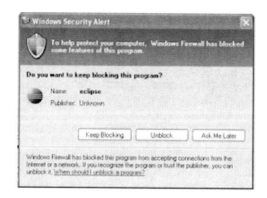

Figure 6.25: Allow Eclipse through the firewall

6.3.2 Seeing the test running

You should see the Selenium window appear. And underneath it the Running Test window.

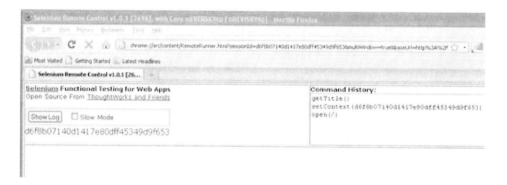

Figure 6.26: The Selenium window shows the commands and any errors that occur

In the Running Test window you can see the actual test execution happening. Of course since it is a small test it may have run too quickly for you to see the details. So we will cover that in the next major section after you check the results.

You should also have seen a bunch of messages appear in your console where you are running Selenium Server.

From the console window you can gain a little insight into how Selenium works. Because we are using Firefox, Selenium creates a new Firefox profile for executing the test. This means that if we have any plugins etc in Firefox then they won't be available to the Selenium test. You can also see each statement in our test `open`, `type`, `click` sent through to the server as a "Command Request" for Selenium RC to execute it within a session and return an `ok` result to the client.

NOTE:
If you didn't see the Selenium browser window then you may have firewall problems. You could check by disabling the firewall while you try to run the test and see if that helps - if it does then you may need to do one or more of the following: open port 4444, add Eclipse, java and the browser to your exclusions list.

```
15:21:22.814 INFO - Started org.openqa.jetty.jetty.Server@18a47c0
15:21:37.335 INFO - Checking Resource aliases
15:21:37.345 INFO - Command request: getNewBrowserSession[*chrome, http://compen
diumdev.co.uk/, ] on session null
15:21:37.345 INFO - creating new remote session
15:21:37.415 INFO - Allocated session 78e11f2da8c44084a8fcd803c9d1306f for http:
//compendiumdev.co.uk/, launching...
15:21:38.797 INFO - Preparing Firefox profile...
15:21:46.909 INFO - Launching Firefox...
15:21:53.128 INFO - Got result: OK,78e11f2da8c44084a8fcd803c9d1306f on session 7
8e11f2da8c44084a8fcd803c9d1306f
15:21:53.148 INFO - Command request: open[/selenium/search.php, ] on session 78e
11f2da8c44084a8fcd803c9d1306f
15:21:54.370 INFO - Got result: OK on session 78e11f2da8c44084a8fcd803c9d1306f
15:21:54.380 INFO - Command request: type[q, Selenium-RC] on session 78e11f2da8c
44084a8fcd803c9d1306f
15:21:54.420 INFO - Got result: OK on session 78e11f2da8c44084a8fcd803c9d1306f
15:21:54.420 INFO - Command request: click[btnG, ] on session 78e11f2da8c44084a8
fcd803c9d1306f
15:21:54.450 INFO - Got result: OK on session 78e11f2da8c44084a8fcd803c9d1306f
15:21:54.470 INFO - Command request: testComplete[, ] on session 78e11f2da8c4408
4a8fcd803c9d1306f
15:21:54.470 INFO - Killing Firefox...
15:21:54.700 INFO - Got result: OK on session 78e11f2da8c44084a8fcd803c9d1306f
```

Figure 6.27: Messages from Selenium Server

The console can prove invaluable when investigating Selenium errors so read the output during your testing to help you continue to learn.

6.3.3   Check the results

After the run you should notice that the JUnit tab is now selected on the right.

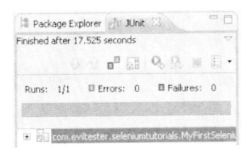

Figure 6.28: JUnit tab after a successful run

This reports that we ran 1 test, with no errors. And the green bar means that all our tests passed. If the test had failed then the bar would be red and we would see the failing tests with a red cross next to them.

6.4   It went too quickly!

We will now use the debugger to run the test slowly and see it in action.

Set a break point by right clicking on the left bar in Eclipse beside your source code on the line with the `.start()` method call.

```
selenium = new DefaultSelenium("localhost", 4444, "*chrome",
                "http://www.compendiumdev.co.uk/");
selenium.start();
```

Choose `Toggle Breakpoint` from the displayed pop-up menu.

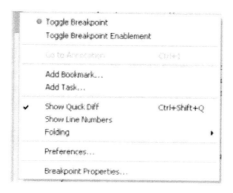

Figure 6.29: Toggle Breakpoint in the context menu

If you now see a round blue circle in the margin next to that line then it means you have set a breakpoint.

```
public void setUp() throws
    selenium = new Default$
    selenium.start();
```

Figure 6.30: A line in Eclipse with a breakpoint set

The breakpoint means that when we run this test in debug mode. The execution of the test will pause when we hit that line and we can manually control the execution of the test.

Add another breakpoint to the line of code that reads:

```
selenium.open("/selenium/search.php");
```

You should see two breakpoints set in your code.

```
@Before
public void setUp() throws Exception {
    selenium = new DefaultSelenium("localhost",
    selenium.start();
}

@Test
public void testExported() throws Exception {
    selenium.open("/selenium/search.php");
    selenium.type("q", "Selenium-RC");
    selenium.click("btnG");
}
```

Figure 6.31: Two breakpoints visible in left info bar

6.4.1   Run the test in debug mode

We want to run the test in debug mode. Switch back to the Package Explorer view by clicking on the Package Explorer tab.

Instead of right clicking on the test class and choosing `Run As\ JUnit Test` we want to choose `Debug As \ JUnit Test`. Or select the test class name in the Package Explorer and press `Alt+Shift+d`, followed by `t`.

The first thing you may notice is a `Confirm Perspective Switch` dialog asking if you want to launch the Debug view. Click the `[x] remember my decision` option and choose `[Yes]`.

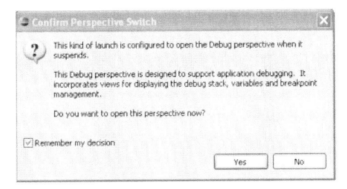

Figure 6.32: Confirm the switch to debug perspective

You should then find yourself in a new window layout of Eclipse. The Debug perspective.

Figure 6.33: The debug toolbar

We will use the toolbar to navigate through the code. Hover the mouse over the button to learn what it does. Each button has a shortcut key equivalent. We will only use two in this tutorial:

71

- Step Over (F6)

- Resume (F8)

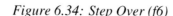

Figure 6.34: Step Over (f6)

Figure 6.35: Resume (F8)

Your test should have stopped executing on the following line:

```
selenium.start();
```

The above line should be highlighted green.

This line has not executed yet.

This will start our Selenium session and start the browser for us. We will step over this line by pressing F6.

Step Over means that it will execute in the debugger but we will not debug through all the lines of code that were written to make .start() happen.

When we step over the code, either by pressing the F6 key, or clicking on the icon, the Selenium Remote Control window should have been displayed. Eclipse now highlights the closing brace in the setUp method in green because this is the next line to be executed.

If you notice the URL in the execution browser you can see that it hasn't yet visited the web page:

- compendiumdev.co.uk/search.php

Also note that it still has a selenium-server command listed:

- http://localhost:4444/selenium-server/core/Blank.html?start=true

Press Step Over (F6) again and you will see a Class File Editor showing TestCase.class. This is a JUnit class and we haven't associated any source code. This is not an error. We can still debug through the test. This is why we set the second breakpoint.

So click the resume button or press F8. And this will execute the code to get to the next line that we are interested in seeing execute under the debugger.

Now you should see the selenium.open("/selenium/search.php"); line selected in green.

72

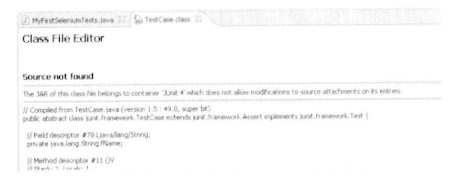

Figure 6.36: JUnit TestCase class code not found

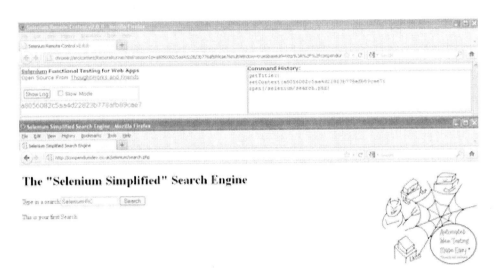

Figure 6.37: The test running

Press `Step Over` (F6) and you should see Selenium execute that command and open the Selenium Simplified Search page in the window below.

Keep pressing `Step Over` (F6) to watch the test execute and when happy that you have seen enough press `Resume` (F8) to skip over the rest of the test code to finish the test.

Click the `[Java]` perspective button in the top right to go back to your more familiar Package Explorer view.

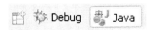

Figure 6.38: Java Perspective Button

6.5   Create and Import some more IDE Converted tests

Just to make sure that we know how to import tests and you can see how easy it will be in the future now that we have done the hard work of setting up the build path.

We will now record and import another test into this class.

Start up Firefox and the Selenium IDE.

Make sure record is on.

Figure 6.39: Record is on

And that you have the Table view showing.

This time record actions where you:

- type `evil tester` into the search box

- and then perform a Search by pressing the `[Search]` button.

You should have a test like the following:

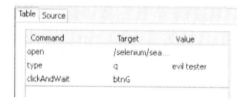

Figure 6.40: Recorded Script in Selenese Table view

Run the test again to make sure you have created something repeatable by clicking the Play button.

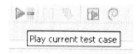

Figure 6.41: Play button on left

If that worked, then we can export to a file with the format to `JUnit 4 (Remote Control)`, load it into a text editor and copy and paste it into Eclipse.

But this time, all we want to copy into Eclipse is the "test" code i.e.

```
@Test
public void testExported() throws Exception {
  selenium.open("/selenium/search.php");
  selenium.type("q", "evil tester");
  selenium.click("btnG");
  selenium.waitForPageToLoad("30000");
}
```

Paste that code into Eclipse beneath the existing test and before the closing brace } of the class.

Then rename the test. i.e. Change testExported to searchForEvilTester

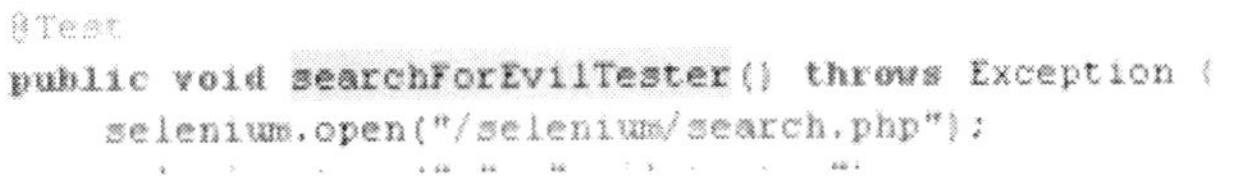

Figure 6.42: The renamed test in Eclipse

NOTE:
If you haven't renamed the earlier test then this is a good time to do it.
If you try and have two methods with the same name and parameter types then you will see an error in eclipse.
By giving your tests unique names, which explain the purpose of the test then you avoid errors and make your test classes more maintainable.

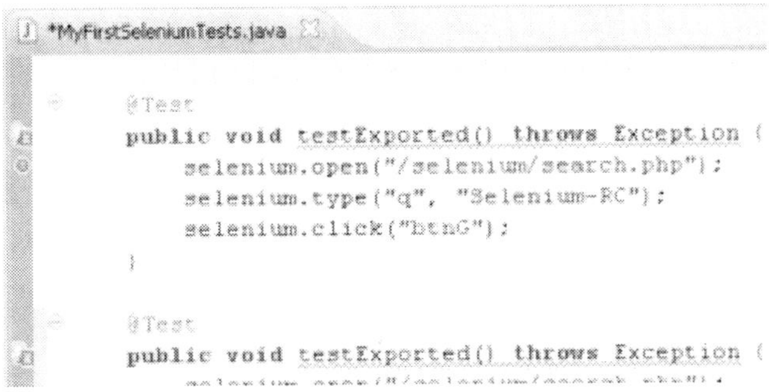

Figure 6.43: Two tests with same name in eclipse

Click on the class and choose run \ JUnit test, then Eclipse will run all the tests in that class.

You should now have enough information to record your own tests and either add them into the existing class, or create new classes to house them.

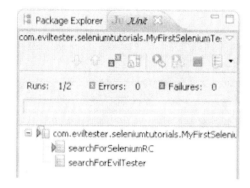

Figure 6.44: JUnit running both tests

We can easily use the IDE to generate the basics for simple tests. In later sections we will see how to identify the locators for the `.type` and `.click` methods, and how you can learn to write tests like this by hand.

Learning to write these tests by hand is important because you well learn how the application hangs together and write robust tests.

Copying code in from the IDE can be quick but we do not want to create all tests like this. In practice I use the IDE to help capture certain actions that I want to do, but may be having difficulty figuring out the exact command sequence, or frames that controls are embedded within.

6.6   Exercises

Create a new class called `MyFirstSetOfExercises` to hold your exercise tests. Create all tests in the IDE and paste them into Eclipse as JUnit tests.

Exercise:

1. search for an term, assert title of page,

2. add an assert that a specific link is present

3. change the value of the search to see the test fail

Chapter 7

The Annotated Generated Test

As we look at the generated test we will learn a lot about Java, Object Oriented programming and how Selenium works.

7.1 Use Attach Source to see the Selenium Driver Source Code

The first thing we will do is configure Eclipse to let us see the source code for the Selenium Driver.

In Eclipse, highlight the text `Selenium` in the line `Selenium selenium=null;` (you can do this by double clicking on the text).

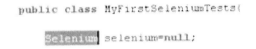

Figure 7.1: Highlighted Selenium Declaration

Then open the declaration in a number of ways, either:

- right click and choose `Open Declaration` from the context menu, or

- press `F3`, or

- press `Ctrl` and click the left mouse button.

Figure 7.2: Open Declaration from Context Menu

`Open Declaration` is a very useful function in Eclipse to take you to the implementation source code for the source item you selected. In this case we want to see the source code for the Class declaration of Selenium.

You should see a Class File Editor window, with the message `Source not found`. This is because we haven't told Eclipse where the source code for the Selenium Java Driver and Server resides on the disk.

77

We can easily fix this by pressing the [Attach Source...] button and navigating to the source code .jar file

- selenium-java-2.0.0-srcs.jar

Figure 7.3: Missing Source Attachment

Click the [Attach Source...] button. And the Source Attachment Configuration dialog appears.

We want to choose a location path by clicking on the [External File...] button.

Using the File Selection dialog that appears. We want to navigate to the directory where we extracted the Selenium Java Client Driver when we installed Selenium.

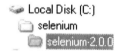

Figure 7.4: Selenium folder

In my case this was in a subdirectory of c:\selenium\

    C:\selenium\selenium-2.0.0

The sources for the client are stored in selenium-java-2.0.0-srcs.jar (where 2.0.0 would be replaced with the version number of Selenium 2.x that you are using). Click on this file to attach it.

Click the [OK] button, and you should see the display change from the Class File Editor to a normal source code editor, the only difference being that the source code is not editable because you are using compiled source in a .jar file, rather than a text file of source code.

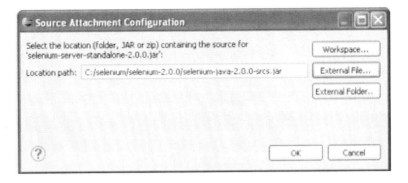

Figure 7.5: Attaching the source jar

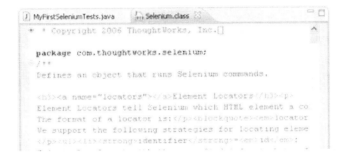

Figure 7.6: Source Code can now be displayed

7.2 Why should we do this?

With Eclipse setup like this, we can start to understand the code that we are using. It is very important to understand as much as possible about the libraries and classes that you are using in your testing. You can start to understand the limitations or restrictions of these classes and learn what you have to build yourself, and what comes for free in the short term to help you get started. If you are just learning programming then you have a whole set of relevant source code to study to look at how other people have used and built the tools. Reading source code is one of the easiest ways for a novice programmer to advance their programming skills.

7.3 How to find line numbers in Eclipse?

To help you find the line number you can:

- switch on line numbering by right clicking on the left margin of the code window (where you set breakpoints) and select `Show line numbers`

79

Figure 7.7: Switch on line numbers from context menu

- press `Ctrl+L` or choose `Navigate \ Goto Line` from the menu

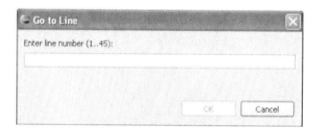

Figure 7.8: Ctrl+L to show "Go to Line" dialog

- Navigate around the code window using the `line : char` indicator on the bottom status bar of the Eclipse window.

Figure 7.9: The line Character Indicator in bottom status bar

7.4 MyFirstSeleniumTests.java Annotated

For a thorough presentation of Java terminology read the official Java documentation on "Learning the Java Language". http://unow.be/rc/javadocs[1]

First, lets start with our tests. We will work through on a line by line basis to understand the code, and drill down into lower levels of the code as necessary.

---

[1]http://java.sun.com/docs/books/tutorial/java/index.html

```
 1  package com.eviltester.seleniumtutorials;
 2
 3  import com.thoughtworks.selenium.*;
 4  import org.junit.After;
 5  import org.junit.Before;
 6  import org.junit.Test;
 7
 8  public class MyFirstSeleniumTests{
 9
10      Selenium selenium=null;
11
12      @Before
13      public void setUp() throws Exception {
14          selenium = new DefaultSelenium("localhost", 4444,
15          selenium.start();
16      }
17
18      @Test
19      public void searchForSeleniumRC() throws Exception {
20          selenium.open("/selenium/search.php");
21          selenium.type("q", "Selenium-RC");
22          selenium.click("btnG");
23      }
24
25      @Test
26      public void searchForEvilTester() throws Exception {
27          selenium.open("/selenium/search.php");
28          selenium.type("q", "evil tester");
29          selenium.click("btnG");
30          selenium.waitForPageToLoad("30000");
31      }
32
33      @After
34      public void tearDown() throws Exception {
35          selenium.stop();
36      }
37  }
```

Figure 7.10: The listing with line numbers to aid detailed explanation

```
1 : package com.eviltester.seleniumtutorials;
```

- First we put the `package` declaration. The package declaration is the first statement
  in the source code file. If we don't add a package statement then the class goes
  into a default `unnamed` package. Packages are a way of grouping classes logically
  as multiple classes in different files can all be declared as belonging to the same
  package. Using packages allows us to ''import'' them later for reuse in different
  classes, packages and applications.

- The package declaration terminates with a semi-colon `;`. All statements in Java
  must end with a `;` as the programmer must tell the compiler where the statement
  ends.

- Packages are covered in the Java documentation http://unow.be/rc/package[2]

```
3 : import com.thoughtworks.selenium.*;
4 : import org.junit.After;
5 : import org.junit.Before;
6 : import org.junit.Test;
```

- Because we want to use classes in the Selenium library, we tell Java to look in the `com.thoughtworks.selenium` package to find the classes we are using e.g. `Selenium`.

- Import statements in Java Documentation http://unow.be/rc/usepkgs[3]

- The other imports on lines 4, 5 and 6 are to allow us to use the JUnit annotations `@After` `@Before` and `@Test`.

```
8 : public class MyFirstSeleniumTests{
```

- For our test code, you can think of Java Classes as collections of tests and helper code to make our tests work. This isn't a particularly good definition in terms of understanding Object Oriented Programming. But in terms of the way that we will use them for our automated tests, this definition will get you started.

- Our test classes are declared as public so that they can be run as part of our test suites.

- This class declaration line ends with `{`. Scope in Java is declared explicitly by putting everything within a pair of `{` and `}`. The scope of the class, or everything declared as part of this class, is contained between the opening `{` on line 8 and the closing `}` on line 37.

- Classes in Java http://unow.be/rc/javaoo[4]

```
10 : Selenium selenium=null;
```

- On line 10 we declare a variable called `selenium` which is of a type `Selenium`. The upper case "S" in `Selenium` tells us that it is a class, and is the class which provides the Selenium API Interface that we use in our automation.

- I initially set it to `null` as it has no object assigned to it.

```
12 : @Before
```

---

[2]http://java.sun.com/docs/books/tutorial/java/package/index.html
[3]http://java.sun.com/docs/books/tutorial/java/package/usepkgs.html
[4]http://java.sun.com/docs/books/tutorial/java/javaOO/index.html

- @Before is an annotation, which means that it provides meta data to the items in the source which follow it. In this case a method called setUp. The @Before annotation means that this setUp method will be called before any method annotated by @Test in the class.

- Since an @Before annotated method runs before each of the tests. And we have a tearDown method annotated with @After when we run MyFirstSeleniumTests.java as a JUnit test, what actually gets executed is the following:

  1. setUp
  2. searchForSeleniumRC
  3. tearDown
  4. setUp
  5. searchForEvilTester
  6. tearDown

- You can verify this for yourself by putting a breakpoint on lines 14, 20, 27, 35 and running the test in debug mode. And at each breakpoint, resuming the test. Note: there is no guarantee that the @Test annotated methods will be run in the order listed, therefore you may see the searchForEvilTester method executed first, but each @Test method will be preceded by the setUp method.

```
13 : public void setUp() throws Exception {
```

- On line 13 we declare a new method called setUp and we are telling Java that under some circumstances it may throw an exception. This means that if something goes wrong in the setup then an exception might be generated rather than the application handling all the problems itself. We will cover exceptions in a later section. But be assured that if you missed this out, Eclipse would prompt you that it was missing.

- You can read about exceptions in the official Java documentation http://unow.be/rc/exceptions[5]

- Again the scope of the method is delimited by { and }. This method consists of the code in lines 14 and 15

```
14: selenium = new DefaultSelenium("localhost", 4444, "*chrome", "http://
    compendiumdev.co.uk/");
```

- On line 14 we assign a DefaultSelenium object to the selenium variable

---

[5]http://java.sun.com/docs/books/tutorial/essential/exceptions/

- We create the variable using the `new` keyword, which creates objects. To do this it calls the "constructor" method on `DefaultSelenium`. This is the method which initialises the object. We tell it that we want it to connect to the Selenium server running on the server `localhost` on port `4444` and using the `*chrome` browser, with a base domain of `http://www.compendiumdev.co.uk`.

- `*chrome` is the browser code for the underlying rendering engine in the Firefox browser. We could have written `*firefox`, and when we write tests ourselves, rather than generating them, we will do that.

- There are a number of browser codes in Selenium: e.g. `*firefox`, `*iexplore`, `*googlechrome` and they all start the browsers in different modes. We will look at this in later sections.

```
16 : }
```

- Line 16 ends the scope of the setUp method started on line 13

```
18 :   @Test
```

- The easiest way of making sure that a class method is run as a JUnit test, is to annotate it with `@Test`. Any method in the class annotated in this way will be treated as a JUnit test.

```
19 :   public void searchForSeleniumRC() throws Exception {
```

- We declare test methods as `public void` thereby allowing the JUnit test runner to execute them.

- And because we are not handling any exceptions that can be thrown by the selenium commands in this method we declare that we may throw an exception.

```
20 :   selenium.open("/selenium/search.php");
```

- This is our first selenium command in the test. Here we are calling the `open` method on the object referenced by the `selenium` variable.

- The `open` method takes the page name as a parameter. Because we used a fully qualified URL in the `setUp` method i.e. `http://www.compendiumdev.co.uk/` when we later pass in a relative URL to the open method, Selenium knows that we want to prefix this with the base URL and actually open the Selenium Search Engine page.

- i.e. http://www.compendiumdev.co.uk/selenium/search.php.

```
21 :    selenium.type("q", "Selenium-RC");
22 :    selenium.click("btnG");
23 : }
```

- I'm going to start explaining blocks of text now, otherwise I'll end up repeating myself, because we have covered all the complicated parts already.

- Again, on line 21, we use a selenium method. This time the `type` method. This takes two parameters. The first is a locator, the second is the text to type. This causes selenium to type `Selenium-RC` into the field named `q`.

- On line 22, we use a selenium method `click` which simulates a mouse click on the button named `btnG`

- On line 23 we end the scope of the test method.

```
25: @Test
26: public void searchForEvilTester() throws Exception {
27:     selenium.open("/selenium/search.php");
28:     selenium.type("q", "evil tester");
29:     selenium.click("btnG");
30:     selenium.waitForPageToLoad("30000");
31: }
```

- There is very little new in this section that we haven't covered.

- On line 25 and 26 we create a new test method called `searchForEvilTester`.

- On lines 30 we use a selenium method `waitForPageToLoad` this takes a single parameter which is a timeout value in milliseconds. Which means that selenium will wait for the page to load and if it hasn't loaded within 30 seconds then it will throw an exception and the test will fail.

- Line 31 ends the scope of the test method

```
33: @After
34: public void tearDown() throws Exception {
35:     selenium.stop();
36: }
```

- Line 33 introduces the `@After` annotation, where the annotated method runs after each `@Test` method.

- Line 35 uses the Selenium `stop` method to stop the Selenium session.

```
37: }
```

85

- Line 37 ends the scope of the class.

Hopefully you have a better idea about what all the lines of code in the test do. Now you are a step closer to learning Java. You will learn more Java throughout this book, but the Java tutorials on the Sun website are a particularly good free online reference.

I included links to relevant portions in the text above but the main web page is http: //unow.be/rc/tutorial[6]

In this book I will not overload you with the definitions of all the pieces of Java and Object Orientation that we cover. I will provide enough information for you to understand the tests you are writing and to help you think about what you are doing. Hopefully the information here will allow you to approach the more detailed explanations in other programming books more easily and understand their more detailed presentation.

7.5   A little about JUnit

JUnit (http://unow.be/rc/JUnit[7]) is a unit test framework for Java. It provides a convenient way of creating ''tests'', running them and having the results tracked in a report. It is also a very simple framework to learn.

We are using it in this text because it is easy to use in Eclipse - it comes as part of the default install. And Selenium IDE supports it as one of the exporting options.

The JUnit Eclipse plugin provides a convenient graphical test runner to show the tests running.

---

[6]http://java.sun.com/docs/books/tutorial/
[7]http://www.JUnit.org/

Chapter 8

Let's get coding

In this section you will learn how to use the tools the way that I think you will choose to use them by default.

8.1   A brief pause, because you have already learned some Java

You have already learned some Java, and some Eclipse tips.

You already know:

- how to recognise an error in Eclipse

- that Eclipse does a lot of error checking for us

- that Eclipse can fix many errors, so left click on that red [x] when it appears - this helps you learn about fixing coding errors in Java

You have also learned:

- Java Classes start with an uppercase letter

- Java Classes are logically organised into packages

- Java Class methods become tests in JUnit by annotating them with `@test`

- Java Class Libraries need adding to our Class path so we can use them

- We need to `import` classes from libraries to use them in our code

8.2   What we will now learn

More about:

- JUnit annotations

- The `DefaultSelenium` class

- Starting and stopping the connection to Selenium server

NOTE:

If we first select MyFirstSeleniumTests.java in the Package Explorer, and then do
File \ New \ Class then you will notice that Eclipse adds the package name into the
New Java Class wizard for us as it assumes we want to keep the new class in the same
logical hierarchy as the one we selected.

8.2.1   Create a New Test From Scratch

Create a new Java class and call this MySecondSeleniumTests.

After using the New Java Class wizard we are going to create a set of test methods from
scratch. So starting with the generated code, we will create a test method within this.

```
package com.eviltester.seleniumtutorials;

public class MySecondSeleniumTests {

}
```

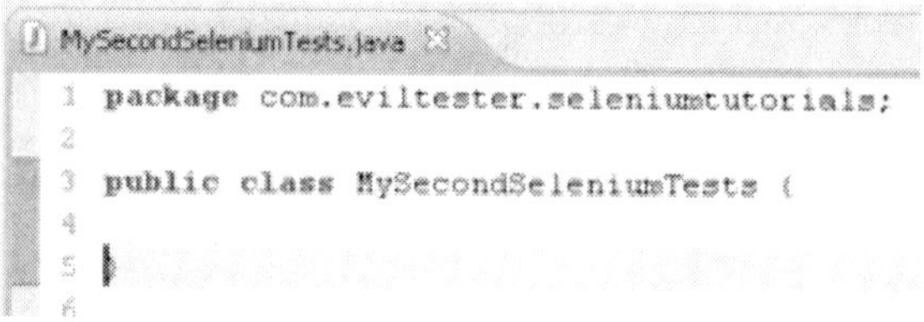

Figure 8.1: Basic declaration for the test

8.2.2   @Test Annotation Turns Methods Into Tests

We write our "tests" as class methods.

Add a new method called initialiseSeleniumRCServer to your class:

```
package com.eviltester.seleniumtutorials;

public class MySecondSeleniumTests {

  public void initialiseSeleniumRCServer(){

  }

}
```

Simply adding a new method does not make it a test.

Java supports annotations to help semantically markup our code.

- http://unow.be/rc/annotationpedia[1]

Add a JUnit `@Test` annotation on the line above the method declaration to allow your method to be used as a JUnit test.

```
package com.eviltester.seleniumtutorials;

public class MySecondSeleniumTests {

  @Test
  public void initialiseSeleniumRCServer(){

  }

}
```

Now you will have noticed that Eclipse has marked that line as an error.

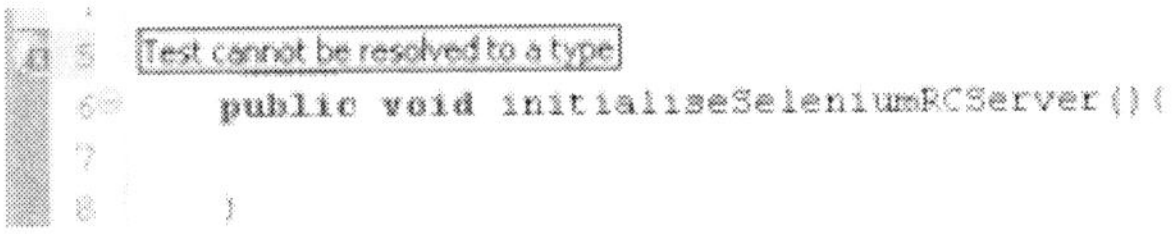

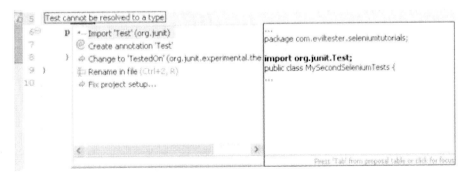

Figure 8.2: Eclipse identified error

By hovering the mouse over the red `[x]` on the left, Eclipse tells us that it doesn't know what a Test is.

```
Test cannot be resolved to a type
```

You can probably guess that this means we have yet to tell Eclipse about JUnit annotations.

If I click on the red `[x]`, then Eclipse will prompt me with ways of potentially resolving this issue: `Import 'Test' (org.junit)`, `Create annotation 'Test'`, etc.

Figure 8.3: Resolve error by clicking on error icon in left border

I want to select `Import 'Test' (org.junit)` because I need to add an import statement for the annotation from JUnit. This will add the import statement into my code.

---

[1]http://en.wikipedia.org/wiki/Java_annotation

```
package com.eviltester.seleniumtutorials;

import org.junit.Test;

public class MySecondSeleniumTests {

  @Test
  public void initialiseSeleniumRCServer(){

  }

}
```

Since I know I'm likely to need more classes and annotations from JUnit, I'm going to pre-empt the fixing of other errors by amending this import to an import statement that matches everything from `org.junit` i.e.

```
import org.junit.*;
```

8.2.3   Back to Our Selenium Test

Add the line below to your test:

```
Selenium selenium = new DefaultSelenium("localhost", 4444, "*firefox",
                       "http://www.compendiumdev.co.uk");
```

Your test will look like this:

```
@Test
public void initialiseSeleniumRCServer(){
  Selenium selenium = new DefaultSelenium("localhost", 4444, "*firefox",
                       "http://www.compendiumdev.co.uk");
}
```

We just added code to create a new Selenium object that we can use to connect to the Selenium RC server.

But, as before we have a red [x] so Eclipse informs us that we have an error here.

```
 7    @Test
 8    public void initialiseSeleniumRCServer(){
 9        Selenium selenium = new DefaultSelenium("localhost", 4444, "*firefox",
10            "http://www.compendiumdev.co.uk");
11    }
```

Figure 8.4: Eclipse reported an error on Selenium

By hovering on the red [x], Eclipse tells us that it doesn't know anything about Selenium with the error:

```
Selenium cannot be resolved to a type
```

Eclipse can fix that for us when we left click on the red [x] and select:

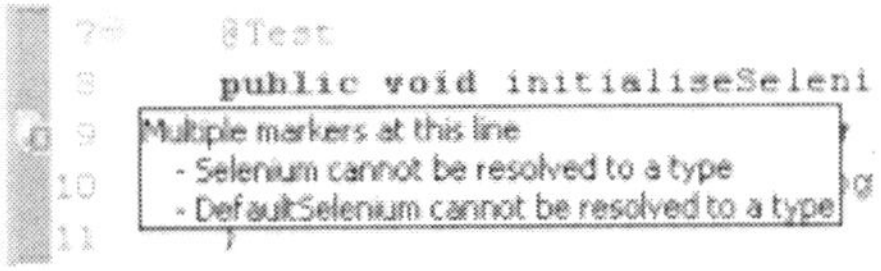

Figure 8.5: Have not defined Selenium

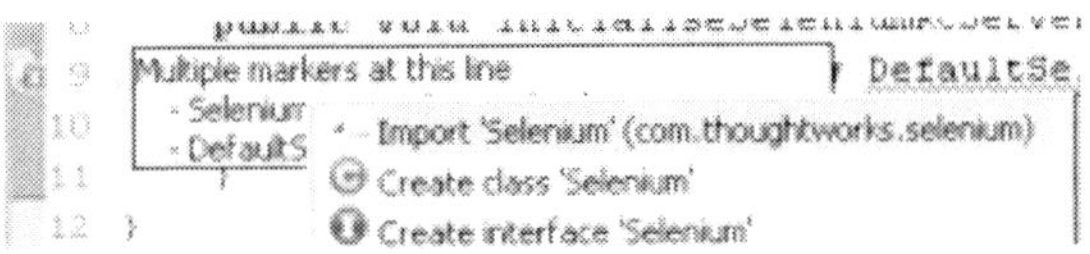

Figure 8.6: Automatically add an import

```
Import Selenium (com.thoughtworks.selenium)
```

from the suggestion pop-up.

Eclipse adds the Selenium Import for us.

```
import com.thoughtworks.selenium.Selenium;
```

But this hasn't fully imported all we need. Eclipse is still telling us that it doesn't know about `DefaultSelenium`.

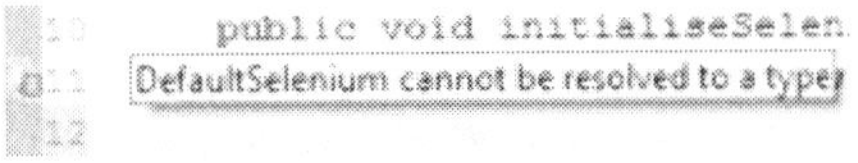

Figure 8.7: DefaultSelenium not defined

Rather than importing `DefaultSelenium`, we may as well do the same regex matching that we did for JUnit and change our selenium import to a wildcard import:

```
import com.thoughtworks.selenium.*;
```

This should remove any future Selenium imports for us as well.

Now our code looks like:

```
package com.eviltester.seleniumtutorials;

import org.junit.*;
import com.thoughtworks.selenium.*;

public class MySecondSeleniumTests {

  @Test
  public void initialiseSeleniumRCServer(){
    Selenium selenium = new DefaultSelenium("localhost", 4444, "*firefox",
        "http://www.compendiumdev.co.uk");
  }
}
```

Figure 8.8: Eclipse warning indicator

Notice that Eclipse has displayed a warning for us.

And if we hover on the yellow `[!]` then we will learn that one of our variables is never read.

```
The local variable selenium is never read
```

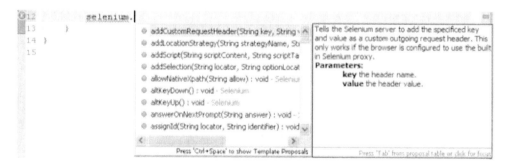

Figure 8.9: Unread local variable

Since we have just started writing our test, that seems fine - if this happens later then we may decide that we don't need the local variable and delete it from our code.

8.2.4 Making Something Happen

Now we are going to start using the local selenium object that we created, so add `selenium.` as the next line in your test method:

```
@Test
public void initialiseSeleniumRCServer(){
    Selenium selenium = new DefaultSelenium("localhost", 4444, "*firefox",
        "http://www.compendiumdev.co.uk");
    selenium.
}
```

When you typed `selenium.` in the above code, you should have noticed a few things, first a red error cross appeared on the line (because we haven't finished the line yet) and a pop up menu appeared.

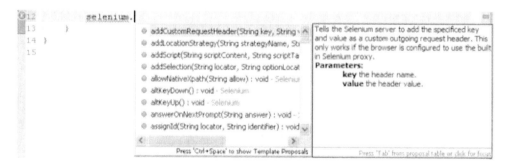

Figure 8.10: Code Completion Dialog

This pop-up menu is the `code completion` dialog and will help you learn the range of Selenium commands available to you. This IDE support is one reason for introducing you to Selenium with Java and Eclipse. Auto completion can be started manually by pressing `Ctrl+Space` and Eclipse will respond with a contextual list of actions or commands based on the text immediately preceding the point you pressed `Ctrl+Space`.

For now we can ignore this and just type the following code.

```
selenium.start();
selenium.open("http://www.compendiumdev.co.uk");
selenium.stop();
```

Save the file. The red [x] should have gone away and you now have a test that does something.

Specifically, we have now created a test which instantiates a `Selenium` object, starts up the session, opens Firefox, visits www.compendiumdev.co.uk, and stops the session.

Run it and see it at work.

8.2.5   Your Final Test Code

One additional thing we will do to the test code before we finish up is to make sure it closes everything that it opened.

Currently it doesn't.

Our basic hierarchy at the moment is:

- start

    - open

- stop

What we really need is to close everything that we open.

- start

    - open
    - close

- stop

So we add the `selenium.close();` statement into the source code, immediately after the `selenium.open(...);`

`selenium.close` will close the Selenium Remote Control window and make sure we leave the test system in the same state we found it and not leave any loose ends that might cause us problems the next time we run the test.

Hopefully if you followed all the instructions then your code looks like the code below:

NOTE:

Starting from version 2.0.0 of Selenium, the `.stop()` closes down the created browser instances. It did not do this in previous versions. I still prefer to make my tests specific and add the `.close()` statements.

```
package com.eviltester.seleniumtutorials;

import org.junit.*;
import com.thoughtworks.selenium.*;

public class MySecondSeleniumTests {

  @Test
  public void initialiseSeleniumRCServer(){
    Selenium selenium = new DefaultSelenium(
              "localhost", 4444, "*firefox",
            "http://www.compendiumdev.co.uk");
    selenium.start();
    selenium.open("http://www.compendiumdev.co.uk");
    selenium.close();
    selenium.stop();
  }
}
```

8.2.6   The DefaultSelenium constructor explained

```
Selenium selenium =
  new DefaultSelenium("localhost", 4444, "*firefox",
        "http://www.compendiumdev.co.uk");
```

The constructor for Selenium has a few key points that you really need to understand.

- `localhost`

    - We are running the Selenium RC server from a separate DOS window. So the Selenium RC server is a separate application running on our machine. `localhost` is the convenient hostname to refer to "this computer". We could use this computers IP address or machine name but `localhost` is a convenient short cut.

    - If our Selenium RC server was running on another machine, or a virtual machine, we would replace `localhost` with the hostname of that computer. Either its machine name or its IP address. We can get this information by running `ipconfig` from the command line - to get the IP address. Running `ipconfig /all` will give more information about the computer - including its Host Name.

94

- `4444`

  – This is the port that Selenium started on. We didn't supply a port name when we entered the initial `java -jar` command so Selenium used the default of `4444`.

  – We could have started Selenium RC using any port we wanted by affixing a `-port` parameter e.g.

  – `java -jar selenium-server-standalone-2.0.0.jar -port 8888`

  – If we get the port wrong then we won't be able to connect to the Selenium RC server process.

- `*firefox`

  – This is the parameter which tells Selenium RC which browser to use. I have told it to use Firefox.

  – The basic browser codes are `*firefox`, `*iexplore` and `*googlechrome`. These refer to Firefox, Internet Explorer and Google Chrome.

- `http://www.compendiumdev.co.uk`

  – This is the parameter which contains the base URL of the site we are testing.

NOTE:

I have put the full url of the page to open as the parameter to the `.open` method. But since we have defined the `baseURL` in the `DefaultSelenium` object I could have used a relative url as the parameter, e.g. for the home page I could have used `""` or `"/"`. Try this in your test and see what difference it makes.

8.3   Retrospectives

8.3.1   Well Done

So if you followed the tutorial this far, you managed to write your first test from scratch (admittedly it didn't do much) and we covered a lot, so a quick recap of what we covered:

- How to recognise an error in Eclipse

- Eclipse does a lot of error checking for us

- Eclipse can fix many errors, so left click on that red [x] when it appears - this helps you learn about fixing coding errors in Java quite quickly

- Java Classes start with an uppercase letter

- Java Classes live in packages

- Java Class Libraries need adding to our Class path so we can use them

- We need to `import` Classes from Libraries to use them in our code

- We add external Java Libraries to the project properties

- To connect to the Selenium server we initialise a `DefaultSelenium` object, then start the session, issue our selenium commands (e.g. `open`), then `close` the session

- How to switch between Java and Debug perspectives

- The Selenium Server displays a lot of logging information in the DOS Window

I think you have most of the infrastructure elements that you need to start writing tests, and you can probably start to follow some of the other Selenium tutorials that are out there on the web now, without too much effort.

8.4 Why did you do that?

In this section I will explain the reasons behind some of the decisions made in the chapter.

8.4.1 Run Selenium RC in a DOS window?

I run Selenium RC in a DOS window so that I can:

- Start it easily

- See the logging messages

- Find the window - changing the title of the DOS window means it appears on my tool bar easily

- Stop and Restart Selenium Easily

Start it easily

You saw how easy it was to start the Selenium Server

```
java -jar selenium-server-standalone-2.0.0.jar
```

Selenium RC also has a bunch of command line parameters. We will discuss these later when we need them.

See the logging messages

I like to view the logging messages from Selenium RC. Sometimes I think the test might have frozen, but a quick glance at the DOS window and I can see that it is processing.

Find The Window

When you change the title of the window you can find it in the Windows task bar much more easily or through your `Alt+Tab` switching. This allows you to easily view the logging messages that Selenium RC displays.

8.4.2 Stop and Restart Selenium Easily

If I am in the DOS window then I can `Ctrl+C` to stop the selenium server.

And I can easily restart it by typing in `java -jar selenium-server-standalone-2.0.0.jar` again or by pressing the cursor up key - up and down cycle through the command history in DOS.

8.5 Final Notes

I want to make it clear -

- You really don't need to know much Java to write automated tests.

- You will learn more Java as and when you need it.

- Eclipse will help you identify the mistakes you make with Java.

- The programmers you work with will happily help you if you are seriously trying to learn.

- Many good books and resources exist to help you learn Java.

Some external links which might help you understand Java:

- Java Basics

    - http://unow.be/rc/pktute[2]

- Official Sun Java Tutorials

---

[2]http://www.perfectknowledgedb.com/Tutorials/H2R/main.htm

- http://unow.be/rc/javadocs[3]

- Thinking in Java 3rd Edition - online edition of a great Java book

  - http://unow.be/rc/tij[4]

- JavaFAQ.nu - examples and tips

  - http://unow.be/rc/javafaq[5]

- Javalessons.com

  - http://unow.be/rc/javalessons[6]

8.6   Back to Eclipse

8.6.1   Removing the Source Code Association

If you ever find that you want to remove the source code association then: from the Package explorer, right click on the correct `.jar` file for the Selenium Server select `properties` from the pop-up menu. e.g. the `selenium-server-standalone-2.0.0.jar` or `selenium-server.jar`

Figure 8.11: Properties menu item from Package Explorer tab

Then delete the text in the `Location Path` field, for the `Java Source Attachment` entry and then click `OK`

---

[3] http://java.sun.com/docs/books/tutorial/java/index.html

[4] http://www.mindviewinc.com/Books/TIJ/

[5] http://www.javafaq.nu/

[6] http://javalessons.com/

Chapter 9

What if it all goes wrong?

Since you are working through these tutorial sections on your own, and things can go wrong. I will try and cover some basic troubleshooting strategies here.

1. Check that Selenium Server is running

2. Close any Selenium RC windows

3. Stop and restart the Selenium RC server

4. Remove any Java threads from the Debug perspective

5. Check for any blocked browser windows

9.1 Check that Selenium Server is running

This is pretty simple, but sometimes we forget to start the Selenium Server.

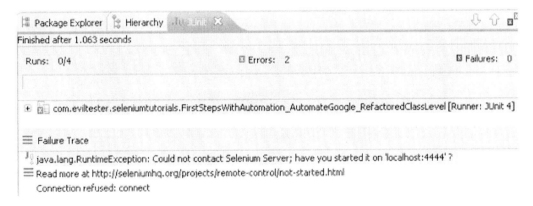

Figure 9.1: JUnit test runner informing us Selenium may not have been started

If this happens then in your JUnit test runner window you'll probably see a message like:

```
java.lang.RuntimeException: Could not contact Selenium Server; have you
    started it?
```

This is pretty easy to resolve. Just follow the instructions we provided earlier to start up the Selenium server.

1. Open a DOS window and change directory to the location of your Selenium server
   .jar file

2. run the server by typing `java -jar selenium-server-standalone-2.0.0.jar`

3. The name of the `.jar` file has changed on different versions and may change in the future, so if the filename listed in the text is not working for you then do a `dir` and check the filename exists, and possibly try some of the other likely files actually listed in your directory.

  - for version 2.0.0
    - `java -jar selenium-server-standalone-2.0.0.jar`
  - for versions prior to 2
    - `java -jar selenium-server.jar`
  - versions above 2.0.0 seem likely to adopt the following naming convention `selenium-server-standalone-versionnumber.jar`. Since this may change, look at the files in the directory and you should be able to work out from the name or from trying to run them `java -jar filename.jar` if they are the server or not.

9.2   Close any Selenium RC windows

Check to see if you have any Selenium RC browser windows open. To do this, just check the browser windows from the taskbar and close any that you don't want.

Figure 9.2: Selenium RC Windows

And if you do, then close them.

This will make sure that nothing is blocking the Selenium server from creating a session window for you.

9.3   Stop and restart the Selenium RC server

Sometimes the Selenium server gets stuck. So, go to your DOS window and press `Ctrl+C` to stop the server running, and then start the server running again, either by retyping `java -jar selenium-server-standalone-2.0.0.jar` or using the up arrow to cycle through the DOS history list to re-run the command.

If that doesn't help and you really think it is a selenium server problem then try closing the DOS window completely and then run the server from scratch in a new DOS window.

You can also issue the HTTP command to stop the server. Open a browser and visit the following URL to stop the selenium server:

`http://localhost:4444/selenium-server/driver/?cmd=shutDownSeleniumServer`

9.4 Remove any Java threads from the Debug perspective

If you have done a bit of work in Eclipse, running, debugging and stopping tests then you may find a few threads running or stopped in the Debug perspective.

Click on the Debug perspective button if the perspective is not open.

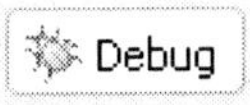

Figure 9.3: Debug Perspective Button

NOTE:
If the button is not present then select `Window \ Open Perspective \ Other...` from the menu, and then select `Debug` from the list of perspectives.

You can see the list of threads and sessions on the left of the screen.

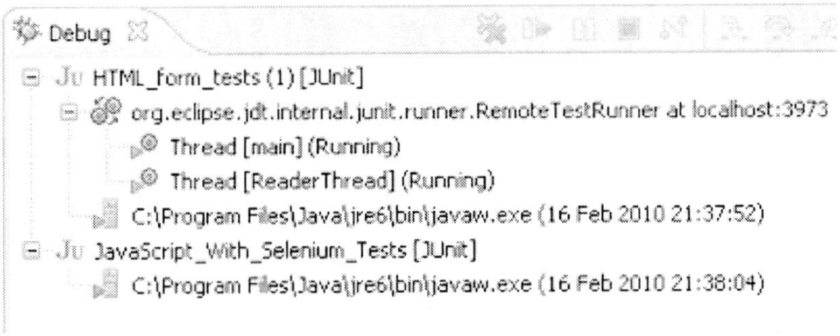

Figure 9.4: Debug view showing multiple sessions

Right click on the sessions and select from the available termination options.

Use `Terminate/Disconnect All` if the option is available. Otherwise just `Terminate and Remove` or simply `Terminate`.

Use the `Remove All Terminated` if available and keep going until your left window is empty of any sessions. This will prevent any rogue connections of sessions interfering with what you are trying to do.

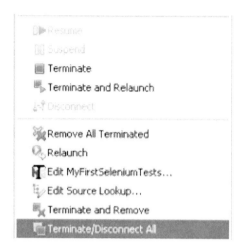

Figure 9.5: Terminate all sessions

9.5   Close any blocked browser windows

By blocked browser window I mean browser windows that may have any pop up dialogs shown, and which can't close because of it.

You may have to `Alt+Tab` through the windows in order to show this.

Or close down any browser windows that you have been using.

9.6   Firefox Update Dialog

If you run a test and are using any of the Firefox browser codes then you might be unlucky enough to see the Firefox updates dialog.

This will prevent your tests from running. So close down all instances of Firefox, check the task manager to ensure you got them all.

Then start up Firefox manually to trigger the update process and then your tests should run without incident.

9.6.1   Summary

I aim to get back to a clean stable state when trying to get Selenium to work again, so I tend to do the following:

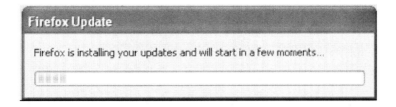

Figure 9.6: The deadly Firefox Update dialog

1. stop the server

2. terminate any debug sessions/threads

3. remove all debug sessions/threads

4. close any Selenium RC browser windows

5. close any blocked browser windows

6. restart the selenium session

If the above steps fail then it may be that your test code is in error so compare it carefully with the code provided in this tutorial.

Hopefully this checklist can help you get back and running if something goes wrong and you can't figure out why Selenium isn't working.

Chapter 10

Essential Firefox Add-Ons

In this section we will look at other free Firefox add-ons that we will use to help us with our Selenium test construction:

- Firebug

- FirePath For Firebug

10.1 Firebug

10.1.1 What is Firebug?

The firebug add-on lets us more easily inspect the web page to:

- explore the DOM,

- the element names and Ids,

- to see the Ajax calls being made and understand the functional flow of the web page

Figure 10.1: Firebug HTML view

10.1.2 Install Firebug

To install Firebug either search for it on the Firefox add-on directory, or visit http://unow.be/rc/getfirebug[1]

- Firefox add-on directory
    - http://unow.be/rc/addons[2]
- Official Firebug Site
    - http://unow.be/rc/getfirebug[3]

As with all Firefox add-ons this will require a browser restart. Once installed you can access firebug from the Tools menu and from the Firefox Web Developer menu.

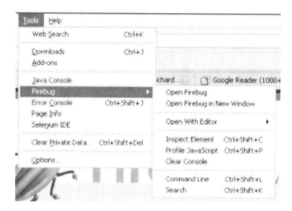

Figure 10.2: Open Firebug from the tools menu

Firebug can also be displayed by clicking on the Firebug icon in the bottom right of the Firefox window.

10.1.3 Basic Firebug Usage

When using firebug with Selenium automation I typically use the `Inspect Element` menu option from the right click context menu that appears after a right mouse button click on an item in a web page.

I will use the "Selenium Simplified" Search Engine as an example:

http://www.compendiumdev.co.uk/selenium/search.php

---

[1] http://www.getfirebug.com/
[2] https://addons.mozilla.org/
[3] http://www.getfirebug.com/

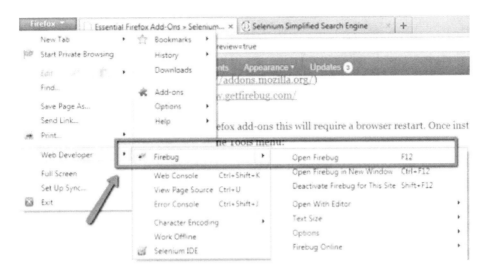

Figure 10.3: Open Firebug from the Web Developer menu

Figure 10.4: Firebug Icon

Figure 10.5: Inspect an Element in Firebug Context Menu

I can get the details of the Search input field by hovering the mouse over the input field. Then right clicking and selecting `Inspect Element`.

This will open Firebug in the `HTML view` and allow me to view the details of the HTML element.

From this I can easily see the identifying attributes and surrounding elements that I can use in my Selenium automation.

Experiment with the Firebug tool as it has a lot of very useful information and editing

Figure 10.6: Selenium Simplified Search Engine

```
<body>
    <img style="float:right" src="cover_small.gif">
    <h1>The "Selenium Simplified" Search Engine</h1>
    <form action="" method="post">
        Type in a search:
        <input type="text" value="Selenium-RC" name="q" title="Search">
        <input type="submit" name="btnG" value="Search">
    </form>
    <script>
```

Figure 10.7: Code for inspected Element

functions that can help with your automation.

10.2   FirePath For Firebug

10.2.1   What is FirePath?

FirePath allows you to type in a CSS Selector or an XPath expression and view the selection results on the page in the browser. You can use this to dynamically optimise and construct your XPath or CSS Selector expressions.

FirePath is a Firebug plugin, so you need to have Firebug installed before you can use this.

10.2.2   Install FirePath

You can install FirePath either from the Firefox add-on directory, or the addon page directly.

- Either search for FirePath on the main directory:

---

[4]https://addons.mozilla.org/en-US/firefox/addon/xpather/
[5]https://addons.mozilla.org/en-US/firefox/addon/firefinder-for-firebug/

NOTE: Over the years I've used a bunch of different plugins to help me. Many of them are no longer compatible with current versions of Firefox. But since FirePath itself might become incompatible, and since some of the other tools might be reworked to become compatible I'll list the best of the rest here:

- XPather : http://unow.be/rc/xpather[4]

- FireFinder : http://unow.be/rc/getfirefinder[5]

- http://unow.be/rc/addons[6]

- or visit the addon page directly:

- http://unow.be/rc/firepath[7]

10.2.3 Basic Usage of FirePath

Once installed you can access it as a tab in Firebug or by right clicking on the browser page and selecting `Inspect in FirePath` from the context menu.

I use FirePath in conjunction with the built in Firebug `Copy XPath` and `Copy CSSPath` functionality.

With FirePath you have a main filter text box where you type either CSS or XPath. Then press the `[Eval]` button to see which items that match that expression.

Items are shown in the browser window with a dotted blue box and are listed in the FirePath source dialog below the expression text box.

My basic steps to create an XPath or CSS selector for an element are:

- Right click on an element in the browser page

- Select `Inspect Element` to open Firebug HTML view

- Right click on the `HTML element view` for the element

- Select `Copy XPath`

- Switch to FirePath

- Paste the XPath statement into FirePath

---

[6]https://addons.mozilla.org/

[7]https://addons.mozilla.org/en-US/firefox/addon/firepath/

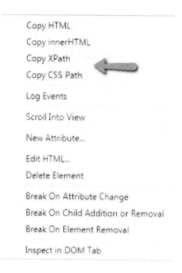

Figure 10.8: Firebug Copy XPath and CSS menu items

- Test and optimise the statement in FirePath

Alternatively:

- Right click on the element and select `Inspect in FirePath` from the context menu.

10.2.4   Optimise XPath with FirePath

Using the "Selenium Simplified" Search Engine as an example.

- I select the search box and choose `Inspect Element`.
- I right click on the selected element text and choose `Copy XPath`.
- I paste this XPath into FirePath and click `[Eval]`.

For the purposes of our testing the XPath supplied by Firebug matches too many items.

`/html/body/form/input`

In expanded form, the above xpath means:

- starting at the root of the document `/`,
- traverse the tree from `html`,
- then `/` down through `body`,

110

- then / down through `form`,

- then / select the `input` elements

We need to learn some basic XPath to use FirePath, and to make our automation more robust. We will cover XPath in more detail in later sections. The description below provides a brief introduction to XPath.

One of the things we want to do with our XPath statements is make them as immune to page changes as we can.

Here our XPath starts from the top of the document, so if the page is restructured then our test is likely to break. Ideally what I want to do is go straight to the input field.

I can see from the results of the filter (and by browsing the Firebug HTML view) that there is only one form on the page. I can tell this from the XPath because `form` text in the XPath does not have an index on it e.g. `form[1]`, or `form[2]`

So I can safely shorten the XPath and still reach the same part of the page.

```
//form/input
```

This shortened XPath means; select the `input` elements where:

- `//` starting anywhere on the page

- `form` elements exist

- `/` which have child

- `input` elements.

Using FirePath I can amend the XPath and click the `[Eval]` button to try out the statement.

Ideally I want the XPath statement to return a single response, but Selenium will use the first one in a list if it finds more than one matching entry.

This statement is better but still dependent on the formatting within the form, and still matches two items.

I really want to go straight to the input field. Which I could do by writing `//input` but I need to find some attributes that uniquely identify the input field.

I could say that I want the first Input, wherever it exists using `//input[1]`.

Evaluating this returns the result I want, but it still seems a little brittle since the page structure might change. I really want a more specific XPath statement.

I do know, from our initial inspection of this field through Firebug that this input field has a number of attributes associated with it:

```
<input type="text" value="Selenium-RC" name="q" title="Search">
```

111

Sadly it doesn't have an `id` which would have guaranteed its uniqueness in the page. But the `name` attribute may be enough to make it unique so I will try an XPath statement that combines the `//input` with a search for the name attribute.

```
//input[@name='q']
```

This returns a single element so I can safely use this XPath.

Chapter 11

Test Automation Thinking 101

11.1   Let's Automate Search

For our first steps in test automation thinking we shall look at a search engine:

http://compendiumdev.co.uk/selenium/search.php

Figure 11.1: Selenium Simplified Search Engine

Not the most famous search engine in the world, but for the purposes of this book, I need an example application which will not change very much between book releases.

The Selenium Simplified Search Engine interface has:

- A big logo

- A title

- A search input box

- A [search] button

So some simple tests would be

- typing in a search string

- press the [search] button

- clicking on the result links

11.2　Start writing some tests

First we shall do a basic search. To do that we need to write some code which does the following:

1. type in some text

2. press the [Search] Button

3. check the results in the page that loads up

Preconditions you need to meet before you work through this section:

- Start up Eclipse, it should open up your project as we left it

- Start up Selenium RC in a DOS window as we learned to do earlier

Our very first test, already opened compendiumdev.co.uk, so we can build on that to do some more work. The first thing I will do is amend the .open statement to use a relative URL rather than the full absolute URL. Remember we can do this because we have used the absolute URL in the call to the DefaultSelenium constructor.

```
@Test
public void initialiseSeleniumRCServer(){

   Selenium selenium = new DefaultSelenium("localhost", 4444, "*firefox",
       "http://www.compendiumdev.co.uk");
   selenium.start();
   selenium.open("/");
   selenium.close();
   selenium.stop();
}
```

11.2.1　Make Selenium Type In Some Text

Copy and paste all that code above, into the code window so that we start another test.

Hopefully you spotted the error symbol when you did this. When we hover over the red [x] we can see the text of the error message:

```
Duplicate method initialiseSeleniumRCServer() in type MySecondSeleniumTests.
```

Because each method in a Java class needs to have a unique name, and we implement each of our tests as a Java method, we need to rename the method.

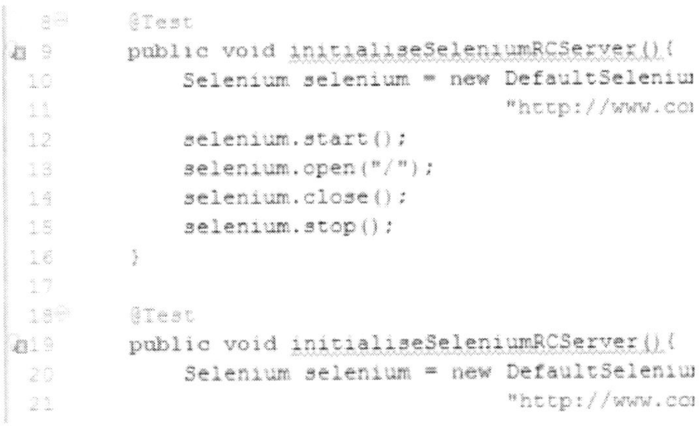

```
 8    @Test
 9    public void initialiseSeleniumRCServer(){
10        Selenium selenium = new DefaultSeleniu
11                        "http://www.co
12        selenium.start();
13        selenium.open("/");
14        selenium.close();
15        selenium.stop();
16    }
17
18    @Test
19    public void initialiseSeleniumRCServer(){
20        Selenium selenium = new DefaultSeleniu
21                        "http://www.co
```

Figure 11.2: Eclipse shows an error for duplicate test method names

Duplicate method initialiseSeleniumRCServer() in type MySecondSeleniumTests

Figure 11.3: Error message for duplicate method names

11.2.2   Fix the duplicate method name

Amend the Java method name so that it reads `typeInASearchTerm`

We also want to amend the relative URL in the `open` method call so that it opens our search engine page.

```
@Test
public void typeInASearchTerm(){

  Selenium selenium = new DefaultSelenium("localhost", 4444, "*firefox",
      "http://www.compendiumdev.co.uk");
  selenium.start();
  selenium.open("/selenium/search.php");
  selenium.close();
  selenium.stop();
}
```

Notice that the error indicators in Eclipse have gone away.

Now we have two methods in our Java class:

- `initialiseSeleniumRCServer`

- `typeInSearchTerm`

11.2.3   Add a Selenium Command

Add a new line of code in the typeInASearchTerm method, beneath:

```
selenium.open("/selenium/search.php");
```

Start the code by typing `selenium`. As soon as you typed the `.` you should see the code completion dialog pop up. This lists all the Selenium RC commands available to us as methods of the Selenium Java object.

The pop-up dialog goes away after a little while, so if we want it back we put our cursor just after the `.` and press `Ctrl+Space`.

We are going to use the type command. Start typing `type` and you should see the number of options in the pop-up dialog reduce.

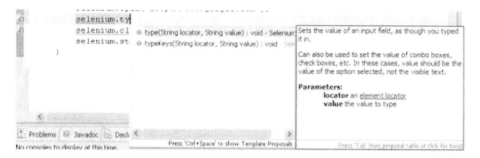

Figure 11.4: Code completion showing fewer Selenium commands

You can choose the `type` method from the pop-up dialog if you want by pressing the `space` key or `return` key, when it is highlighted in the list.

If you do this Eclipse will add the code for you `selenium.type(locator, value)`

Add a `;` to the end of the line since all Java statements terminate with a semi-colon.

Eclipse reports an error on the line because it doesn't know what `locator` or `value` are.

Eclipse added these into the code because the `type` method takes two arguments, both strings.

11.2.4   The "type" method

The `type` method takes two arguments:

- the first argument (`locator`) is a string that tells Selenium where to type the text

- the second argument (`value`) is the text to type

We will cover locator strings in more depth as we go on. But for now we just need to know that the locator string helps Selenium find the HTML element on the page that we are looking for.

116

11.2.5 Find the locator with Firebug

I use Firebug when constructing automated Selenium tests.

After installing Firebug do the following:

- open www.compendiumdev.co.uk/selenium/search.php in Firefox

Click on the input field so that the cursor is in the main search box, then right click the mouse and choose `Inspect Element` from the pop-up menu.

Figure 11.5: The Firebug Inspect Element function from right click context menu

You should see the Firebug window displayed with the input element details visible.

You can also click the ''inspect'' icon in the top left of the Firebug menu bar. This will highlight on the page the elements and display them in the Firebug window.

Having Inspected it, we now have the details we need to automate it.

I could use the name field to identify it by simply typing `q` as the locator, or `name=q`.

But I will use a more fully constructed XPath to make the test more robust.

11.2.6 A brief introduction to XPath

XPath is a standard language for querying XML data. The DOM can be queried by XPath as well.

117

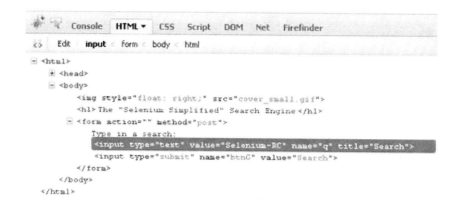

Figure 11.6: Element is highlighted and displayed in Firebug's HTML Frame

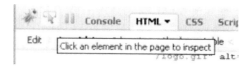

Figure 11.7: Inspect Icon with tooltip

- XPath specification: http://unow.be/rc/xpath[1]

- XPath on Wikipedia: http://unow.be/rc/xpathpedia[2]

We will cover XPath in more detail later on in the document but we will use it gradually throughout this tutorial so that you start to learn how to use it through exposure, rather than just reading the definitions about it.

The locator that we will use will look like this:

```
//input[@name='q']
```

This means:

- `//` - find (anywhere in the document)

- `input` - an input element

- `[` - which has

  - `@` - an attribute
  - `name` - called name
  - `='q'` - with a value of `q`

- `]`

---

[1]http://www.w3.org/TR/xpath
[2]http://en.wikipedia.org/wiki/XPath

NOTE:

I could have used the locator q which would try and match something with the id of q or the name of q, or been even more specific and used the locator `name=q`.

But both of these methods are brittle. In HTML a name does not have to be unique, so additional elements with the name q might get added to the page at a later date, making the test fail.

Learning how to use XPath to make your tests more robust will serve you well in the future.

11.2.7   Add the locator into the code

So add this XPath statement into your code:

```
selenium.type("xpath=//input[@name='q']", value);
```

We can tell Selenium that the locator is an XPath statement by writing `xpath=` before the XPath statement.

NOTE:

We can leave out the `xpath=` when we use an XPath starting with `//` because selenium will treat it as an XPath string.

e.g. `selenium.type("//input[@name='q']", "Selenium-RC");`

And all that remains now is to search for something, so change `value` to read `"Selenium-RC"`.

```
selenium.type("xpath=//input[@name='q']", "Selenium-RC");
```

When you do this you should also notice that Eclipse no longer reports an error against this line because we have written a valid Java statement.

11.2.8   Check that it works

If you want, you could run this now by:

- first adding the `@Ignore` annotation alongside the existing `@Test` annotation on the method `initialiseSeleniumRCServer`, so we only run the `typeInASearchTerm` test.

```
@Ignore @Test
public void initialiseSeleniumRCServer(){
```

NOTE:

We want to do this because JUnit will run any of the methods annotated as `@Test`, and since we are only interested in one at the moment it makes sense to not have the other one annotated at the moment.

We could also have deleted the `@Test` annotation but by adding `@Ignore` to the test, we make sure that we remember that the method is actually a test and not a helper method on the class. We should get in the habit of investigating ignored tests because we only want to use `@Ignore` as a temporary measure.

We can also add comments to our `@Ignore` annotation.

e.g.

```
@Ignore("temporarily exclude, only run typeInASearchTerm")
@Test
```

This is the better approach because we have declared why we are ignoring the test and don't have to struggle to remember later.

- putting a debug statement on the `selenium.close();` line,

- right click on the test class and choose to `Debug As \ JUnit Test`,

- you should see the Selenium test open up the search page and perform a search. Notice that the commands we have used e.g. `selenium.open`, get displayed in the top right hand corner of the `Selenium Remote Control` browser window that appears,

- finish off the debug process by clicking the resume button,

- click on the `Java perspective` toolbar button to go back to our source code view

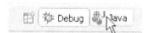

Figure 11.8: Java Perspective button

11.2.9   Now make it Click on the Search Button

We will follow a similar process for the search button:

- start adding the Selenium code

- find the button on the page

- create an XPath so that selenium can locate it

- add the XPath details to our source code

11.2.10   Selenium "Click" Method

Start adding a new command after the `type` statement.

By using code completion we can see that the Selenium command we need to use is the `click` command.

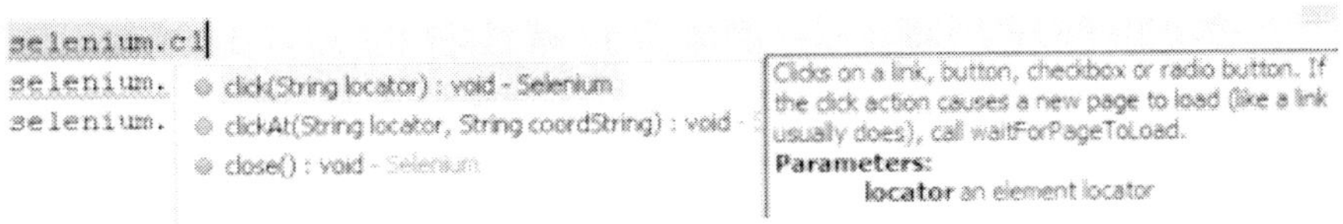

Figure 11.9: Click command code completion

The click command takes a single argument (`locator`), the location of the HTML element we want to click on.

So use the code completion context menu to have Eclipse write our basic code for us. Remembering to add the `;` to the end of the line.

```
selenium.click(locator);
```

11.2.11   Locate the button with Firebug

Use the Inspect icon and click on the `[Search]` button. And the details for the button are displayed in the source code window.

```
<input type="submit" value="Search" name="btnG" />
```

11.2.12   Create an XPath so that selenium can locate it

A very similar XPath to the last one, but this time we will use two attributes to identify the button:

```
//input[@name='btnG' and @type='submit']
```

Here we are using the `and` conditional operator to match items with the name `btnG` and a type of `submit`.

We could just use the name to find it, but here you are learning that we can use multiple attributes and longer conditional statements to create more specific locator strings.

11.2.13   Add the XPath details to our source code

Overwrite the `locator` in your source code so that the click statement line looks like this:

```
selenium.click("xpath=//input[@name='btnG' and @type='submit']");
```

11.2.14   One last thing to do

When Selenium clicks on the button, the request will be submitted and a new page will load. I will add a wait for the page to load after the click:

```
selenium.waitForPageToLoad("30000");
```

This will wait 30 seconds for the page to load, and if it hasn't loaded by the time 30 seconds roll around it will timeout with an exception and the test will fail.

11.2.15   Now check that it works

Now run the test in debug mode to make sure that it does what you expected.

- Make sure there is a breakpoint on `selenium.stop();`.

- Right click on `MySecondSeleniumTests.java` in the Package Explorer and choose `Debug As \ JUnit test`.

- Hopefully you saw the `Selenium Remote Control` window actually do the search.

- Back in Eclipse, press `F8` or click on the `[Resume]` button in the debug toolbar to finish your test.

- Click on the `Java perspective` toolbar button to go back to your source code.

11.2.16   Quick Summary

Great, you made Selenium RC do something, and you did it by writing code.

So just to remind you of what you learned:

- the Selenium `type` command

- the Selenium `click` command

- some XPath

- use of `xpath=` or `//` to create XPath selenium locators

- `@Ignore` to prevent tests from running

- Selenium uses locator strings to find items on a page

- how to use the Firebug and FirePath to find items on a page

- more familiarity with Debugging tests

- using Eclipse to swap perspectives

And just to remind you what the test you wrote looked like if you followed the instructions:

```
@Test
public void typeInASearchTerm(){

    Selenium selenium = new DefaultSelenium("localhost", 4444, "*firefox",
        "http://www.compendiumdev.co.uk");
    selenium.start();
    selenium.open("/selenium/search.php");
    selenium.type("xpath=//input[@name='q']", "Selenium-RC");
    selenium.click("xpath=//input[@name='btnG' and @type='submit']");
    selenium.waitForPageToLoad("30000");
    selenium.close();
    selenium.stop();
}
```

11.3   But is it a test if we don't check any results?

Back when we started this session the basic test we were going to write was:

1. `type` in some text

2. `click` the `[search]` Button

3. check the results in the page that loads up

We have managed to implement the first two items.

But is it a ''test'' if we don't check the results?

We ultimately want these tests to run without us watching them, and have the tests report accurately the passes and failures.

At the moment these tests might fail for some of the following reasons:

- The names of the input fields on the form changed so our locators stopped working and Selenium could not find the elements

- compendiumdev.co.uk servers got slow and the pages timed out

They would not fail if:

- The search suddenly started performing random searches so instead of searching for ''Selenium-RC'' like we asked it to, it searched for ''Surrealism DC'' - our test would not know.

We need to add some code to check for basic acceptance conditions.

11.3.1 But we can't control the data

We have the complication here that, we don't control the data that the search engine searches against so we can't guarantee the results it will return.

Therefore we cannot adopt the strategy of checking each of the links returned and making sure they match the data we expect to have returned.

What can we do?

Well, we know that the search engine does a pretty good job of returning results that match your searches. We should probably expect to see the Selenium Remote Control homepage in the list of results on the first page.

Certainly when I did the search it was on the first page, and was in fact the first item returned.

So one acceptance criteria we can use is:

- Selenium Remote Control homepage listed in returned results

By looking at the returned page we can see a few things that will help determine if the search engine has done the search we asked for.

Figure 11.10: Selenium-RC in title

The search box on the page has the search term we typed in so I can check that too.

Figure 11.11: Selenium-RC was added to the search input field

So the full list of acceptance criteria that I will automate for this "test" are:

- Selenium Remote Control homepage listed in returned results

- Page title has "Selenium-RC" in it

- Search box on the page has "Selenium-RC" in it

11.4 Acceptance Criteria: Selenium Remote Control homepage listed in returned results

We have a number of ways of checking for the homepage as a result in the page.

1. have selenium look for text we know is on the home page

2. get the source code for the page and scan it for the text we want

3. look for a specific URL in the page

The third item will turn out to be the most robust but I think it is important for you to understand alternative strategies as well. Some of these may be suboptimal in this situation, but may help you in the future.

11.4.1 Look for text in the page

Of all the options this one is the weakest and most likely to break or provide a false positive result. A false positive result is when the test passes, but the condition that you wanted tested fails.

But sometimes looking for text may be exactly what you want to do so we'll explore it here.

It only takes one command to check if the text is present on the page.

```
selenium.isTextPresent(pattern);
```

The `isTextPresent` method takes a single argument, the string you want to search for.

Based on the results of the search we could pick out some of the returned text.

- seleniumhq.org/projects/remote-control

  Selenium Remote-Control Selenium RC comes in two parts. A server which automatically launches and kills browsers, and acts as a HTTP proxy for web requests from them.

Figure 11.12: Examine the search results for text to check for

And check for the text using the `isTextPresent` method.

```
selenium.isTextPresent(
  "Selenium Remote-Control Selenium RC comes in two parts." +
  " A server which automatically");
selenium.isTextPresent(
  "launches and kills browsers, and acts as" +
  " a HTTP proxy for web requests from them.");
```

125

This method of checking is pretty brittle since the Selenium Remote Control homepage content is highly likely to change and any time you are testing something with variable content where you embed that content in your test then you better expect a few things to happen:

- increased test maintenance effort

- frequent failures of your automated test pack

So consider carefully if this is a strategy that you really want to pursue. It may be exactly what you want, but you have to be aware of the brittleness that you are building into your test pack.

Initially we might expect the test that uses this method to look like this:

```
@Test
public void typeInASearchTermAndAssertThatHomePageTextIsPresent(){
  Selenium selenium = new DefaultSelenium(
    "localhost", 4444, "*firefox", "http://www.compendiumdev.co.uk");
  selenium.start();
  selenium.open("/selenium/search.php");
  selenium.type("xpath=//input[@name='q']", "Selenium-RC");
  selenium.click("xpath=//input[@name='btnG' and @type='submit']");
  selenium.waitForPageToLoad("30000");
  selenium.isTextPresent(
    "Selenium Remote-Control Selenium RC comes in two parts." +
    " A server which automatically");
  selenium.isTextPresent(
    "launches and kills browsers, and acts as" +
    " a HTTP proxy for web requests from them.");
  selenium.close();
  selenium.stop();
}
```

Edit your tests so that you create a new test like the above and run it through in debug mode and see if it works.

Your test passed right? So now change the text you were checking the presence of and see if the test fails.

```
selenium.isTextPresent("Selenium Remote-Control Selenium RC blah blah blah");
```

I suspect that text is not on the page. So running it now, did the test fail?

Mine didn't. But the text is not present on the page. So what went wrong?

Use assertions to make the test fail on error

Some methods in Selenium will throw exceptions if they don't work properly, and that will cause the test to fail - which is what we want since we want to know if the test hasn't run properly. e.g. open, close, type, click.

126

But some methods return values which we can use in our test e.g. `isTextPresent` returns a boolean value: `true`, or `false`.

We need to check the returned value from `isTextPresent` and fail the test if it is not what we expect.

To do this we are going to use an `assert`.

An assert is a statement which ''makes an assertion that something will be a specific way'' (read that with your most authoritative inner voice), and it throws an exception if the world is not the way it expects it to be.

We can use one of the asserts built into JUnit e.g. `assertEquals`, `assertTrue`, `assertFalse`. At the moment all we want to do is check that a value is true so we will use `assertTrue`.

The assertion wrapped `isTextPresent` method should look like this:

```
assertTrue(selenium.isTextPresent(
   "Selenium Remote-Control Selenium RC comes in two parts." +
   " A server which automatically"));
assertTrue(selenium.isTextPresent(
   "launches and kills browsers, and acts as" +
   " a HTTP proxy for web requests from them."));
```

What we have just written here means:

- assert that (the value returned from the `selenium.isTextPresent` method) is true

And if you typed those lines into your source code then you will notice that Eclipse reports an error against these lines, because we haven't told it about the `assertTrue` method in JUnit.

```
The method assertTrue(boolean) is undefined for the type
   MySecondSeleniumTests
```

Eclipse should be able to fix this error because we have told it about JUnit, but the assert methods have to be statically imported.

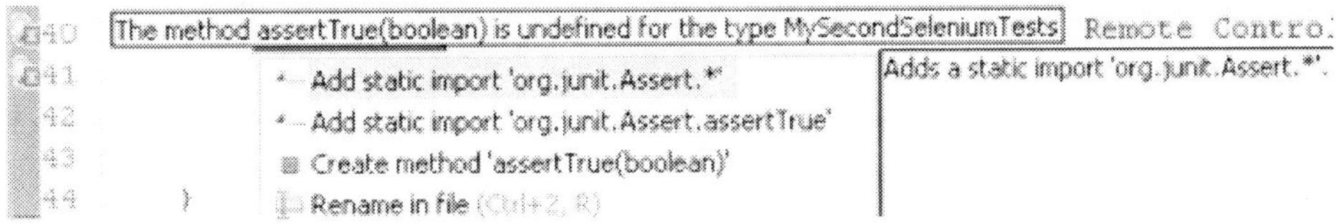

Figure 11.13: Tool tip explaining the error associated with assertTrue

Select `Add static import 'org.junit.Assert.*'`

Eclipse will add a static import to our code.

```
import static org.junit.Assert.*;
```

This will allow us to use any of the Asserts which JUnit provides.

If you followed the instructions as intended then Eclipse should be showing an error free source code. And if we run the test now with the correct text it should pass, and if we change the text to be text which is not on the page, it should fail.

Now that you have a failing test we should have a quick look at how to debug a failing test.

Debugging a Failing Test

When you ran the test with the incorrect text, hopefully you saw the JUnit tab display a red bar, and identify a failing test.

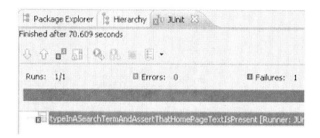

Figure 11.14: The test runner showing a failed test

The big red bar across the top tells us that a test failed.

The crosses on the tree tell us which tests in the hierarchy failed.

The window on the bottom, when we select one of the failing tests, shows us the Java Stack trace for the test execution. The Java stack trace is the list of error messages that we use to work out what went wrong.

Look at the error reported, and scroll to the right so you can see the error code. It fails with an assertion error.

If we double click on the line in the stack trace then we will jump to the line of code that generated the exception, allowing us to debug and fix it.

NOTE:
Because the test failed before we reached the `selenium.close();` and `selenium.stop();` statements, the selenium browser windows will be left open.
We will see how to handle this side-effect later by using the `@After` and `@AfterClass` annotations in our refactoring sections.

Our final test with assertions

Our final test should look like the following:

```
@Test
public void typeInASearchTermAndAssertThatHomePageTextIsPresent(){
   Selenium selenium = new DefaultSelenium(
       "localhost", 4444, "*firefox",
       "http://www.compendiumdev.co.uk");
   selenium.start();
   selenium.open("/selenium/search.php");
   selenium.type("xpath=//input[@name='q']", "Selenium-RC");
   selenium.click("xpath=//input[@name='btnG' and @type='submit']");
   selenium.waitForPageToLoad("30000");
   assertTrue(selenium.isTextPresent(
     "Selenium Remote-Control Selenium RC comes in two parts." +
     " A server which automatically"));
   assertTrue(selenium.isTextPresent(
     "launches and kills browsers, and acts as" +
     " a HTTP proxy for web requests from them."));
   selenium.close();
   selenium.stop();
}
```

NOTE:

In JUnit, all assert methods can take a description as the first parameter e.g.

`assertTrue("false is not true", false);`

Using these textual descriptions can make understanding the stack trace a little easier. Without the description you have to get used to clicking through to the code to see the line in error.

You will see usage of this approach later in this chapter.

For JUnit `assertTrue` in particular the error message can seem confusing:

```
JUnit.framework.AssertionFailedError: null at
    JUnit.framework.Assert.fail(Assert.java:47) at
    JUnit.framework.Assert.assertTrue(Assert.java:20) at
    JUnit.framework.Assert.assertTrue(Assert.java:27)
```

The `null` is the description of the error, but since we didn't add add a description, JUnit reported it as `null`.

11.4.2   Scan the page source code

Selenium's `getHtmlSource()` method will return the HTML source code of the page so we can parse it and compare it using normal java tools.

In some instances this can speed up our tests. For example, every time we use a Selenium RC command we are:

129

- sending a message from Java to the Selenium RC server

- the Selenium RC server is communicating with the Selenium Remote Control browser

- the Selenium Remote Control browser is using JavaScript to manipulate the browser DOM

Any results that come back have to come back through that chain as well.

This can make Selenium slow if you do a lot of query commands.

So one strategy we might choose to use is a single command to return the HTML source code and then parse that ourselves.

For our particular purpose here this is overkill, but I'll recreate the `isTextPresent` test above using this method.

```
@Test
public void typeInASearchTermAndAssertThatHomePageTextIsPresentInSource(){
   Selenium selenium = new DefaultSelenium("localhost", 4444, "*firefox",
       "http://www.compendiumdev.co.uk");
   selenium.start();
   selenium.open("/selenium/search.php");
   selenium.type("xpath=//input[@name='q']", "Selenium-RC");
   selenium.click("xpath=//input[@name='btnG' and @type='submit']");
   selenium.waitForPageToLoad("10000");
   String pageSource = selenium.getHtmlSource().toLowerCase();
   assertTrue(pageSource.contains(
       ("Selenium Remote-Control Selenium RC comes in two parts." +
       " A server which automatically").toLowerCase()));
   assertTrue(pageSource.contains(
       ("launches and kills browsers, and acts as" +
       " a HTTP proxy for web requests from them.").toLowerCase()));
   selenium.close();
   selenium.stop();
}
```

You can see the changes I had to make pulled out in the listing below.

```
String pageSource = selenium.getHtmlSource().toLowerCase();
assertTrue(pageSource.contains(
    ("Selenium Remote-Control Selenium RC comes in two parts." +
    " A server which automatically").toLowerCase()));
assertTrue(pageSource.contains(
    ("launches and kills browsers, and acts as" +
    " a HTTP proxy for web requests from them.").toLowerCase()));
```

I wrap the string concatenation code `"" + ""` in parenthesis so that the joined string is used for the `.toLowerCase()` method.

I create a new variable, `pageSource`, which is a Java `String` object that will store the source code returned by selenium's `getHtmlSource` method.

Then I directly replaced the `selenium.isTextPresent` with `pageSource.contains`

`contains()` is a method of a Java `string` object which returns true if the object contains the string passed as argument into the method.

Try it and see if this works in the same way as the previous test.

Did yours work?

Mine didn't.

And this illustrates one of the dangers of using the source code directly. The HTML page doesn't display the raw text. Look at the screenshot and we can see that our Search Engine has added formatting in the text to make bold the first words in the search results paragraph.

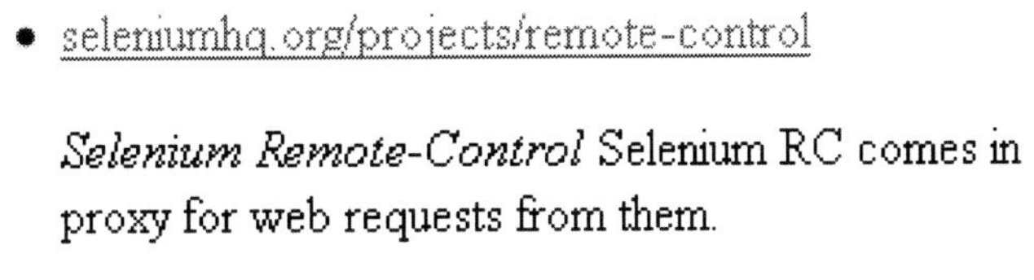

- seleniumhq.org/projects/remote-control

  Selenium Remote-Control Selenium RC comes in proxy for web requests from them.

Figure 11.15: The search text has HTML formatting

If we look at the source code of the page we can see that there are embedded HTML commands in the page so we might try and search for:

- ''Selenium Remote-Control Selenium RC comes in two parts. A server which automatically''

- ''launches and kills browsers, and acts as a HTTP proxy for web requests from them.''

If you look at the source-code for the test you will see that I have added a `.toLowerCase()` when retrieving the page source-code and in the assert on our snippet. Internet Explorer and Firefox store the source code differently internally. Internet Explorer capitalises the HTML commands internally, but not when displaying the source so this would fail in Internet Explorer if we did not convert it to lowercase.

Every time you use the source code directly you run into these potential problems. Also since HTML ignores white space when rendering you may find that you have to add additional new lines into your comparison strings.

So for our purposes getting the source code is not really what we want to do.

11.4.3 Look for a specific URL in the page

Since we know that the homepage for the Selenium RC project is:

- http://seleniumhq.org/projects/remote-control

Then we could just check for the presence of an `href` with this on the page.

But it might equally be:

- `http://seleniumhq.org/projects/remote-control/`

- `http://seleniumhq.org/projects/remote-control/index.html`

Also, in a recent re-organisation of the Selenium site. `http://selenium-rc.seleniumhq.org` redirects to `http://seleniumhq.org/projects/remote-control/`

So if we consider all these valid alternatives and are happy if any one of them appears on the page then we can use XPath to help us do that.

We will use the selenium method. `getXpathCount` which returns a Java `Number` object representing the number of times the XPath matches something on the page.

An XPath which would match the first URL is:

```
//a[@href='http://seleniumhq.org/projects/remote-control']
```

- which means: find any anchor elements with an href attribute matching the url in single quotes. e.g.

```
<a href='http://seleniumhq.org/projects/remote-control'>Selenium Home</a>
```

`getXpathCount` takes an XPath statement as an argument. Which means that we don't write `xpath=` at the start of the string when we pass the XPath string in as an argument.

If the URL `http://seleniumhq.org/projects/remote-control` was on the page 3 times, then the `getXpathCount` would return a decimal object of 3.

```
getXpathCount("//a[@href='http://seleniumhq.org/projects/remote-control']");
```

In order to use the returned value, we really want it to be an integer so we will convert it to an integer using the `.intValue()` method of the `Number` class e.g.

```
getXpathCount("//a[@href='http://seleniumhq.org/projects/remote-control']").
   intValue();
```

The test code looks as follows, I have added inline java comments so you can understand the code:

```
@Test
public void typeInASearchTermAndAssertThatHomePageURLExists(){
   Selenium selenium = new DefaultSelenium(
           "localhost", 4444, "*firefox",
           "http://www.compendiumdev.co.uk");
   selenium.start();
   selenium.open("/selenium/search.php");
```

```
selenium.type("xpath=//input[@name='q']", "Selenium-RC");
selenium.click("xpath=//input[@name='btnG' and @type='submit']");
selenium.waitForPageToLoad("10000");

/* create a new variable called matchingCountTotal to calculate
   the total number of times our xpath matches, initially setting
   it to 0   */
int matchingCountTotal = 0;

// call getXpathCount with our first xpath for the url and
// add the intValue version to the total
matchingCountTotal += selenium.getXpathCount(
    "//a[@href='http://selenium-rc.seleniumhq.org']").intValue();
matchingCountTotal += selenium.getXpathCount(
    "//a[@href='http://selenium-rc.seleniumhq.org/']").intValue();

// call the getXpathCount again with our next url and add
// the returned intValue to the total
matchingCountTotal += selenium.getXpathCount(
    "//a[@href='http://seleniumhq.org/projects/remote-control']").intValue
        ();

// call the getXpathCount again with our next url and add
// the returned intValue to the total
matchingCountTotal += selenium.getXpathCount(
    "//a[@href='http://seleniumhq.org/projects/remote-control/index.html']"
        ).intValue();

// call getXpathCount with our last url xpath and add
// the returned intValue to the total
matchingCountTotal += selenium.getXpathCount(
    "//a[@href='http://seleniumhq.org/projects/remote-control/']").intValue
        ();

assertTrue("No homepage URL found",matchingCountTotal>0);

selenium.close();
selenium.stop();
}
```

So a few things to note in the above test:

- In Java anything after `//` is treated as a comment in the line and not as code.

- You can also comment blocks of text by adding `/*` to start the comment and `*/` to end it

- We do not have to prefix arguments to `getXpathCount` with `xpath=`

- We convert the results of `getXpathCount` to an integer to use it easily

- `a += b` in Java means add the value of `b` to the variable `a` (the same as `a = a + b`)

- We have used a different form of `assertTrue`, this time we have added an error message to display if the assert fails, this will make it easier to debug the test.

Try that test out and see how you get on. If it passed then you might want to amend it to make it fail so that you can see the benefit of adding text strings to your assertions. To make it fail, amend the `assertTrue` statement to read:

```
assertTrue("No homepage URL found",matchingCountTotal==-1);
```

Running it now, you should notice a few things:

- The Selenium Remote Control window did not close

- The assertion error in the console window and in the JUnit stack trace is more readable

The Selenium Remote Control window did not close because we did not reach the line with the `.close()` command.

```
selenium.close();
```

This is one reason for spending some time in the "What if it all goes wrong?" section, as you may find yourself having to tidy up after failing tests. We will look at some JUnit functionality which can help us tidy up our environment, even in the face of failing tests, in a later section. The assertion error in the stack trace now displays `No homepage URL found` so it is much easier to see why the test failed when an assertion is not met.

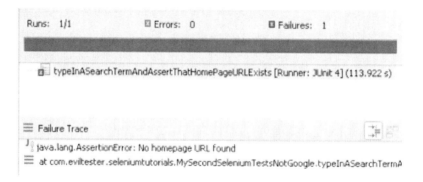

Figure 11.16: Annotation message makes error easier to debug

A quick note on XPath optimisation

XPath is a programming language and it is possible to write a single XPath statement which finds all the versions of the homepage URL by using the starts-with function in XPath, since some of our URLs start with the same string. e.g.

```
"//a[starts-with(@href,'http://seleniumhq.org/projects/remote-control')]"
```

Then the test would look as follows:

134

```
@Test
public void typeInASearchTermAndAssertThatHomePageURLExistsWithFewerXpath(){
  Selenium selenium = new DefaultSelenium(
        "localhost", 4444, "*firefox",
                  "http://www.compendiumdev.co.uk");
  selenium.start();
  selenium.open("/selenium/search.php");
  selenium.type("xpath=//input[@name='q']", "Selenium-RC");
  selenium.click("xpath=//input[@name='btnG' and @type='submit']");
  selenium.waitForPageToLoad("10000");

  // create a new variable called matchingCountTotal to calculate
  // the total number of times our xpath matches, initially setting
  // it to 0
  int matchingCountTotal = 0;

  // call getXpathCount with our xpath for the url and
  // add the intValue version to the total
  matchingCountTotal += selenium.getXpathCount(
      "//a[starts-with(@href,'http://selenium-rc.seleniumhq.org')]").intValue
         ();
  matchingCountTotal += selenium.getXpathCount(
    "//a[starts-with(@href,'http://seleniumhq.org/projects/remote-control')]"
         ).intValue();

  assertTrue("No homepage URL found",matchingCountTotal>0);

  selenium.close();
  selenium.stop();
}
```

11.4.4   Most Robust Method

Of the 3 methods we have just looked at for finding the homepage URL in the page:

- text in the page

- scanning the source code

- look for a specific URL

I think that looking for the specific URL is the most robust:

- The URL is less likely to change than text on the home page

- The source code method is horribly brittle and cross browser testing is harder

11.5   Acceptance Criteria: Page title has "Selenium-RC" in it

Selenium has a command to return the page title:

135

- `getTitle()`

`getTitle` takes no arguments and returns a `String` assigned with the title of the page in it.

```
String pageTitle = selenium.getTitle();
assertTrue("Page Title does not contain Selenium-RC search term: " +
    pageTitle, pageTitle.contains("Selenium-RC"));
```

So we end up with a test like the following:

```
@Test
public void typeInASearchTermAndCheckPageTitleHasSearchTermInIt(){
    Selenium selenium = new DefaultSelenium(
            "localhost", 4444,
            "*firefox", "http://www.compendiumdev.co.uk");
    selenium.start();
    selenium.open("/selenium/search.php");
    selenium.type("xpath=//input[@name='q']", "Selenium-RC");
    selenium.click("xpath=//input[@name='btnG' and @type='submit']");
    selenium.waitForPageToLoad("30000");

    String pageTitle = selenium.getTitle();
    assertTrue("Page Title does not contain Selenium-RC search term: " +
        pageTitle, pageTitle.contains("Selenium-RC"));

    selenium.close();
    selenium.stop();
}
```

11.6   Acceptance Criteria: Search box on the page has Selenium-RC in it

The search box on the web page is a form element. Selenium has a command called `getValue` to return the value of form elements.

By going through a process of finding the XPath of the search box form element as we did previously we can construct an XPath locator to use with the `getValue` statement.

```
String searchTerm = selenium.getValue(
        "xpath=//input[@name='q' and @title='Search']");
```

Our test looks like the following.

```
@Test
public void typeInASearchTermAndCheckSearchInputHasSearchTermInIt(){
    Selenium selenium = new DefaultSelenium("localhost", 4444,
            "*firefox", "http://www.compendiumdev.co.uk");
    selenium.start();
    selenium.open("/selenium/search.php");
    selenium.type("xpath=//input[@name='q']", "Selenium-RC");
    selenium.click("xpath=//input[@name='btnG' and @type='submit']");
    selenium.waitForPageToLoad("30000");
    String searchTerm = selenium.getValue(
        "xpath=//input[@name='q' and @title='Search']");
    assertTrue("Search Input does not contain Selenium-RC : " + searchTerm,
```

```
        searchTerm.equals("Selenium-RC"));
    selenium.close();
    selenium.stop();
}
```

11.7 One test to rule them all

By taking all the above code for the acceptance criteria. We could choose to leave all the individual tests. Or we could roll all the acceptance criteria into a single test.

```
@Test
public void typeInASearchTermAndCheckResultsPage(){
    Selenium selenium = new DefaultSelenium("localhost", 4444,
            "*firefox", "http://www.compendiumdev.co.uk");
    selenium.start();
    selenium.open("/selenium/search.php");
    selenium.type("xpath=//input[@name='q']", "Selenium-RC");
    selenium.click("xpath=//input[@name='btnG' and @type='submit']");
    selenium.waitForPageToLoad("30000");

    String searchTerm = selenium.getValue(
      "xpath=//input[@name='q' and @title='Search']");

    assertTrue("Search Input does not contain Selenium-RC : " + searchTerm,
        searchTerm.equals("Selenium-RC"));
    String pageTitle = selenium.getTitle();
    assertTrue("Page Title does not contain Selenium-RC search term: " +
        pageTitle,
        pageTitle.contains("Selenium-RC"));

    int matchingCountTotal =
      selenium.getXpathCount(
      "//a[starts-with(@href,'http://seleniumhq.org/projects/remote-control')]"
        ).intValue();

    matchingCountTotal += selenium.getXpathCount(
        "//a[starts-with(@href,'http://selenium-rc.seleniumhq.org')]").intValue
            ();
    assertTrue("No homepage URL found ",matchingCountTotal>0);

    selenium.close();
    selenium.stop();
}
```

In favour of this approach we have:

- A single test to maintain

- All the acceptance criteria have to be met for the functional implementation to pass anyway

- Removed duplication in the set of tests

Against this approach we have:

- Not quite as readable from the test title what is being tested

- If one assert fails, the whole test fails. But there might be a number of problems that we would only find by running the test multiple times i.e. after each fix.

It is a matter of style for your project which you prefer. We will cover techniques for reducing the amount of repeated code later. Personally I like to have test titles which describe the purpose of the test. I would keep the smaller multiple tests, and if the number of tests started to grow too large I might then merge the tests.

11.8   Summary

You have now learned the following Selenium methods:

`waitForPageToLoad, isTextPresent, getHtmlSource, getXpathCount, getTitle, stop, open, type, click,`

You also learned a little more Java: inline comments, `+=` , variables - both `String` and `int`, Java `Number` object .

You have also learned:

- JUnit assertions, specifically `assertTrue` and making assert statements more readable to aid debugging

- debugging failing tests and using the stack trace

- using local variables for readability and aid debugging

In addition you have learned some pros and cons for a variety of acceptance criteria checking strategies. All of the strategies are valid, experiment with them to learn which ones work best for you.

Next, we will refactor this code and use JUnit functionality to remove code duplication.

NOTE:

In this section we used @ignore to avoid running all the tests. It is possible, from Eclipse, to run a single test. In the Package Explorer, expand the test class to show all the tests then right click on an individual test method, you can then choose to run that individual method as a JUnit test.

Chapter 12

First Steps with Automation Refactored

12.1 Introducing Refactoring

Refactoring refers to the process of changing the structure of code without changing the basic behaviour. We refactor to improve e.g. increase readability, simplify structure, make code more maintainable, etc.

We have written 4 tests:

- `typeInASearchTermAndAssertThatHomePageTextIsPresent`

- `typeInASearchTermAndAssertThatHomePageURLExistsWithFewerXpath`

- `typeInASearchTermAndCheckPageTitleHasSearchTermInIt`

- `typeInASearchTermAndCheckSearchInputHasSearchTermInIt`

All of which use a common pattern:

- Start the test and go to Search page

- Implement the acceptance criteria

- Tidy up the test

We can refactor the tests to:

- reduce the amount of repeated code

- make the test more readable

I will start by refactoring the block of code before the acceptance criteria into a new method to setup the test. I can do this automatically to help avoiding making any manual errors.

12.2 Automatically refactoring the start up code into a new method

Select the code to refactor into a new method. Start by refactoring the start code common to the tests.

```
Selenium selenium = new DefaultSelenium(
        "localhost", 4444,
        "*firefox", "http://www.compendiumdev.co.uk");
selenium.start();
selenium.open("/selenium/search.php");
selenium.type("xpath=//input[@name='q']", "Selenium-RC");
selenium.click("xpath=//input[@name='btnG' and @type='submit']");
selenium.waitForPageToLoad("10000");
```

```
@Test
public void typeInASearchTermAndCheckPageTitleHasSearchTermInIt(){
    Selenium selenium = new DefaultSelenium(
            "localhost", 4444,
            "*firefox", "http://www.compendiumdev.co.uk");
    selenium.start();
    selenium.open("/selenium/search.php");
    selenium.type("xpath=//input[@name='q']", "Selenium-RC");
    selenium.click("xpath=//input[@name='btnG' and @type='submit']");
    selenium.waitForPageToLoad("30000");

    String pageTitle = selenium.getTitle();
    assertTrue("Page Title does not contain Selenium-RC search term: " +

    selenium.close();
    selenium.stop();
}
```

Figure 12.1: Highlight code ready to refactor it into a new method

Right click and from the pop-up menu choose Refactor \ Extract Method...

Figure 12.2: Extract Method in the Refactor contextual menu

In the wizard that follows, I enter the method name as startSeleniumAndSearchForSeleniumRC.

Because the source code is repeated across all the tests, Eclipse has identified that it can replace a number of occurrences:

```
Replace 3 occurrences of statements with method
```

This means that Eclipse will amend all the tests to use this new start up method.

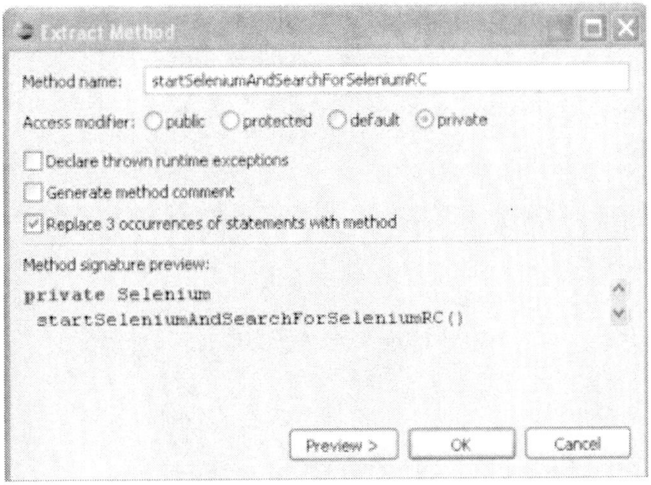

Figure 12.3: The Extract Method Wizard

NOTE:

Amending all instances only works when the code is repeated exactly throughout the class (as would happen if copy and pasted). So sometimes before an extract method refactor, I do minor code edits to get the code the same throughout the source.

I set the method as private, as I only want to use it with the tests of this class at the moment.

After completing this step my test code has reduced in size and I have a new method containing common code:

```
@Test
public void typeInASearchTermAndCheckPageTitleHasSearchTermInIt(){
    Selenium selenium = startSeleniumAndSearchForSeleniumRC();

    String pageTitle = selenium.getTitle();
    assertTrue("Page Title does not contain Selenium-RC search term: " +
        pageTitle,
        pageTitle.contains("Selenium-RC"));

    selenium.close();
    selenium.stop();
}

private Selenium startSeleniumAndSearchForSeleniumRC() {
    Selenium selenium = new DefaultSelenium("localhost", 4444,
            "*firefox", "http://www.compendiumdev.co.uk");
    selenium.start();
    selenium.open("/selenium/search.php");
    selenium.type("xpath=//input[@name='q']", "Selenium-RC");
    selenium.click("xpath=//input[@name='btnG' and @type='submit']");
    selenium.waitForPageToLoad("30000");
```

```
        return selenium;
    }
```

And all the tests now follow this pattern.

12.3 Automatically refactor the tear down code into a new method

We can then do the same thing with the tear down code:

```
    selenium.close();
    selenium.stop();
```

Select this code and refactor it into a new method called `stopSeleniumAndCloseBrowser`.

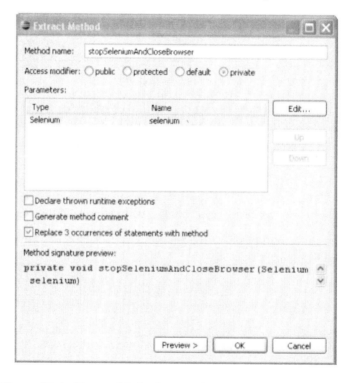

Figure 12.4: Extract Method Wizard with multiple occurrences

Eclipse identifies that, not only can it do this to the other occurrences, but that it needs to create a parameter so that we can pass in the `selenium` object.

This refactoring creates a new method:

```
    private void stopSeleniumAndCloseBrowser(Selenium selenium) {
        selenium.close();
        selenium.stop();
    }
```

And our test now looks much cleaner and more readable:

```
@Test
public void typeInASearchTermAndCheckPageTitleHasSearchTermInIt(){
   Selenium selenium = startSeleniumAndSearchForSeleniumRC();

   String pageTitle = selenium.getTitle();
   assertTrue("Page Title does not contain Selenium-RC search term: " +
      pageTitle,
      pageTitle.contains("Selenium-RC"));

   stopSeleniumAndCloseBrowser(selenium);
}
```

The source code is now much more readable and maintainable.

(See `MySecondSeleniumTests_Refactored.java` in `com.eviltester.seleniumtutorials.chap12` in the downloadable source-code.)

Using some JUnit functionality we can actually do much better than this and create proper setup and tear down code, to remove the repeated code from each of the test methods.

12.4   JUnit @Before and @After

JUnit supports a number of Java annotations that help us do the same thing for the different test automation events that we encounter when running tests.

JUnit has before and after annotations for:

- Method

- Class

A JUnit Method is anything in your code annotated with `@Test`

Any Java method annotated with:

- `@Before` will be run before every JUnit `@Test` method

- `@After` will be run after every JUnit `@Test` method

- `@BeforeClass` will be run once before any methods in that class

- `@AfterClass` will be run once after all methods in the class

12.4.1 Refactoring Plan and Analysis

With our test code looking like the following:

```
@Test
public void typeInASearchTermAndCheckPageTitleHasSearchTermInIt(){
  Selenium selenium = startSeleniumAndSearchForSeleniumRC();

  String pageTitle = selenium.getTitle();
  assertTrue("Page Title does not contain Selenium-RC search term: " +
    pageTitle,
    pageTitle.contains("Selenium-RC"));

  stopSeleniumAndCloseBrowser(selenium);
}
private void stopSeleniumAndCloseBrowser(Selenium selenium) {
  selenium.close();
  selenium.stop();
}
private Selenium startSeleniumAndSearchForSeleniumRC() {
  Selenium selenium = new DefaultSelenium("localhost", 4444,
        "*firefox", "http://www.compendiumdev.co.uk");
  selenium.start();
  selenium.open("/selenium/search.php");
  selenium.type("xpath=//input[@name='q']", "Selenium-RC");
  selenium.click("xpath=//input[@name='btnG' and @type='submit']");
  selenium.waitForPageToLoad("30000");
  return selenium;
}
```

I want to create a method which sets up Selenium and goes to the search engine. This is currently done by the line:

```
Selenium selenium = startSeleniumAndSearchForSeleniumRC();
```

I will move this into a method of its own and annotate it @Before. I also want to annotate stopSeleniumAndCloseBrowser with the @After.

But first, because the stopSeleniumAndCloseBrowser method takes a parameter I will first have to move selenium into a field instead of a variable local to the method.

So my plan is:

- remove the parameter from stopSeleniumAndCloseBrowser

- move setup code into a new method and annotate it with @Before

- remove the setup code from each @Test method

- annotate stopSeleniumAndCloseBrowser with @After

- remove the tear down code from each @Test method

144

NOTE:
A field is a variable at the class level which is accessible by all methods in the class.

12.4.2 Remove parameter from stopSeleniumAndCloseBrowser

Eclipse does not have an automated refactoring for the way we have written this code. So I manually delete the parameter, and I can see from the errors in the source code, what additional changes I need to make.

```
private void stopSeleniumAndCloseBrowser() {
    selenium.close();
    selenium.stop();
}
```

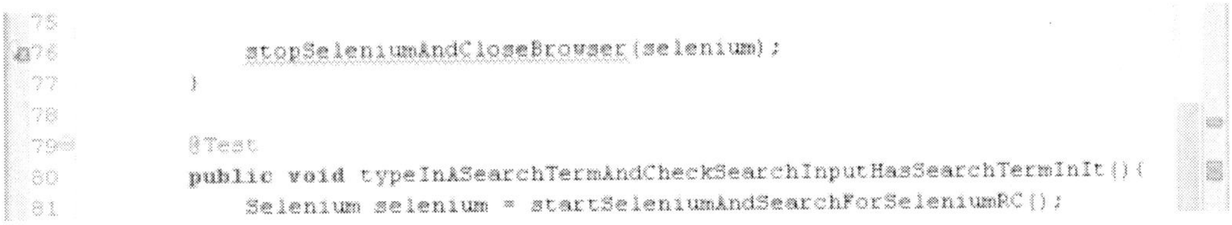

Figure 12.5: Eclipse marks errors in left info bar and right info bar

Errors are highlighted by red crosses on the left border, and by red rectangles on the right border.

First I will remove the selenium parameter from each of the `stopSeleniumAndCloseBrowser` calls.

This clears up many of the errors.

But the errors against `selenium.close();` and `selenium.stop();` remind me that I still have to introduce the field.

I can add this field by clicking the mouse on the red error cross next to the `selenium.close();` statement and selecting `Create field 'selenium'` from the pop-up menu.

12.4.3 Move setup code into a new method

Once I do this. Eclipse reports no errors against the source code. But at this point we have introduced an error. You can see the error in the following source code snippet:

```
private Selenium selenium;
private Selenium startSeleniumAndSearchForSeleniumRC() {
    Selenium selenium = new DefaultSelenium("localhost", 4444, "*firefox",
            "http://www.compendiumdev.co.uk");
    selenium.start();
```

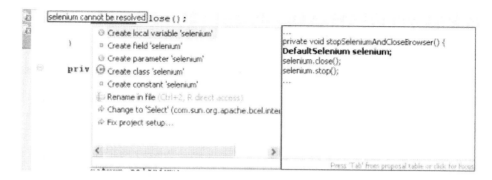

Figure 12.6: Automatically fix errors through Eclipse context menus

```
selenium.open("/selenium/search.php");
selenium.type("xpath=//input[@name='q']", "Selenium-RC");
selenium.click("xpath=//input[@name='btnG' and @type='submit']");
selenium.waitForPageToLoad("30000");
return selenium;
}
```

Our last fix introduced the field which you can see at the top of the source code snippet `private Selenium selenium;`. This field variable can be used by any of the methods in the class.

But we still have the local declaration of selenium in the test methods e.g.:

```
Selenium selenium = startSeleniumAndSearchForSeleniumRC();
```

If I don't amend this line then each method will create a local instance of the selenium variable and negate the effect of trying to move the test setup into an `@Before` method.

I will fix this by creating a method called `automateTestSetup` which I annotate with `@Before`.

```
@Before
public void automateTestSetup(){
  selenium = startSeleniumAndSearchForSeleniumRC();
}
```

12.4.4   Remove the setup code from each @Test method

Now our source code has no displayed errors, but we haven't finished fixing the source code yet. We still have to remove the repeated code from each of the `@Test` methods.

So delete all the `Selenium selenium = startSeleniumAndSearchForSeleniumRC();` lines from each of the `@Test` methods.

I also need to amend the `startSeleniumAndSearchForSeleniumRC` method to use the class variable:

I do this by removing the declaration and leaving the assignment.

146

```
selenium = new DefaultSelenium("localhost", 4444, "*firefox",
              "http://www.compendiumdev.co.uk");
```

Since I've done so many changes. I'm just going to run the tests and make sure they still run.

All of my tests still run.

I get more nervous about manual refactoring than I do about automated refactoring so I needed to run the tests to convince me that I hadn't broken anything before doing anything else.

12.4.5   Annotate stopSeleniumAndCloseBrowser with @After

I add `@After` to `stopSeleniumAndCloseBrowser`.

```
@After
private void stopSeleniumAndCloseBrowser() {
  selenium.close();
  selenium.stop();
}
```

12.4.6   Remove the tear down code from each @Test method

All that remains now is to remove the `stopSeleniumAndCloseBrowser();` line from each of the `@Test` methods.

I will do this manually by deleting the line throughout.

And then run the tests to make sure they still run and tidy up after themselves.

Our tests should have failed when we did that, because JUnit expects all `@After` and `@Before` annotated methods to be made public.

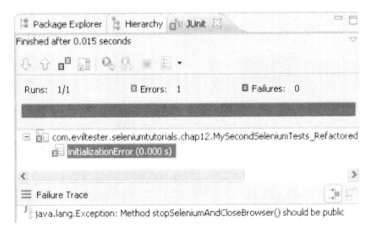

Figure 12.7: JUnit Test Runner showing our error

To fix this, change the declaration of `stopSeleniumAndCloseBrowser` to public.

```
@After
public void stopSeleniumAndCloseBrowser() {
  selenium.close();
  selenium.stop();
}
```

Running the tests should now result in them all passing.

12.4.7   The Refactored Code

```
package com.eviltester.seleniumtutorials;
import static org.junit.Assert.*;
import org.junit.*;
import com.thoughtworks.selenium.*;

public class MySecondSeleniumTests{

  private Selenium selenium;

  @Before
  public void automateTestSetup(){
    selenium = startSeleniumAndSearchForSeleniumRC();
  }

  private Selenium startSeleniumAndSearchForSeleniumRC() {
    selenium = new DefaultSelenium("localhost", 4444, "*firefox",
          "http://www.compendiumdev.co.uk");
    selenium.start();
    selenium.open("/selenium/search.php");
    selenium.type("xpath=//input[@name='q']", "Selenium-RC");
    selenium.click("xpath=//input[@name='btnG' and @type='submit']");
    selenium.waitForPageToLoad("30000");
    return selenium;
  }

  @Test
  public void typeInASearchTermAndAssertThatHomePageTextIsPresent(){
    assertTrue(selenium.isTextPresent(
      "Selenium Remote-Control Selenium RC comes in two parts." +
      " A server which automatically"));
    assertTrue(selenium.isTextPresent(
      "launches and kills browsers, and acts as" +
      " a HTTP proxy for web requests from them."));
  }

  @Test
  public void typeInASearchTermAndAssertThatHomePageURLExistsWithFewerXpath()
      {
    // create a new variable called matchingCountTotal to calculate
    // the total number of times our XPath matches, initially setting
    // it to 0
    int matchingCountTotal = 0;

    // call getXpathCount with our xpath for the url and
    // add the intValue version to the total
    matchingCountTotal += selenium.getXpathCount(
```

```
      "//a[starts-with(@href,'http://selenium-rc.seleniumhq.org')]").intValue()
          ;

      matchingCountTotal += selenium.getXpathCount(
      "//a[starts-with(@href,'http://seleniumhq.org/projects/remote-control')]"
          ).intValue();

      assertTrue("No homepage URL found",matchingCountTotal>0);
  }

  @After
  public void stopSeleniumAndCloseBrowser() {
    selenium.close();
    selenium.stop();
  }

  @Test
  public void typeInASearchTermAndCheckPageTitleHasSearchTermInIt(){
    String pageTitle = selenium.getTitle();
    assertTrue("Page Title does not contain Selenium-RC search term: " +
        pageTitle, pageTitle.contains("Selenium-RC"));
  }

  @Test
  public void typeInASearchTermAndCheckSearchInputHasSearchTermInIt(){
    String searchTerm = selenium.getValue(
        "xpath=//input[@name='q' and @title='Search']");
    assertTrue("Search Input does not contain Selenium-RC : " + searchTerm,
      searchTerm.equals("Selenium-RC"));
  }
}
```

The refactored code has the following advantages:

- Smaller

- Less code duplication

- `@Test` methods concentrate on the test and not the environment configuration

We have less code duplication because our setup and tear down code is in a single place. This makes the tests easier to maintain since we only have to make changes in a single place.

Having the `@Test` methods concentrate only on what needs to be done for the test makes them easier to read, understand and maintain.

A common practice in automated testing is to have a setup and tear down process. JUnit supports us in this by allowing us to do setup and tear down at multiple levels. We are currently only using the method level.

12.4.8 @BeforeClass & @AfterClass

`@Before`, and `@After` execute the methods before and after every test method. This means that we start and stop the server and the browser before every test. This makes the test execution slower than we need.

149

We can use the `@BeforeClass` and `@AfterClass` methods so that we start and stop the server once for the entire set of test methods in the class.

Unfortunately using the `@BeforeClass` and `@AfterClass` annotations requires a few more amendments to our code. We can't simply replace `@Before` with `@BeforeClass` and `@After` with `@AfterClass`.

In order to make the methods accessible at the class level the methods have to become static.

So make the following changes:

- The declaration of the selenium variable must become static

```
static Selenium selenium;
```

- The `automateTestSetup` method must become static

```
@BeforeClass
static public void automateTestSetup(){
  selenium = startSeleniumAndSearchForSeleniumRC();
}
```

- The `stopSeleniumAndCloseBrowser` must also become static

```
@AfterClass
static public void stopSeleniumAndCloseBrowser() {
  selenium.close();
  selenium.stop();
}
```

- And lastly the private method `startSeleniumAndSearchForSeleniumRC` must also be declared as static

```
static private Selenium startSeleniumAndSearchForSeleniumRC() {
  selenium = new DefaultSelenium("localhost", 4444, "*firefox",
      "http://www.compendiumdev.co.uk");
  selenium.start();
  selenium.open("/selenium/search.php");
  selenium.type("xpath=//input[@name='q']", "Selenium-RC");
  selenium.click("xpath=//input[@name='btnG' and @type='submit']");
  selenium.waitForPageToLoad("30000");
  return selenium;
}
```

After making these changes you should see a massive execution speed improvement to the tests.

This speed improvement comes because we only start up the browser once for all the tests, and only connect to Selenium server once for all the tests. The tests themselves have always run quickly, it was only the environmental setup that caused them to run slowly.

---

[1]http://java.sun.com/docs/books/tutorial/java/javaOO/classvars.html

NOTE:

Static means that no matter how many objects of a class are a created, they all share the same variables or methods marked as static. i.e. If I create a method as static then each call to the method on any object, calls the same code. If I update a static variable, then it will be updated on all objects of the class.

Static fields and methods are common to all object instances of a class. For more information on static you might wish to read the official documentation.

http://unow.be/rc/classvars[1]

Our refactored code

```
package com.eviltester.seleniumtutorials;
import static org.junit.Assert.*;
import org.junit.*;
import com.thoughtworks.selenium.*;

public class MySecondSeleniumTests {

  static Selenium selenium;

  @BeforeClass
  static public void automateTestSetup(){
    selenium = startSeleniumAndSearchForSeleniumRC();
  }

  static private Selenium startSeleniumAndSearchForSeleniumRC() {
    selenium = new DefaultSelenium("localhost", 4444, "*firefox",
          "http://www.compendiumdev.co.uk");
    selenium.start();
    selenium.open("/selenium/search.php");
    selenium.type("xpath=//input[@name='q']", "Selenium-RC");
    selenium.click("xpath=//input[@name='btnG' and @type='submit']");
    selenium.waitForPageToLoad("30000");
    return selenium;
  }

  @Test
  public void typeInASearchTermAndAssertThatHomePageTextIsPresent(){
    assertTrue(selenium.isTextPresent(
      "Selenium Remote-Control Selenium RC comes in two parts." +
      " A server which automatically"));
    assertTrue(selenium.isTextPresent(
      "launches and kills browsers, and acts as" +
      " a HTTP proxy for web requests from them."));
  }

  @Test
  public void typeInASearchTermAndAssertThatHomePageURLExistsWithFewerXpath()
      {
    // create a new variable called matchingCountTotal to calculate
    // the total number of times our xpath matches, initially setting
    // it to 0
```

151

```
    int matchingCountTotal = 0;

    // call getXpathCount with our xpath for the url and
    // add the intValue version to the total
    matchingCountTotal += selenium.getXpathCount(
    "//a[starts-with(@href,'http://selenium-rc.seleniumhq.org')]").intValue()
        ;
    matchingCountTotal += selenium.getXpathCount(
    "//a[starts-with(@href,'http://seleniumhq.org/projects/remote-control')]"
        ).intValue();

    assertTrue("No homepage URL found",matchingCountTotal>0);
}

@AfterClass
static public void stopSeleniumAndCloseBrowser() {
    selenium.close();
    selenium.stop();
}

@Test
public void typeInASearchTermAndCheckPageTitleHasSearchTermInIt(){
    String pageTitle = selenium.getTitle();
    assertTrue("Page Title does not contain Selenium-RC search term: " +
        pageTitle, pageTitle.contains("Selenium-RC"));
}

@Test
public void typeInASearchTermAndCheckSearchInputHasSearchTermInIt(){
    String searchTerm = selenium.getValue(
        "xpath=//input[@name='q' and @title='Search']");
    assertTrue("Search Input does not contain Selenium-RC : " + searchTerm,
        searchTerm.equals("Selenium-RC"));
}
}
```

NOTE:
You can find this code in the downloadable source-code packages
com.eviltester.seleniumtutorials.chap12 in the class MySecondSeleni-
umTests_Refactored_BeforeClass_AfterClass

12.5 Automatically create JUnit Test Structure

Eclipse has a useful wizard to create a basic test skeleton: `File \ New \ JUnit Test Case`

The `New JUnit Test Case` Wizard will display.

We would need to overwrite the name of the test to rename it. By Default the wizard uses
the last value you put in and appends `Test` to it.

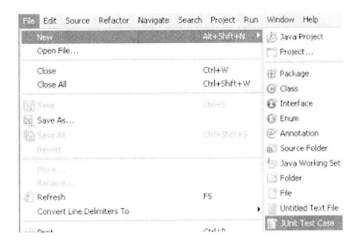

Figure 12.8: Start the New JUnit Test Case Wizard

JUnit Test Case

Select the name of the new JUnit test case. You have the options to specify the class under test and on the next page, to select methods to be tested.

○ New JUnit 3 test   ◉ New JUnit 4 test

Source folder: InitialSeleniumTests/src

Package: com.eviltester.seleniumtutorials

Name: AutomaticallyGeneratedTestCaseClass

Superclass: java.lang.Object

Which method stubs would you like to create?
☑ setUpBeforeClass()   ☑ tearDownAfterClass()
☑ setUp()   ☑ tearDown()
☐ constructor

Do you want to add comments? (Configure templates and default value here)
☐ Generate comments

Class under test: com.eviltester.seleniumtutorials.FirstStepsWithAutomation_AutomateGoogle_RefactoredClassLevelTest

Figure 12.9: The JUnit Test Case Wizard Dialog

You can amend the package and source folder to organise your tests, and choose the version of JUnit you want to create a skeleton for.

You would then choose which method stubs to create:

- `setUpBeforeClass()` creates a static method with that name with the `@BeforeClass` annotation

- `tearDownAfterClass()` creates a static method annotated with `@AfterClass`, this can only be selected if you have chosen to create a `setUpBeforeClass()` method

153

- `setUp()` creates a method annotated with `@Before`. It is called `setUp` because this is the naming convention used when extending the JUnit `TestCase` class, you can rename it.

- `tearDown()` creates a method named `tearDown` annotated with `@After`. Again you can rename it to anything you choose.

- You could choose to generate comments but these don't add much value and you are better off adding your own comments later if you need them.

The generated code:

```
package com.eviltester.seleniumtutorials;

import org.junit.After;
import org.junit.AfterClass;
import org.junit.Before;
import org.junit.BeforeClass;

public class AutomaticallyGeneratedTestCaseClass {

    @BeforeClass
    public static void setUpBeforeClass() throws Exception {
    }

    @AfterClass
    public static void tearDownAfterClass() throws Exception {
    }

    @Before
    public void setUp() throws Exception {
    }

    @After
    public void tearDown() throws Exception {
    }
}
```

You then need to add your references to Selenium add your code. Using this approach can prove a time saver. I usually start with the `@Before` and `@After` annotated setUp and tearDown methods and manually refactor to `@BeforeClass` and `@AfterClass` methods later.

12.6   Summary

You have learned the following: Java Class Variables vs Local Variables, Automatic Refactoring in Eclipse. A number of basic principles: Run tests after refactoring, Separate setup and tear down from tests. The JUnit annotations: `@Before` and `@After`, `@BeforeClass` and `@AfterClass`. Also the New JUnit Test Case wizard

You might want to flip back through the pages and compare the various code snippets to see how much more understandable, and easier to read, the code is now compared to our original version.

Chapter 13

How to upgrade Selenium

Occasionally you will encounter issues with Selenium that have been fixed in the newest version. So how do you upgrade your server?

13.1   First Download the New Version

Follow the earlier instructions to download and extract the Selenium distribution from http://unow.be/rc/getSelenium[1].

You will have to draw hints from the download page regarding what you need to download. Prior to version 2.0, Selenium was distributed as a single archive file that you downloaded. At the time of writing, with Selenium 2.0. There are two files to download.

- the server,

- the associated client.

This may change in the future, so learn to read the download page carefully.

13.2   Configure Eclipse Project

Then configure your project in Eclipse to use the new `.jar` files.

- Select the project in the Package Explorer and then either press `Alt+Enter` or select `Properties` from the `Project` menu.

- Change the referenced libraries on the Java Build Path.

    1. Select Java Build Path on the properties tree
    2. Select Libraries from the tab
    3. Remove the current Selenium .jar libraries
    4. Select `[Add External Jars...]` and add the new the jar files associated with the distribution from the new path where you unarchived the new version

---

[1]http://seleniumhq.org/download/

Figure 13.1: Amend the project properties

13.3   Remember to re-attach the source

In one of your tests, select one of the selenium commands and press F3, you should be prompted to re-attach the source. Navigate to the .jar file containing the source and re-attach it as you did previously.

Chapter 14

Basic HTML Theory

This chapter will provide you with a basic understanding of HTML. Just enough to cover the basic requirements for writing Selenium tests.

If you visit a web page in your browser, and then view source on that page. You will see that an HTML page has a very simple structure.

Figure 14.1: A very simple HTML page

Open http://www.compendiumdev.co.uk/selenium/basic_web_page.html in a browser and view the source code and you will see a very simple set of markup.

```
<!DOCTYPE html PUBLIC "-//W3C//DTD XHTML 1.0 Strict//EN"
    "http://www.w3.org/TR/xhtml1/DTD/xhtml1-strict.dtd">
<html>
  <head>
    <title>Basic Web Page Title</title>
  </head>
  <body>
        <p id="para1">A paragraph of text</p>
    <p id="para2">Another paragraph of text</p>
  </body>
</html>
```

14.1   Page Structure

An HTML page has a very simple structure.

- A doctype to help the browser identify what to do with the file

- an `<html>` block which contains the page code

– a `<head>` section

– a `<body>` section

14.2   Elements & Tags

HTML consists of nested elements. Elements are represented by an opening tag: e.g. `<p>`, followed by the corresponding closing tag `</p>`.

In a well formed XHTML document each opening tag has a corresponding closing tag. Some older doctypes allow you to leave off the closing tag and let the browser try and work out where an element finishes.

Some elements do not have any content, so don't have an open and close tag, they are self contained e.g. `<br />`.

Because elements are nested, an HTML document can be viewed as a tree. This allows XPath to be used to traverse it.

14.3   Attributes

Elements can have attributes e.g. The `id` in `<p id="para1">`

Attributes help to specify display styles, code, and in the case of `id` - a unique identifier for the element in the document.

14.4   Expanded

Just to be clear, in the line:

```
<p id="para1">A paragraph of text</p>
```

- The paragraph element is: `<p id="para1">A paragraph of text</p>`

- The paragraph element content (or text) is: `A paragraph of text`

- The tags are: `<p>` `</p>`

- The attribute is: `id`

- The attribute value is: `para1`

158

Chapter 15

Basic XPath Theory

This chapter will provide you with a basic understanding of XPath. Just enough to cover the basic requirements for writing Selenium tests.

XPath is the XML Path Language. Since all HTML, once loaded into a browser, becomes well structured and can be viewed as an XML tree, we can use XPath to traverse it.

XPath is a full programming language so you can perform calculations (e.g. `last()-1`), and use boolean operations (e.g. `or`, `and`).

NOTE:
To help follow this section you might want to visit the web page:
http://compendiumdev.co.uk/selenium/basic_web_page.html
With the page loaded, use the Firebug plugin FirePath to try out the XPath statements listed.

I'll include the listing of the XHTML for the basic_web_page.html here so you can follow along:

```
<!DOCTYPE html PUBLIC "-//W3C//DTD XHTML 1.0 Strict//EN"
            "http://www.w3.org/TR/xhtml1/DTD/xhtml1-strict.dtd">
<html>
        <head>
                <title>Basic Web Page Title</title>
        </head>
        <body>
            <p id="para1" class="main">A paragraph of text</p>
            <p id="para2" class="sub">Another paragraph of text</p>
        </body>
</html>
```

15.1   XPath Expressions

XPath expressions select ''nodes'' or ''node-sets'' from an XML document.

e.g. The XPath expression `//p` would select the following node-set from the example in the ''Basic HTML Theory'' section:

```
<p class="main" id="para1">A paragraph of text</p>
<p class="sub" id="para2">Another paragraph of text</p>
```

15.2   Node Types

XPath has different types of nodes. In the example XHTML these are:

- Document node (the root of the XML tree): `<html>`

- Element node e.g.:

    - `<head><title>Basic Web Page Title</title></head>`
    - `<title>Basic Web Page Title</title>`
    - `<p id="para1">A paragraph of text</p>`

- Attribute node e.g.

    - `id="para1"`

15.3   Selections

15.3.1   Start from root

Start selection from the document node with `/`, this allows you to create absolute path expressions e.g.

- `/html/body/p`

Matches all the paragraph element nodes.

```
assertEquals(2,selenium.getXpathCount("/html/body/p"));
```

15.3.2   Start from Anywhere

Start selection matching anywhere in the document with `//`, this allows you to create relative path expressions. e.g.

- `//p`

Matches all paragraph element nodes.

```
assertEquals(2,selenium.getXpathCount("//p"));
```

15.3.3   By Element Attributes

Select attribute elements with @ followed by an attribute name. e.g.

- `//@id`

Would select all the id attribute nodes.

```
assertEquals(2,selenium.getXpathCount("//@id"));
```

15.4   Predicates

Predicates help make selections more specific and are surrounded by square brackets.

15.4.1   Predicates can be indexes

- `//p[2]`

Matches the second p element node in the node-set

```
assertEquals("Another paragraph of text",selenium.getText("//p[2]"));
```

- `//p[1]`

Matches the first p element node.

```
assertEquals("A paragraph of text",selenium.getText("//p[1]"));
```

15.4.2   Predicates can be attribute selections

- `//p[@id='para1']`

Matches the p element node where the value of the attribute id is para1

```
assertEquals("A paragraph of text", selenium.getText("//p[@id='para1']"));
```

- `//p[@class='main']`

Matches the p element node where the value of the attribute class is main.

```
assertEquals("A paragraph of text",
             selenium.getText("//p[@class='main']"));
```

15.4.3   Predicates can be XPath functions

- `//p[last()]`

Select the last paragraph.

```
assertEquals("Another paragraph of text",selenium.getText("//p[last()]"));
```

15.4.4   Predicates can be comparative statements

- `//p[position()>1]`

This returns all but the first `p` element.

```
assertEquals("Another paragraph of text",
   selenium.getText("//p[position()>1]"));
assertEquals("A paragraph of text",
   selenium.getText("//p[position()>0]"));
```

15.5   Combining Match Queries

You can combine several selections by using `|` e.g.

- `//p | //head`

Match any paragraph element node and also get the `head` element node.

```
assertEquals(3,selenium.getXpathCount("//p | //head"));
```

15.6   Wild Card Matches

You can also use wild cards:

15.6.1   node()

`node()` matches any type of node (document, element, attribute) e.g

- `//node()[@id='para1']`

This matches any node with an `id` of `para1`.

```
assertEquals(1,selenium.getXpathCount("//node()[@id='para1']"));
```

`//node()` matches all the nodes (try it, you may not get the results you expect).

`//body/node()` matches all the nodes in the body (again, try it to see if you get the value you expect).

162

15.6.2 *

Match anything depending on its position with * e.g.

- `@*`

Matches any attribute.

- `//p[@*='para1']`

Would match the first paragraph

```
assertEquals(1,selenium.getXpathCount("//p[@*='para1']"));
```

* can match nodes e.g.

- `//*[@*]`

Matches anything with any attribute

```
assertEquals(2,selenium.getXpathCount("//*[@*]"));
```

- `//*[@id]`

Matches anything with an `id` attribute.

```
assertEquals(2,selenium.getXpathCount("//*[@id]"));
```

- `/html/*`

Matches all children of the document node.

```
assertEquals(2,selenium.getXpathCount("/html/*"));
```

15.7   XPath Functions

Since XPath is actually a programming language it has built in functions which we can
use in our XPath statements. Some common XPath functions are listed below.

15.7.1   contains()

`contains()` allows you to match the value of attributes and elements based on text anywhere in the comparison item e.g.

- `//p[contains(.,'text')]`

Match any paragraph with text in the main paragraph e.g. Both our paragraphs. The . matches the current node, in this case the paragraph text.

```
assertEquals(2,
    selenium.getXpathCount("//p[contains(.,'text')]"));
```

- `//p[contains(.,'Another')]`

Match any paragraph with `Another` in the paragraph text, in our example this would match the second paragraph.

```
assertEquals("Another paragraph of text",
    selenium.getText("//p[contains(.,'Another')]"));
```

- `//p[contains(@id,'1')]`

This would match any paragraph where the `id` had `1` in it, in our example this is the first paragraph

```
assertEquals("A paragraph of text",
    selenium.getText("//p[contains(@id,'1')]"));
```

15.7.2   starts-with()

`starts-with()` allows you to match the value of attributes and elements based on text at the start of the comparison item e.g.

- `//*[starts-with(.,'Basic')]`

Would match any node where the contents of that node start with `Basic`, in our example this would match the title.

```
assertEquals("Basic Web Page Title",
            selenium.getText("//*[starts-with(.,'Basic')]"));
```

- `//*[starts-with(@id,'p')]`

This would match any node where the id name started with `p`, in our example this would match the paragraphs.

```
assertEquals("Basic Web Page Title",
            selenium.getText("//*[starts-with(.,'Basic')]"));
```

15.7.3   Many More

There are many XPath functions available to you, I have just picked a few of the most common ones that I use. I recommend that you visit some of the web sites below to learn more about XPath functions, and experiment with them.

Recommended web sites for function references:

- http://unow.be/rc/w3xpath[1]

- http://unow.be/rc/msxpathref[2]

- http://unow.be/rc/pitstop1[3]

15.8   Boolean Operators

You can setup matches with multiple conditions.

15.8.1   and

- `//p[starts-with(@id,'para') and contains(.,'Another')]`

Find all paragraphs where the `id` starts with `para` and the text contains `Another` i.e. the second paragraph.

```
assertEquals("Another paragraph of text",
        selenium.getText(
        "//p[starts-with(@id,'para') and contains(.,'Another')]"));
```

15.8.2   or

- `//*[@id='para1' or @id='para2']`

Find any node where the `id` is `para1` or the `id` is `para2` i.e. our two paragraphs.

```
assertEquals(2,
    selenium.getXpathCount("//*[@id='para1' or @id='para2']"));
```

---

[1]http://www.w3schools.com/XPath/xpath_functions.asp
[2]http://msdn.microsoft.com/en-us/library/ms256115.aspx
[3]http://www.xmlpitstop.com/ListTutorials/DispContentType/XPath/PageNumber/1.aspx

15.9   XPath optimisation

For our testing we typically want to get the shortest and least brittle XPath statement to identify elements on a page.

Some XPath optimisation strategies that I have used are:

- use the `id`,

- use a combination of attributes to make the XPath more specific,

- start at the first unique element

We have to make a trade off between handling change and false positives. So we want the XPath to return the correct item, but don't want the test to break when simple changes are made to the application under test.

15.9.1   Use the ID

If the element has a known `id` then use that e.g.

- `//*[@id='p2']`

Or you probably want to be even more specific and state the type e.g.

- `//p[@id='p2']`

15.9.2   Use the attributes

If it doesn't have an id, but you can identify it with a combination of attributes then do that. Our example XHTML doesn't have enough nodes to make this clear, but we did this with our initial Search Engine testing.

e.g. `//input[@name='q' and @title='Search']`

15.9.3   Start at the first unique element

If there is really nothing to distinguish the element then look up the Ancestor chain and find the first unique element.

e.g. `//form/table[1]/tbody/tr[1]/td[2]/input[2]`

This approach starts to introduce the chance of false positives since a new input might be added before the one we want, and the test would start using that instead because the input we actually want would now be indexed as `input[3]`.

15.10 Selenium XPath Usage

Selenium uses XPath in locators to identify elements e.g.

```
selenium.isElementPresent("xpath=//p[@id='p1']")
```

Because only XPath locators start with `//` it is possible to write XPath locators without adding `xpath=` on the front. e.g.

```
selenium.isElementPresent("//p[@id='p1']")
```

The specific XPath command `getXpathCount` expects an XPath statement as its argument so you should not use `xpath=` in front of the XPath locator. e.g.

```
selenium.getXpathCount("//p"); //return a count of the p elements
```

This might provide a good reason for not using `xpath=` in any of your locators, but each of us has personal coding styles so you get to choose the style you prefer.

You can combine the XPath statement in the `getAttribute` statement to get specific attributes from elements e.g.

```
assertEquals("p2", selenium.getAttribute("xpath=//p[2]@id"));
assertEquals("p2",selenium.getAttribute("//p[2]@id"));
```

The `@id` (or more specifically @<attribute-name>) means that the statement is not valid XPath but Selenium parses the locator and knows to split off the `@id` on the end before using it.

NOTE:
The source code for tests illustrating these XPath commands can be found in the source code archive described in Chapter 31 and in the package com.eviltester.seleniumtutorials.chap15

167

Chapter 16

Basic CSS Selector Theory

XPath statements can slow down your tests as they evaluate slowly in Internet Explorer. CSS selectors run faster than the equivalent XPath. As you become more experienced with Selenium, you will probably gravitate towards using CSS selectors as your locators.

16.1　FirePath for Firebug

I use ''FirePath'' to help me with my CSS Selectors.

By typing a CSS selector as the input, and pressing the `[Eval]` button. You can see the elements in the page which match the CSS selector - this allows you to check if your CSS selector constrains the search results enough.

16.2　CSS Selector Expressions

In Selenium, you prefix a CSS locator with `css=` e.g. The CSS selector `css=p` would match all the paragraphs in a web page.

NOTE:
When using FirePath, you do not add the `css=` prefix. Only use this in Selenium.

NOTE:
As with the XPath chapter. Most of the examples in this section will use the simple page at http://www.compendiumdev.co.uk/selenium/basic_web_page.html

16.3　Selenium and CSS

Selenium uses CSS in locators to identify elements e.g.

```
selenium.isElementPresent("css=p[id='p1']")
```

You can also use the CSS statement in the `getAttribute` statement to get specific attributes from elements e.g.

```
assertEquals("p2", selenium.getAttribute("css=p.main@id"));
```

Selenium does not provide a `getCSSCount` function, like the `getXPathCount` function, but we can create a simple `getCSSCount` function using the `getEval` command that we will explain later.

```
// based on http://www.ivaturi.org/home/addgetcsscountcommandtoselenium
private int getCSSCount(String aCSSLocator){
  String jsScript =
  "var cssMatches = eval_css(\"%s\", window.document);cssMatches.length;";
  return Integer.parseInt(
    selenium.getEval(String.format(jsScript, aCSSLocator)));
}
```

NOTE:

`String.format` is a particularly useful Java command for avoiding concatenating strings together. `String.format` has the following form:

```
String.format(<a format string>,<list of arguments>);
```

For the format string, you create a string e.g. ''hello there %s, I have %d for sale'' and then add the replacement items for the `%` markers as arguments:

```
String name = "alan";
int amount=10;
String.format("hello there %s, I have %d for sale",name,amount);
```

This allows you to have constants which you can add values into without concatenating lots of variables together.

For more information on String.format visit:

- http://unow.be/rc/stringFormat[1]

If you want to use `getCSSCount` in the short term then add it as a private method in the test class, and you can use it in your tests as follows.

```
@Test
public void someCounts(){
  assertEquals(2,getCSSCount("p"));
  assertEquals(6, getCSSCount("*"));
  assertEquals(2, getCSSCount("body > *"));
  assertEquals(1,getCSSCount("p[id='para1']"));
}
```

---

[1]http://java.sun.com/j2se/1.5.0/docs/api/java/util/Formatter.html#summary

16.4   Selections

CSS selectors, use a hierarchical definition much like XPath to match elements on the page.

16.4.1   Direct Descendents and Absolute Paths

In XPath we use `/` to build a path to an element on the page e.g. `//head/title`
With CSS selectors we use the `>` notation e.g.

* `head > title`

```
assertEquals("Basic Web Page Title", selenium.getText("css=head > title"));
```

16.4.2   Sub Elements and Relative Paths

In XPath we can chain `//` constructs to match any depth in the tree. e.g. `//html//title` to find all `title` elements anywhere below an `html` element
In CSS, add white space between the elements e.g.

* `html title`

```
assertEquals("Basic Web Page Title", selenium.getText("css=html title"));
```

16.5   Attribute and Index matching

16.5.1   Attribute Matching

CSS selectors support a variety of notation for making selections more specific. There is a very close equivalent to the XPath `[]` notation with CSS.

We can use `[]` to match attribute selections in both CSS and XPath e.g.

* `p[id='para1']`

    – selects the `p` element where the value of the `id` attribute is `para1`

```
assertEquals("A paragraph of text", selenium.getText("css=p[id='para1']"));
```

* `p[class='main']`

171

- selects the `p` element where the value of the `class` attribute is `main`

```
assertEquals("A paragraph of text", selenium.getText("css=p[class='main']"));
```

- `p[id]`

    - select all `p` elements with an `id` attribute
    - although this matches more than one element, Selenium will always use the first

```
assertEquals("A paragraph of text", selenium.getText("css=p[id]"));
```

16.5.2 Special attribute selectors

Some of the attributes are so commonly used that they have special notation to help make the CSS selectors shorter:

- ID: for `id`'s we can use the shortcut notation `#`

    - `p#para1`

        * we can use `#` to select an element with a specific `id`
    - `#para1`

        * we can also find something using just the `id`, equivalent to the XPath statement `//*[@id='para1']`
- Class: for class we can use the shortcut notation ".."

    - `p.main`

        * will match the `p` element with the class `main`

16.5.3 Indexed Matching

CSS Selectors also supports Indexed matching. The w3c specification lists all the indexing predicates, these are called pseudo classes in the w3c specification e.g.

- `first-child`, matches the first child of an element e.g.

    - `body *:first-child`

        * matches the first child of the body element

```
assertEquals("A paragraph of text",
    selenium.getText("css=body *:first-child"));
```

172

- `last-child`, matches the last child of an element e.g.

  - `body *:last-child`, matches the last child of the body element

```
assertEquals("Another paragraph of text",
    selenium.getText("css=body *:last-child"));
```

- `nth-child()`, matches the nth child of an element

  - `body *:nth-child(1)`
    * match the first child of any type
  - `body *:nth-child(2)`
    * match the first child of type p
  - `body *:nth-child(2)`
    * match the 2nd child of any type

```
assertEquals("A paragraph of text",
        selenium.getText("css=body *:nth-child(1)"));
assertEquals("A paragraph of text",
        selenium.getText("css=body p:nth-child(1)"));
assertEquals("Another paragraph of text",
        selenium.getText("css=body *:nth-child(2)"));
```

- `nth-last-child()`, matches the nth child of an element counting backwards from the last child

  - `body p:nth-last-child(1)`
    * returns the last child for the body element
  - `body:nth-last-child(2)`
    * returns the second last child for the body element

```
assertEquals("Another paragraph of text",
   selenium.getText("css=body p:nth-last-child(1)"));
assertEquals("A paragraph of text",
   selenium.getText("css=body p:nth-last-child(2)"));
```

The Selenium documentation describes support for all css1, css2 and css3 selectors. With the following exceptions:

- CSS3 Name spaces,

- the following pseudo classes(:nth-of-type, :nth-last-of-type, :first-of-type, :last-of-type, :only-of-type, :visited, :hover, :active, :focus, :indeterminate)

173

- Also no support for the pseudo elements(::first-line, ::first-letter, ::selection, ::before, ::after).

The following blog post by Santiago Ordonez on the Sauce Labs Blog suggests that the css support is improving and different browsers will support additional methods. You may want to experiment with the exceptions as they may work in your environment.

- http://unow.be/rc/jquery-css[2]

16.6   Advanced

16.6.1   Combining Matches

You can combine several selections by chaining them in a comma separated list, the items are not guaranteed to returned in the order listed e.g.

- `p , title`

    - get any paragraph element and the title element

This might be useful as an alternative count mechanism using the `getCSSCount` method listed earlier.

```
assertEquals(3, getCSSCount("title, p"));
assertEquals(3, getCSSCount("p, title"));
```

16.6.2   Wild Card Matches

CSS has a universal selector `*` which matches any element type

- `*` matches all elements in the page

```
assertEquals("Basic Web Page Title A paragraph of text\n Another paragraph of
    text", selenium.getText("css=*"));
```

- `body > *`

    - matches all children under body
    - Since 2 elements get returned, Selenium will use the first one

```
assertEquals("A paragraph of text", selenium.getText("css=body > *"));
```

---

[2]http://saucelabs.com/blog/index.php/2011/01/why-jquery-in-selenium-css-locators-is-the-way-to-go/

16.6.3 Attribute Substring matching

There are three attribute selectors which match substrings in the value of the attribute:

- `^=`

    - matches the prefix
    - `p[class^='ma']`
        * would match any paragraph which has a `class` name starting with `ma`

```
assertEquals("A paragraph of text",
            selenium.getText("css=p[class^='ma']"));
```

- `$=`

    - matches a suffix
    - `p[class$='n']`
        * would match any paragraph with a `class` name ending in `n`

```
assertEquals("A paragraph of text",
            selenium.getText("css=p[class$='n']"));
```

- `*=`

    - matches a substring anywhere in the attribute value
    - `p[class*='u']`
        * would match any paragraph with `u` in the `class` name

```
assertEquals("Another paragraph of text",
            selenium.getText("css=p[class*='u']"));
```

16.6.4 Boolean Operators

You can setup matches with multiple conditions e.g.

- `p[class='main'][id='para1']`

    - match any paragraph with a `class` of `main` and an `id` of `para1`

```
assertEquals("A paragraph of text",
            selenium.getText("css=p[class='main'][id='para1']"));
```

You can negate conditions e.g.

175

- `p:not([class='main'])[id^='para']`

    - would match any paragraph which does not have the `class main` and the `id` starts with `para`

```
assertEquals("Another paragraph of text",
            selenium.getText("css=p:not([class='main'])[id^='para'] "));
```

- `p:not([class='main'])[id^='para']:not([class='sub'])`

    - you can have multiple negations in the selector
    - would match any paragraph which does not have the `class main` and the `id` starts with `para` and does not have the `class sub` - in our example this would match no elements

```
assertEquals(0, getCSSCount(
    "p:not([class='main'])[id^='para']:not([class='sub'])"));
```

16.6.5 Sibling Combinators

As well as traversing a hierarchy with " " and ">" we can also check for siblings before and after a particular element e.g.

- +

    - match an element immediately following another element e.g.
    - p + p
        * match a paragraph that immediately follows another paragraph

```
assertEquals("Another paragraph of text", selenium.getText("css=p + p"));
```

- ~

    - match an element, following, but not immediately following another item

16.7 Useful Links

- http://unow.be/rc/csscompat[3]

    - A page that lists browser compatibility with various CSS selectors.

---

[3]http://kimblim.dk/css-tests/selectors/

- http://unow.be/rc/firepathgcode[4]

  - Homepage for FirePath with links to the support google group and instructions on its use.

- http://unow.be/rc/w3css3[5]

  - The official W3C selectors specification

  - The W3C specification, has an excellent summary of the CSS selection patterns

- http://unow.be/rc/css-vs-xpath[6]

  - A Sauce Labs blog post and video on speed of css versus XPath. Blog post contains reference to an XPath to css conversion script.

NOTE:
The source code for tests illustrating these CSS examples can be found in the source code archive described in Chapter 31 and in the package com.eviltester.seleniumtutorials.chap16

---

[4]http://code.google.com/p/firepath/
[5]http://www.w3.org/TR/css3-selectors/
[6]http://saucelabs.com/blog/index.php/2011/05/why-css-locators-are-the-way-to-go-vs-xpath/

Chapter 17

Learning The Selenium API

Now that you have learned the basics of the JUnit test framework, Eclipse and simple Java. It is time to start learning the Selenium API.

Selenium has a very simple and unstructured API. Basically a long list of methods on the Selenium object. This makes the API large and unwieldy, but it also makes it very simple for beginners which is one reason why you don't need to know much Java to get started.

The most up to date documentation for the API is found in the Selenium source code, and since it is added as JavaDoc comments it will appear in Eclipse as the comments in the code completion documentation.

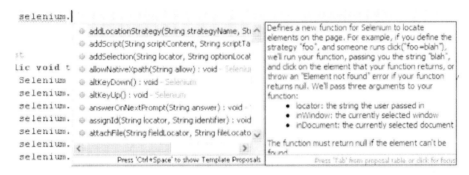

Figure 17.1: JavaDoc displayed as code completion contextual help

In the following few chapters we will build some familiarity with the API methods by using them to complete common tasks that you will encounter when testing web sites.

17.1 Tips for Learning

We have detailed sections to help you learn but the following tips can help you learn faster, and boost your learning in these sections:

- Associate the Selenium source code with your project to benefit from code completion documentation.

- Explore the methods available on the Selenium objects by using ctrl+space code completion.

- Read through the Selenium Source code. Independently of the code completion, this can be daunting to start with, but you will learn Selenium capabilities and see an example of a large java project.

179

- Read the official documentation. This guide is intended to complement the official documentation. It may cover some details that this text does not.

Chapter 18

Testing HTML Forms

When testing websites we often have to input data which we send to the server.

This is typically done by using POST commands initiated from Forms.

To help I have created a simple form on the web at http://www.compendiumdev.co.uk/ selenium/basic_html_form.html

This contains all the common HTML Form Elements so we can manipulate them in a safe and simple environment.

Figure 18.1: An HTML form

18.1   An HTML Form

You can recognise an HTML form in the source code for a web page by looking for a form element.

```
<form name="HTMLFormElements" action= "http://www.compendiumdev.co.uk/
    selenium/form_processor.php"
    method="post" id="HTMLFormElements">
```

Forms have the following child elements which capture the input for the form:

- Single Line Text

```
<input type="text" name="username" size="15" />
```

- Passwords

```
<input type="password" name="password" size="15" />
```

- Multi-line text

```
<textarea cols="40" name="comments" rows="6">
```

- Files

```
<input type="file" name="filename" size="35" />
```

- Hidden Fields

```
<input type="hidden" name="hiddenField" value="Hidden Field Value" />
```

- Check Box Items

```
<input type="checkbox" name="checkboxes[]" value="cb1" />
```

- Radio Buttons

```
<input type="radio" name="radioval" value="rd1" />
```

- Multi-Select Items

```
<select multiple="multiple" name="multipleselect" size="4">
    <option value="ms1">
        Selection Item 1
    </option>
    <option value="ms2">
        Selection Item 2
    </option>
</select>
```

- Dropdown selection items

```
<select name="dropdown">
    <option value="dd1">
            Drop Down Item 1
        </option>
        <option value="dd2">
            Drop Down Item 2
        </option>
</select>
```

- Submit Button

```
<input type="submit" name="submitbutton" value="submit" />
```

We need to learn how to handle all of these form elements with Selenium to test forms effectively.

18.2   Submit a Form with Default Values

The easiest way of learning how to do something simple in Selenium is to record it through the IDE. So we will use the IDE to visit the web form and submit it.

Use Firefox to visit http://www.compendiumdev.co.uk/selenium/basic_html_form.html

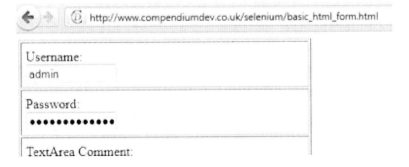

Figure 18.2: The URL to access an HTML form you can use for learning

Start up the Selenium IDE.

Figure 18.3: Submit Button

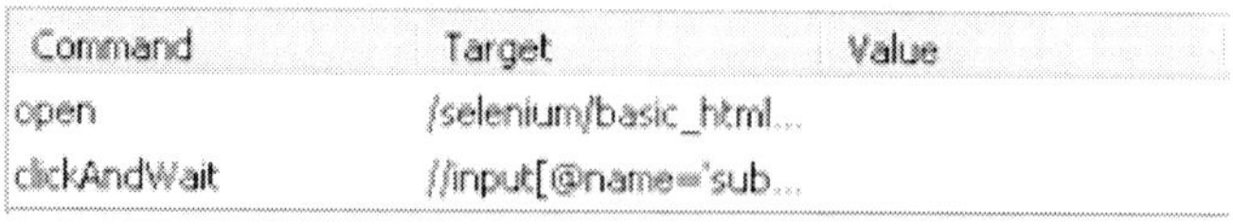

Command	Target	Value
open	/selenium/basic_html...	
clickAndWait	//input[@name='sub...	

Figure 18.4: A simple Selenese Script

After making sure that the IDE is recording, click the `[Submit]` button on the Form.

You should now see the IDE showing a simple Selenese Script.

Exporting the test to a text file, named `testUntitled` as you did before.

Now, use `File \ New \ JUnit Test Case` in Eclipse to create a new JUnit Test Case called `HTML_form_tests`. Automatically generate the `setUpBeforeClass`, `tearDownAfterClass` and `setUp` methods.

NOTE:
I changed the package so that these tests were stored in `com.eviltester.seleniumtutorials.chap18` as this will help you locate the tests in the downloadable source code (as covered in Appendix "Playing along at home")

Copy in only the `@Test` annotated `testUntitled()` method with the test details in it, to the Eclipse IDE. Rename the test method to:

`test_submit_form_with_default_values`

Before we can run the test, we need to:

- add `import org.junit.Test;`

- create the code in our `@BeforeClass` and `@AfterClass` methods,

- and make references to Selenium

- all our tests will be done on the `basic_html_form.html` so I will move the `selenium.open` statement into the `@Before` method

- and I know we will be adding asserts so I also add an import for those

```
import static org.junit.Assert.*;
```

To make the test look like this:

```
package com.eviltester.seleniumtutorials.chap18;
import org.junit.AfterClass;
import org.junit.BeforeClass;
import org.junit.Test;
import static org.junit.Assert.*;
import com.thoughtworks.selenium.DefaultSelenium;
import com.thoughtworks.selenium.Selenium;

public class HTML_form_tests {
  private static Selenium selenium;
  @BeforeClass
  public static void setUpBeforeClass() throws Exception {
    selenium = new DefaultSelenium("localhost", 4444,
        "*firefox", "http://www.compendiumdev.co.uk");
    selenium.start();
  }

  @AfterClass
  public static void tearDownAfterClass() throws Exception {
    selenium.close();
    selenium.stop();
  }

  @Before
  public void setUp() throws Exception {
    selenium.open("/selenium/basic_html_form.html");
  }

  @Test
  public void test_submit_form_with_default_values(){
    selenium.click("//input[@name='submitbutton' and @value='submit']");
    selenium.waitForPageToLoad("30000");
  }
}
```

The steps I took to get the code to this point were:

- First add the `private Selenium selenium;` command. When I added this code, Eclipse automatically added in the necessary `import` statements.

- Manually added the code to start selenium in `setUp`.

- Manually added the close and stop calls in `tearDownAfterClass`.

18.2.1 Commands Used

First we had to open the page which we wanted.

Submitting a form requires the use of the click command on the submit button element.

The IDE did a good job of constructing the XPath statement that uniquely identifies the button on our form so there is no need to change that.

Also note that since we expect the click action to open a new page we also use the `waitForPageToLoad` command to pause the test until a new page is loaded.

18.2.2 Submit Form without clicking button

Some forms allow you to submit them without clicking a button, e.g. A search field.

Selenium has the `submit` command for these particular situations. e.g.

```
selenium.submit("//form[@id='HTMLFormElements']");
```

This doesn't work exactly the same way as clicking the button since the name and value of the button will not be part of the request sent to the server.

If you try this on the example application we are using for testing then you will notice that in the results page, text is displayed saying that you did not click the button. So this may prove useful for some applications but it probably should not be your default submit process.

```
@Test
public void test_submit_form_without_clicking_submit(){
    selenium.submit("//form[@id='HTMLFormElements']");
    selenium.waitForPageToLoad("30000");
}
```

18.3   Amend a Text, Password, TextArea or File Field

Useful Commands: `type`, `typeKeys`

18.3.1   Text Fields

We can enter values into a text field using the `type` command. e.g.

```
selenium.type("username", "eviltester");
```

`type` takes a locator (''username'') and a value to type (''eviltester'');

For this form we can use ''username'' as the locator because the source of the input field is:

```
<input type="text" size="15" name="username"/>
```

Selenium is smart enough to use the name attribute to find the element to use. We could also have used a more complicated XPath to achieve the same results e.g.

```
//input[@name="username"]
```

A test which types in a username and submits the form would look like:

```
@Test
public void test_submit_form_with_new_username() throws Exception {
  selenium.type("username","eviltester");
  selenium.click("//input[@name='submitbutton' and @value='submit']");
  selenium.waitForPageToLoad("30000");
}
```

18.3.2   type vs typekeys

Selenium provides us with two commands for typing in data.

`type`, simulates the typing of values into the field.

`typekeys`, triggers the `keyDown`, `keyPress`, and `keyUp` events for each character that it inputs. This can be useful when entering data into javaScript enabled fields.

For most forms you will get by with the `type` command.

18.3.3   Password Fields

Password fields are basically just text fields but the value typed in is not visible to the user.

Use the same `type` or `typekeys` command covered above.

To type "myPassword" in to the password field we would use:

```
selenium.type("password","myPassword");
```

e.g.

```
@Test
public void test_submit_form_with_new_password(){
  selenium.type("password","myPassword");
  selenium.click("//input[@name='submitbutton' and @value='submit']");
  selenium.waitForPageToLoad("30000");
}
```

18.3.4   TextArea Fields

TextArea fields are essentially big text fields so we would use the type command again.

But we will probably want to take advantage of the multi-line nature of the textarea.

To do this we insert a \n into the string we pass to the `type` command. e.g.

```
selenium.type("comments", "a multiline\ncomment\nin the TextArea");
```

This would enter:

```
a multiline
comment
in the TextArea
```

187

NOTE:

In java putting \ into a string does not add \ it sets java up to expect an escape character.

Java escape characters:

\b - backspace

\t - tab

\n - newline

\f - form feed

\r - carriage return

\" - double quote

\' - single quote

\\ - backslash

\uHHHH - unicode escape where HHHH is a hex value encoding

(for more on hex value encoding see http://unow.be/rc/utf8de[1])

Here we are using the Java escape characters.

Example:

```
selenium.type("comments",
              "\\\n\t\"I said, give me your pound sign\"\u00A3");
```

Would type a forward slash, a new line and a tab, and then the string and pound sign.

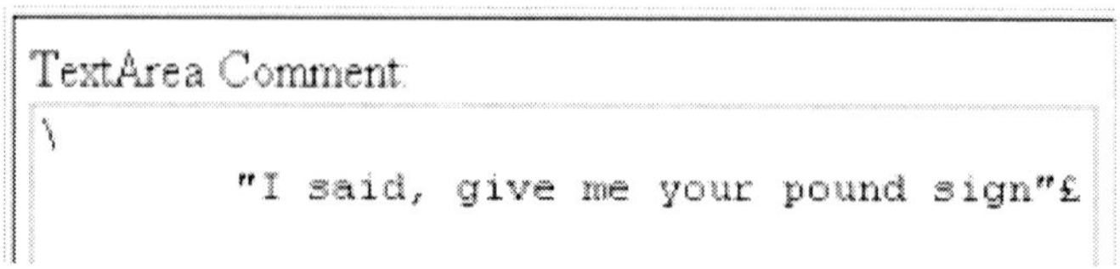

Figure 18.5: Escaped Chars added to a Text Area

You can still use escape characters in a normal text field and they will be passed through in the form, but you won't see the effect of new lines in the text box. e.g.

```
@Test
public void test_submit_form_with_html_escaped_text(){
  selenium.type("comments", "\\\n\t\"I said, give me your pound sign\"\u00A3"
      );
  selenium.click("//input[@name='submitbutton' and @value='submit']");
  selenium.waitForPageToLoad("30000");
}
```

188

NOTE:

File element automation no longer works reliably because browsers are more secure against JavaScript hacks.

If you use the WebDriverBackedSelenium (covered later) then you may have more success with typing into File fields. However during the editing of this book as Selenium moved between versions 2.1.0 and 2.17.0, and Firefox advanced to version 9. I found neither the type method, nor attachFile, to provide a reliable means of automating this HTML form element.

File uploads are still a tricky area of web applications to work with. I tend to use Java HTTP libraries directly and build tests specifically around the file processing, using Selenium to test the GUI elements but not the file uploading. I consider the technicalities behind this too advanced for this introductory book so I leave you with the warning that the File element is likely give you problems.

For this reason you will find the File upload tests annotated with @ignore in the download source code, and I will not cover file attachments and automation beyond this section.

Figure 18.6: Browse Button

18.3.5 File Field

If you have ever used the browse button on IE or Firefox to upload a file then you might wonder how Selenium handles the pop-up dialog box that appears.

On older browsers e.g. IE6 and Firefox below 3.5, the common way of avoiding this was to use the type command to add the full path name of a file into the File field.

```
selenium.type("filename", "C:\\Selenium\\readme.txt");
```

The above statement fills the filename box with: c:\selenium\readme.txt

Note the use of the escape characters to add \ into the string.

```
@Test
public void test_submit_form_with_filename(){
  selenium.type("filename", "C:\\Selenium\\readme.txt");
  selenium.click("//input[@name='submitbutton' and @value='submit']");
  selenium.waitForPageToLoad("30000");
}
```

This is still the recommended approach taken when using the WebDriverBackedSelenium, although it may not work on all browsers.

---

[1]http://www.utf8-chartable.de/

Attachfile command

The `attachFile` command is typically used when your server is not running on the same box as your client, or in a grid scenario. The Attach file command differs because it takes the URL of a file as its argument. i.e.

```
attachFile(locator, url)
```

If I want to use `attachFile` for a local file then I would have to use

```
selenium.attachFile("filename", "file://c:/selenium/readme.txt");
```

NOTE:
I have found the url required changes between releases. I used to be able to use the filename directly e.g. `c:\\selenium\\readme.txt`
Later I had to change this to a `file://` URL. e.g. `file://c:/selenium/readme.txt`.
If you find that the attachFile command does not work then you may need to experiment with different URL formats to find the local file.

Note also that in the file box, the file path is not `c:\selenium\readme.txt` it is a temporary file location e.g.

```
C:\DOCUME~1\Alan\LOCALS~1\Temp\se-567909924.txt
```

We see a temporary file location because the file has had to be transferred from the client, to the server.

Selenium Documentation lists this as only supporting the Firefox `*chrome` browser mode for Selenium, so it would not work in `*iexplore` or `*googlechrome`.

18.4   Amending Checkboxes and Radio Items

Checkboxes and radio boxes use exactly the same commands either:

- `click`

- `check`

- `uncheck`

18.4.1 Click

Differences in behavior with click are only apparent on the browser.

So for a checkbox:

- If selected then `click` on it will unselect it.

- If unselected then `click` on it will select it.

For a radio button:

- `click` will always select it

e.g.

```
selenium.click("//input[@name='checkboxes[]' and @value='cb3']");
selenium.click("//input[@name='radioval' and @value='rd2']");
```

`click` will only raise an exception if it cannot click on the element. i.e. If the element is not found or not visible or not enabled.

In a checkbox group, multiple items can be selected.

In a radio button group, only one radio button can be selected at a time. As soon as you `click` on one of the radio buttons, whichever of the others that was previously selected, will be unselected.

```
@Test
public void test_submit_form_with_click_check_and_radio(){
   selenium.click("//input[@name='checkboxes[]' and @value='cb2']");
   selenium.click("//input[@name='checkboxes[]' and @value='cb3']");
   selenium.click("//input[@name='radioval' and @value='rd3']");
   selenium.click("//input[@name='submitbutton' and @value='submit']");
   selenium.waitForPageToLoad("30000");
}
```

18.4.2 Check

`check` will make sure that the item is checked after the action has run.

In the following scenario where checkbox 3 is selected, and checkbox 2 is not selected.

Figure 18.7: Checkbox 3 Selected

If I run:

191

```
selenium.check("//input[@name='checkboxes[]' and @value='cb2']");
selenium.check("//input[@name='checkboxes[]' and @value='cb3']");
```

Then the end result would be checkbox 3 selected and checkbox 2 selected.

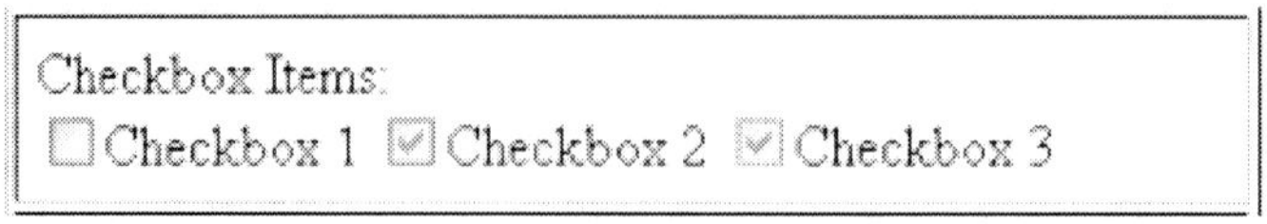

Figure 18.8: Two Checkboxes selected

To contrast this with the `click` method, starting from the same point.

```
selenium.click("//input[@name='checkboxes[]' and @value='cb2']");
selenium.click("//input[@name='checkboxes[]' and @value='cb3']");
```

Had I used `click` then I would have ended up with checkbox 2 selected, but because checkbox 3 was selected prior to the `click`, checkbox 3 would have been unselected.

Figure 18.9: No checkboxes selected

For radio buttons `check` works much the same as `click` since you can't uncheck a radio button by clicking on it, only by selecting another radio button in the group.

18.4.3   Uncheck

`uncheck` guarantees that whatever the status of the element before we issue the `uncheck` command it will be unchecked afterward.

So in the following scenario for checkboxes where checkbox 3 is selected:

Figure 18.10: A Single Checkbox selected

Running

```
selenium.uncheck("//input[@name='checkboxes[]' and @value='cb3']");
selenium.uncheck("//input[@name='checkboxes[]' and @value='cb1']");
```

```
```

Figure 18.11: After deselecting the checkbox

Would result in no checkboxes being selected. Since cb3 would be unchecked and cb1 would remain unchecked.

`uncheck` has a different effect on radio buttons and allows you to bypass normal browser functionality.

Given the situation where Radio button 2 was selected.

Figure 18.12: A single radio button selected

If I were to `click` on any of the items, then that item and only that item would be selected.

If I were to `check` any of the items then that item and only that item would be selected.

If I were to `uncheck` any unselected item then it will remain unselected.

But if I `uncheck` a selected item I can `uncheck` that item and have the situation where none of the radio buttons are selected. Something you can't do normally in the browser. e.g.

```
selenium.uncheck("//input[@name='radioval' and @value='rd2']");
```

The above code would result in the view below:

Figure 18.13: All radio buttons unchecked

18.5   Amending Multiple Select Values

Selenium provides commands for working with multiple selection items.

- `removeSelection` - deselects a selected item

- `removeAllSelections` - deselect every selected item

- `addSelection` - adds an unselected item to the selection

`addSelection` and `removeSelection` take 2 arguments (locator, optionLocator):

- `locator` - a locator for the selection element itself

- `optionLocator` - the item in the selection element

So in on our example page we have

```
<select multiple="multiple" name="multipleselect[]" size="4">
  <option value="ms1">
        Selection Item 1
    </option>
    <option value="ms2">
          Selection Item 2
    </option>
  <!- some stuff removed -->
</select>
```

I can select an item using the following code:

```
selenium.addSelection("multipleselect[]", "label=Selection Item 1");
```

If I `addSelection` an item that is already selected then it remains selected and no exception is thrown.

And I can remove a selection with:

```
selenium.removeSelection("multipleselect[]", "label=Selection Item 4");
```

If I `removeSelection` on an item that is not selected then the item remains unselected and no exception is thrown.

Alternatively I could remove all the selected items:

```
selenium.removeAllSelections("multipleselect[]");
```

I am not limited to using ''label'' as my locator for the option element, I could just as easily have used the ''value''.

```
selenium.addSelection("multipleselect[]", "value=ms2");
```

So If I start with the following situation:

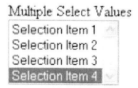

Figure 18.14: A Multiple Selection Item

And run the following test:

```
@Test
public void test_submit_form_with_multiple_select_values(){
  selenium.removeSelection("multipleselect[]", "label=Selection Item 3");
  selenium.addSelection("multipleselect[]", "label=Selection Item 4");
  selenium.addSelection("multipleselect[]", "label=Selection Item 1");
  selenium.removeSelection("multipleselect[]", "label=Selection Item 4");
  selenium.addSelection("multipleselect[]", "value=ms2");
  selenium.click("//input[@name='submitbutton' and @value='submit']");
  selenium.waitForPageToLoad("30000");
}
```

We will end up with the following form submitted through to the application:

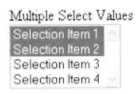

Figure 18.15: Two Items Selected

18.6   Amending Dropdown Elements

Drop down elements have a very similar html syntax to the multi-select box above, but because of the absence of the attribute multiple="multiple". They are displayed as a drop down.

```
<select name="dropdown">
  <option value="dd1">
        Drop Down Item 1
    </option>
    <option value="dd2">
          Drop Down Item 2
    </option>
</select>
```

Figure 18.16: A dropdown item

Because only one item can be selected in a dropdown, Selenium provides us with a single command for manipulating dropdown elements:

- `select`

`select` takes two attributes (selectLocator, optionLocator):

- selectLocator - a locator for the select element

- optionLocator - a locator for the option element

The following code selects ''Drop Down Item 1''.:

```
selenium.select("dropdown", "label=Drop Down Item 1");
```

Dropdown:

Drop Down Item 1

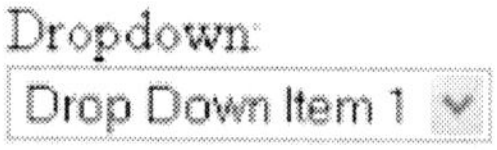

Figure 18.17: Item1 selected in dropdown

As this test code demonstrates:

```
@Test
public void test_submit_form_with_dropdown_values(){
  // by default 3 is selected, so select item 1
  selenium.select("dropdown", "label=Drop Down Item 1");
  selenium.click("//input[@name='submitbutton' and @value='submit']");
  selenium.waitForPageToLoad("30000");
}
```

18.7   Amending Hidden Field Values

Amending a hidden field value is unlikely to be something that you will often want to do in your automated tests. Although it is something that we frequently want to do in our manual tests.

The Selenium API does not have a method designed for this specific task. But it does have a very generic method for executing arbitrary JavaScript. And so, by supplementing our learning of Java with a little JavaScript we can do more things to the web application than we can through Selenium alone.

The command we will use here, since we just want to execute a small snippet of JavaScript is: getEval

getEval allows us to pass in some JavaScript which Selenium will execute in the browser on our behalf and return the value of the script. e.g.

```
selenium.getEval(
    "this.browserbot.findElement(\"name=hiddenField\").value=\"amended value
        \"");
```

To amend a hidden field we will take advantage of the fact that Selenium creates an object in the Browser context called browserbot. So I can use browserbot to find the element I want to amend and then use normal JavaScript DOM manipulation to amend the value of the element. e.g.

```
@Test
public void test_submit_form_with_hidden_field(){
  selenium.getEval(
  "this.browserbot.findElement(\"name=hiddenField\").value=\"amended value\""
    );
  selenium.click("//input[@name='submitbutton' and @value='submit']");
  selenium.waitForPageToLoad("30000");
}
```

18.8 Checking the Values of the Input Fields

Simply issuing the commands to change form values is not good enough when writing automated tests so we need the ability to query the values of the form items. Either:

- before we change them to take action based on the default state of the form, or

- after we change them to make sure that our actions did what we expected.

Selenium provides a number of methods for this. Some very general like `getValue` which we can apply to many of the elements. And others more specific for working with `<select>` items.

18.8.1 Text, Password, TextArea

For all these items we use getValue to give us the value of the elements. e.g.

```
selenium.getValue("username");    // will return the text entered as the
    username
```

As illustrated by the following test. The test types in some values for the text items then uses assertions to check if the value entered is the same as the value that we typed in.

```
@Test
public void test_check_text_entered_values(){
  selenium.type("username","eviltester");
  selenium.type("password","myPassword");
  selenium.type("comments", "simple text");

  assertEquals("username not as entered",
      "eviltester",selenium.getValue("username"));
  assertEquals("password not as entered",
      "myPassword",selenium.getValue("password"));
  assertEquals("comments not as entered",
      "simple text",selenium.getValue("comments"));
}
```

18.8.2   CheckBox & Radio Items

For Checkboxes and Radio Items we have two commands that we can use:

- getValue, which returns the string "off" or "on" depending on the state of the checkbox/radio button.

- isChecked, which returns a boolean true or false depending on the state of the checkbox/radio button. isChecked takes a single parameter locator to identify the item you want to check.

e.g. The following tests use both getValue and isChecked to query the default settings of the checkboxes and radio buttons and then, after selecting them, checks the values again.

```
@Test
public void test_check_checkbox_values(){

    assertEquals("by default checkbox 1 is not selected", "off",
        selenium.getValue("//input[@name='checkboxes[]' and @value='cb1']"));
    assertEquals("by default checkbox 2 is not selected", "off",
        selenium.getValue("//input[@name='checkboxes[]' and @value='cb2']"));
    assertEquals("by default checkbox 3 is selected", "on",
        selenium.getValue("//input[@name='checkboxes[]' and @value='cb3']"));

    selenium.check("//input[@name='checkboxes[]' and @value='cb2']");
    selenium.uncheck("//input[@name='checkboxes[]' and @value='cb3']");

    assertFalse("checkbox 1 is still not selected",
        selenium.isChecked("//input[@name='checkboxes[]' and @value='cb1']"));
    assertTrue("checkbox 2 is now selected",
        selenium.isChecked("//input[@name='checkboxes[]' and @value='cb2']"));
    assertFalse("default checkbox 3 is no longer selected",
        selenium.isChecked("//input[@name='checkboxes[]' and @value='cb3']"));
}

@Test
public void test_check_radio_values(){

    assertEquals("by default radio 1 is not selected", "off",
        selenium.getValue("//input[@name='radioval' and @value='rd1']"));
    assertEquals("by default radio 2 is selected", "on",
        selenium.getValue("//input[@name='radioval' and @value='rd2']"));
    assertEquals("by default radio 3 is not selected", "off",
        selenium.getValue("//input[@name='radioval' and @value='rd3']"));

    selenium.check("//input[@name='radioval' and @value='rd1']");

    assertTrue("radio 1 is now selected",
        selenium.isChecked("//input[@name='radioval' and @value='rd1']"));
    assertFalse("radio 2 is no longer selected",
        selenium.isChecked("//input[@name='radioval' and @value='rd2']"));
    assertFalse("radio 3 is not selected",
        selenium.isChecked("//input[@name='radioval' and @value='rd3']"));
}
```

18.8.3   Multiple Select & DropDown

MultiSelect boxes and DropDowns use the same commands (since they are essentially the same html markup that should not come as too much of a surprise).

- `getValue`

- `isSomethingSelected`

- `getSelectedId`

- `getSelectedIds`

- `getSelectedIndex`

- `getSelectedIndexes`

- `getSelectedLabel`

- `getSelectedLabels`

- `getSelectedValue`

- `getSelectedValues`

- `getSelectOptions`

A quick reminder of the syntax of a Select element

- Multiple Select

```
<select multiple="multiple" name="multipleselect" size="4">
    <option value="ms1">
        Selection Item 1
    </option>
    <option value="ms2">
        Selection Item 2
    </option>
</select>
```

- Dropdown Select

```
<select name="dropdown">
    <option value="dd1">
        Drop Down Item 1
    </option>
    <option value="dd2">
        Drop Down Item 2
    </option>
</select>
```

getValue

`getValue` is useful for drop downs where a single item can be selected, but less so for multi selection items. For single dropdown items `getValue` returns the value attribute of the item selected.

For the default on our test page it is ''dd3'' : e.g.

```
selenium.getValue("dropdown")
```

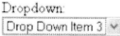

Figure 18.18: Item 3 selected by default

isSomethingSelected

`isSomethingSelected` returns a boolean value which tells us if at least one item has been selected in either the dropdown or the multi-select element. e.g.

```
selenium.isSomethingSelected("dropdown")
```

getSelectedId & getSelectedIds

`getSelectedId` returns the `id` attribute of the selected option in a dropdown.

In the markup of our test page we have no id values so this will return an empty string.

In order to return a value we would need markup like the following:

```
<option id="selectedbydefault" value="dd3" selected="selected">
        Drop Down Item 3
</option>
```

With this markup, if dd3 were selected then `getSelectedId` would return a string with the value `selectedbydefault`.

`getSelectedIds` returns a string array of the `id` attributes of any selected options. If, as is the case in our example page, there are no ids, then you will receive an array with 1 item which is an empty string.

getSelectedIndex & getSelectedIndexes

`getSelectedIndex` returns a string containing the index value of the selected item. e.g.

```
selenium.getSelectedIndex("dropdown")
```

On our example page the third item is selected by default and `getSelectedIndex` returns ''2'' because the Indexes of the option elements start at 0. So ''dd1'' is at index 0.

`getSelectedIndexes` returns a string array containing the index values of the selected items. This can be used on both drop down and multi-selects e.g.

```
System.out.println("dropdown getSelectedIndexes:");
for (String item : selenium.getSelectedIndexes("dropdown")) {
  System.out.println(item);
}

System.out.println("multiselect getSelectedIndexes:");
for (String item : selenium.getSelectedIndexes("multipleselect")) {
  System.out.println(item);
}
```

This would print out:

```
dropdown getSelectedIndexes:
2
multiselect getSelectedIndexes:
3
```

If more items were selected in the multi-select then they would all be printed out.

getSelectedLabel & getSelectedLabels

`getSelectedLabel` returns a string containing the label of selected item (the text displayed in the dropdown). e.g.

```
selenium.getSelectedLabel("dropdown")
```

For our example page this would return ''Drop Down Item 3'' which is the text for the selected option. e.g.

```
<option value="dd3" selected="selected">
     Drop Down Item 3
</option>
```

`getSelectedLabels` returns a string array containing the labels of all the selected items. This can be used on both dropdown and multi-selects e.g.

```
System.out.println("dropdown getSelectedLabels:");
for (String item : selenium.getSelectedLabels("dropdown")) {
  System.out.println(item);
}

System.out.println("multiselect getSelectedLabels:");
for (String item : selenium.getSelectedLabels("multipleselect")) {
  System.out.println(item);
}
```

This would print out:

```
dropdown getSelectedLabels:
Drop Down Item 3
multiselect getSelectedLabels:
Selection Item 4
```

getSelectedValue and getSelectedValues

`getSelectedValue` returns a string containing the value attribute of selected item e.g.

```
selenium.getSelectedValue("dropdown");
```

For our example page this would return ''dd3'', the value attribute in the defining HTML e.g.:

```
<option value="dd3" selected="selected">
  Drop Down Item 3
</option>
```

`getSelectedValues` returns a string array containing the values of all the selected items. This can be used on both drop down and multi-selects e.g.

```
System.out.println("dropdown getSelectedValues:");
for (String item : selenium.getSelectedValues("dropdown")) {
  System.out.println(item); // dd3
}

System.out.println("multiselect getSelectedValues:");
for (String item : selenium.getSelectedValues("multipleselect")) {
  System.out.println(item); // ms4
}
```

This would printout:

```
dropdown getSelectedValues:
dd3
multiselect getSelectedValues:
ms4
```

getSelectOptions

`getSelectOptions` applies to both drop downs and multi select elements, and it returns a string array of all the option labels. e.g.

```
System.out.println("dropdown getSelectOptions:");
for (String item : selenium.getSelectOptions("dropdown")) {
  System.out.println(item); // all the labels of items in the drop down
}

System.out.println("multiselect getSelectOptions:");
for (String item : selenium.getSelectOptions("multipleselect")) {
  System.out.println(item); // all the labels of items in the multi select
}
```

displays:

```
dropdown getSelectOptions:
Drop Down Item 1
Drop Down Item 2
Drop Down Item 3
Drop Down Item 4
Drop Down Item 5
Drop Down Item 6
```

```
multiselect getSelectOptions:
Selection Item 1
Selection Item 2
Selection Item 3
Selection Item 4
```

Put It All Together

To consolidate our learning we can put this all together into an example test.

This test will go to the page and randomly select an item from the drop down, while making sure that it does not reselect the value that was there by default.

Many people don't use random values in tests because they want the tests to be ''repeatable''. For some tests that is important. But sometimes we can increase the data coverage of our tests by using random selections and expose bugs after repeated runs of the test, thereby increasing the bug finding potential of the tests.

This example covers the dropdown, but the multi-select code is much the same.

```
@Test
public void test_randomly_select_value_from_dropdown(){

    // get all options in the dropdown
    String dropDownOptions[] = selenium.getSelectOptions("dropdown");

    // get the index of the currently selected item in the dropdown
    String currentDropDownItem = selenium.getSelectedIndex("dropdown");
    int previouslySelectedIndex =Integer.valueOf(currentDropDownItem);

    // randomly choose an item in the dropdown
    Random generator = new Random(); // requires import java.util.Random to be
        added
    int dropDownIndex = generator.nextInt(dropDownOptions.length);

    // make sure it isn't the same as the current one
    if(dropDownIndex==previouslySelectedIndex){
      // it is the same, so add one
      dropDownIndex++;
      // but this might push it out of bounds so modulus it
      dropDownIndex = dropDownIndex % dropDownOptions.length;
    }

    // select this new one
    selenium.select("dropdown", "label=" + dropDownOptions[dropDownIndex]);

    // check that something is selected
    assertTrue(selenium.isSomethingSelected("dropdown"));

    // check that what we wanted is selected
    assertEquals(dropDownIndex,
      Integer.valueOf(selenium.getSelectedIndex("dropdown")).intValue());

    //double check we didn't select the same thing
    assertTrue(dropDownIndex!=previouslySelectedIndex);
  }
```

A few explanations for readers with less Java experience:

- Since `getSelectedIndex` returns a String, I have to convert it to an Integer to allow us to do the arithmetical comparisons which I do with the `Integer.valueOf` method which converts the String `currentDropDownItem` into an integer

```
Integer.valueOf(currentDropDownItem);
```

- I use the standard Java `Random` class to generate a random number between 0 and the length of the `dropDownOptions` string array. So if the array is 6 in length, then I get a random number from 0 to 5 inclusive. I also have to add a new import statement to the head of my `.java` file: `import java.util.Random;`.

- Since we are making the test random and expect the test to last the lifetime of the application. I have taken the precaution that the default value might change.

  - Currently the default value is 4 out of 6 possible items. But a later change may make ''Drop Down Item 6'' the default, and if that happens then adding 1 in the event of a conflict would create an array index of 6 and push it out of bounds.

  - After adding 1 to it, I use the modulus operator `%`, which acts as a remainder operation.

  - In the event of choosing 6 we do `6%6`. The result of `6%6` is 0 which is the first item in the array.

  - If the random value conflicts but does not push it out of bounds e.g. 4, then the result of `4%6` is 4 , so we get the value we wanted.

Chapter 19

Testing Static HTML

By static HTML I mean the standard HTML markup commands:

e.g. `<h1>` `<p>` `<li>` `<ul>` etc.

Ignoring Forms (which we covered) and ignoring JavaScript, which we will cover later.

Despite the large amount of HTML markup elements (see http://unow.be/rc/HTMLelement[1]). Selenium handles these the same way.

Much of the time when we test applications we check if the page has displayed values that we want to see displayed, and traverse through links on the site. Most of this type of processing is done via static HTML commands and we can get by with a minimal set of Selenium commands and an understanding of XPath or CSS selectors.

In this section we will cover the following commands:

- Most Used

    - click

    - getText

    - getTitle

    - getXPathCount

    - isElementPresent

    - isTextPresent

- Used Less

    - assignid

    - getAttribute

    - getBodyText

    - getHTMLSource

    - highlight

    - goBack

---

[1]http://en.wikipedia.org/wiki/HTML_element

19.1 A Basic Static HTML Test

In this example we will submit a form and check some basic results on the processor page, then navigate back to the form, change it, and check that our changes were passed through.

First I create a new class called `Static_HTML_tests.java`.

In package `com.eviltester.seleniumtutorials.chap19` with the following code:

```java
package com.eviltester.seleniumtutorials.chap19;

import static org.junit.Assert.*;
import org.junit.AfterClass;
import org.junit.Before;
import org.junit.BeforeClass;
import org.junit.Test;
import com.thoughtworks.selenium.DefaultSelenium;
import com.thoughtworks.selenium.Selenium;

public class Static_HTML_tests {

  private static Selenium selenium;

  @BeforeClass
  public static void setUpBeforeClass() throws Exception {
    selenium = new DefaultSelenium("localhost", 4444,
        "*firefox", "http://www.compendiumdev.co.uk");
    selenium.start();
  }

  @AfterClass
  public static void tearDownAfterClass() throws Exception {
    selenium.close();
    selenium.stop();
  }


  @Before
  public void setUp() throws Exception {
    selenium.open("/selenium/basic_html_form.html");
  }

  @Test
  public void submit_form_with_values_and_check_static_html(){
    // add test details in here
  }
}
```

The first thing I do in the test is fill details into the form and then submit it. We have covered this in the previous section so no real explanation is required:

```java
@Test
public void submit_form_with_values_and_check_static_html(){
  selenium.type("username","eviltester");
  selenium.type("password","myPassword");
  selenium.click("//input[@name='submitbutton' and @value='submit']");
  selenium.waitForPageToLoad("30000");
}
```

I want to investigate the resulting page to help me build my test results.

So I will manually goto http://www.compendiumdev.co.uk/selenium/basic_html_form.html, type in the username and password above, and then press the [submit] button.

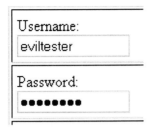

Figure 19.1: Username and Password fields

When I submit the form I see the form processed page which is static HTML generated by the PHP application.

Based on what I can see here I will check:

- that the title is as I expect
- the username I typed in
- the password I typed in
- a comment was added by default
- no filename was entered
- the number of checkboxes was as I expected

Then I will click the Go back to the main form link.

In the form, amend the checkboxes, and add a filename.

Then resubmit the form and check those details.

19.1.1   getTitle - Check the page title

Selenium comes with a command to return the title of the page as a String:

- getTitle

getTitle takes no arguments and I will add it to the test directly in an Assert.

```
assertEquals("Processed Form Details",selenium.getTitle());
```

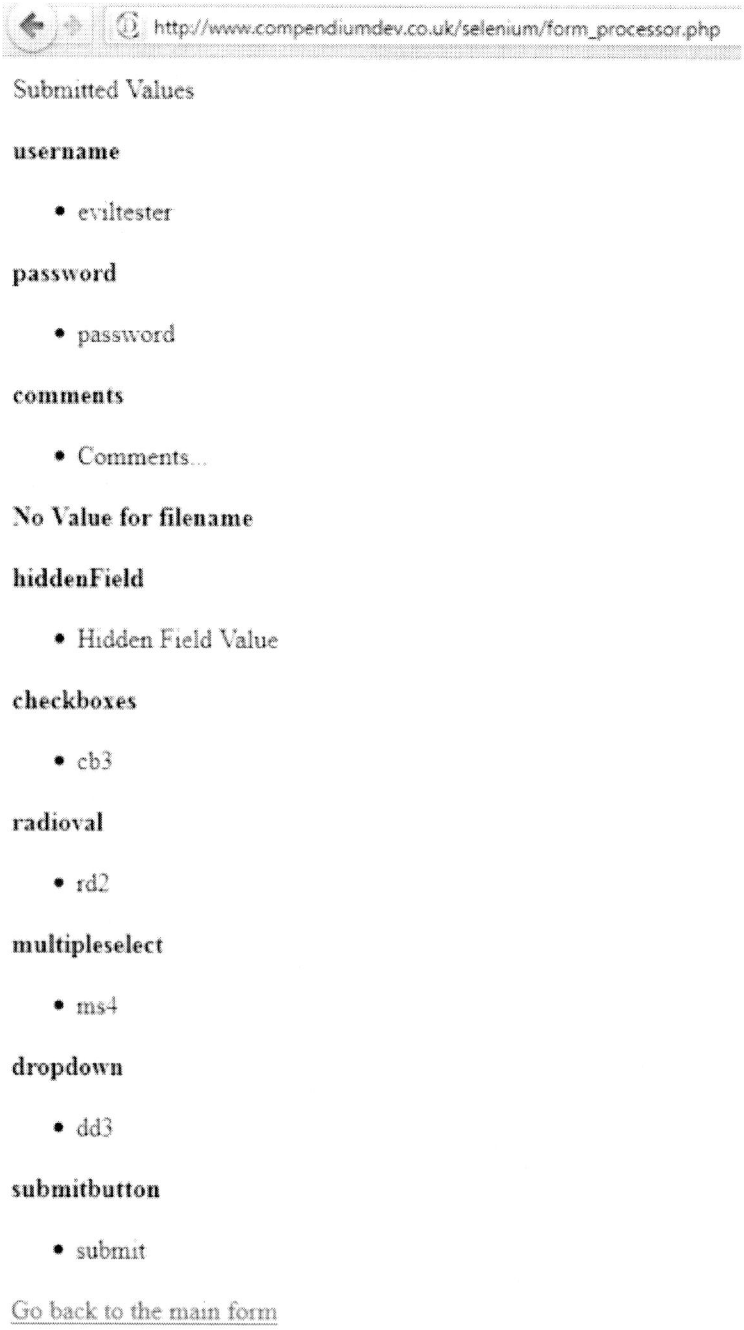

Submitted Values

username

- eviltester

password

- password

comments

- Comments...

No Value for filename

hiddenField

- Hidden Field Value

checkboxes

- cb3

radioval

- rd2

multipleselect

- ms4

dropdown

- dd3

submitbutton

- submit

Go back to the main form

Figure 19.2: Results of form submission

So how did I know what text to add as my expected result text?

Well, I can see it displayed at the top of the browser, so I could type it into the test from there.

Or I can more accurately view the page source and copy it from there.

In Firefox, to view the page source I right click on the page and select `View Page Source`

Figure 19.3: View Source

Then in the resulting source display, select the text in the `<title>` element

Figure 19.4: Source Displayed

By putting the check inside the `AssertEquals`, if the page title is not as I expect then the test will throw an assertion exception and fail.

19.1.2   getText - Check the username

Selenium's `getText` command allows us to retrieve the text for any element.

- `getText(String locator)`

`getText` takes a String as an argument the locator for the element we want to get the text for.

So if we look at the page in Firefox I can right click on the username text and (using the Firebug plugin which we installed) choose the `Inspect Element` contest menu entry to see its details.

I can see that the `<li>` element for the username has an `id` of `_valueusername`.

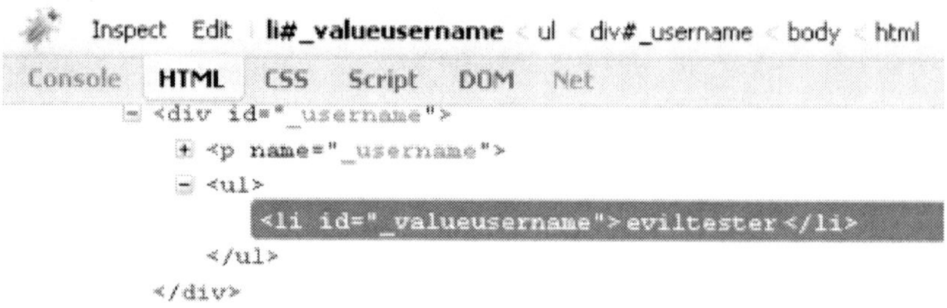

Figure 19.5: Username field inspected

I can use that `id` directly as my locator string. And again I will use this directly within an `Assert` statement.

```
assertEquals("eviltester", selenium.getText("_valueusername"));
```

NOTE:

I can use the `getText` method to access the text of any element. I could have used `getText` instead of `getTitle` (had Selenium not provided that command) by using:

```
selenium.getText("//head/title")
```

If you want to confirm this for yourself, try the following test:

```
@Test
public void getText_equals_getTitle() {
  selenium.open("/selenium/basic_html_form.html");
  assertEquals("HTML Form Elements",selenium.getTitle());
  assertEquals(selenium.getTitle(),selenium.getText("//head/title"));
}
```

19.1.3   isTextPresent - check the heading

Since our example page has the text ''Submitted Values'' at the top, I will do a quick check to make sure that the text is present on the page.

- `isTextPresent(String pattern)`

`isTextPresent` takes a single String as an argument and this can be written in 5 different ways:

- Submitted Values

    - note: with no prefix (as above) this defaults to glob pattern matching so you can use `*` and `?` as wild cards.

- `glob:Sub*d V?lu?s`

    - prefix the string with `glob:` to use this format deliberately
    - `*` stands for any sequence of characters
    - `?` stands for any single character
    - also known as ''wildmat'' pattern matching (http://unow.be/rc/wildmat[2])

- `regexp:S..m.tted V(.)*s`

    - prefix with `regexp:` to use JavaScript regular expression patterns
    - for more details see http://unow.be/rc/jskit[3] and http://unow.be/rc/jsreg[4]

- `regexpi:s..m.tted v(.)*s`

    - prefix with `regexpi:` to use a case insensitive JavaScript regular expression patterns

- `exact:Submitted Values`

    - find the string exactly on the page with no wild card processing

In our test I will use a glob search but with no wild cards.

```
assertTrue(selenium.isTextPresent("Submitted Values"));
```

19.1.4   isElementPresent - check comments and filename

Sometimes we want to check if an HTML Element is present on the page or not, and we can use Selenium's `isElementPresent` command to do this:

- `isElementPresent(String locator)`

```
□ <body>
       <p> Submitted Values </p>
   ⊞ <div id=" username">
   ⊞ <div id=" password">
   □ <div id=" comments">
       ⊞ <p name=" comments">
       □ <ul>
               <li id=" valuecomments"> Comments... </li>
           </ul>
       </div>
   ⊞ <p>
   ⊞ <div id=" hiddenField">
   ⊞ <div id=" checkboxes">
```

Figure 19.6: HTML for a simple page structure

`isElementPresent` takes a locator as the argument and if found returns a boolean value of `True`.

The example static HTML for the form processing has a very simple structure.

Each field that I submitted in the form is contained in a div with an `id` of `_fieldname` and within the div is a descriptive paragraph with the `name` of the field and an unordered list, where each list item has the value entered in the field and an `id` of `_value<insertfieldname>`.

When a form field was not entered there is no div; simply an unidentified paragraph with text describing the missing field.

```
□ <p>
       <strong> No Value for filename </strong>
   </p>
```

Figure 19.7: No Value for filename Paragraph

I will check for the presence of the div for `_comments` and for the absence of the div for `_filename` with the following code:

```
assertTrue(selenium.isElementPresent("_comments"));
assertFalse(selenium.isElementPresent("_filename"));
```

19.1.5   getXPathCount - count the checkboxes entered

XPath is an incredibly powerful mechanism for querying the HTML page returned. A basic understanding of XPath will go a long way in helping you construct robust automated

---

[2]http://en.wikipedia.org/wiki/Wildmat
[3]http://www.javascriptkit.com/javatutors/redev.shtml
[4]http://www.regular-expressions.info/javascript.html

tests.

XPath can be used in locators by prefixing a locator with `xpath=` but we can use XPath statements directly in the `getXPathCount` method.

```
getXPathCount(string xpath)
```

No need to prefix the string passed into `getXPathCount` with `xpath=`, if you do then getXPathCount will fail.

e.g. Because I know that all the checkbox values are rendered as list items within an unordered list within the `_checkboxes` div I can use the following XPath statement to select them all from the HTML document: `//div[@id='_checkboxes']/ul/li`

Our code for counting the number of checkboxes selected reads:

```
assertEquals(1,selenium.getXpathCount("//div[@id='_checkboxes']/ul/li").
    intValue());
```

`getXPathCount` returns a `Number` so I convert that into an `integer` for comparing in the `Assert` because I know that for our first test, we expect to have 1 checkbox item selected.

19.1.6   click - navigate to the form

HTML pages have hyperlinks to move between pages using the anchor tags in the document.

As users we click on these to navigate to another page. As automators we use the selenium command `click`.

- `click(String locator)`

`click` takes, as the argument, the locator for the anchor we wish to click on.

By examining the source code using Firebug in Firefox we can see that the link has an id of `back_to_form` so we can use this directly as our locator string.

```
selenium.click("back_to_form");
selenium.waitForPageToLoad("30000");
```

19.1.7   The rest of the test

- For the rest of the test I want to check that the click takes me back to the form, by checking the title of the form page.

```
assertEquals("HTML Form Elements",selenium.getTitle());
```

- Then I will check all the checkboxes.

213

```
selenium.check("//input[@name='checkboxes[]' and @value='cb1']");
selenium.check("//input[@name='checkboxes[]' and @value='cb2']");
selenium.check("//input[@name='checkboxes[]' and @value='cb3']");
```

- Then resubmit the form

```
selenium.click("//input[@name='submitbutton' and @value='submit']");
selenium.waitForPageToLoad("30000");
```

- Check that the count for the checkboxes has increased to 3

```
assertEquals(3, selenium.getXpathCount("//div[@id='_checkboxes']/ul/li").
    intValue());
```

19.1.8   The full test and summary

In the preceding test we used the following commands:

- click

- getTitle

- isTextPresent

- isElementPresent

- getXpathCount

- getText

These represent the core of the commands for working with static HTML so here is the
full test

```
@Test
public void submit_form_with_values_and_check_static_html(){
  selenium.type("username","eviltester");
  selenium.type("password","myPassword");
  selenium.click("//input[@name='submitbutton' and @value='submit']");
  selenium.waitForPageToLoad("30000");

  // check the title on the page
  assertEquals("Processed Form Details",selenium.getTitle());

  // check the username entered
  assertEquals( "eviltester",selenium.getText("_valueusername"));

  // check the submitted values text is on the page
  assertTrue(selenium.isTextPresent("Submitted Values"));

  //isElementPresent to check comments and filename
```

```
assertTrue(selenium.isElementPresent("_comments"));
assertFalse(selenium.isElementPresent("_filename"));

// use getXPathCount to check the number of checkboxes
assertEquals(1
  ,selenium.getXpathCount("//div[@id='_checkboxes']/ul/li").intValue());

// click to go back to the form
selenium.click("back_to_form");
selenium.waitForPageToLoad("30000");

// check the page title with getTitle
assertEquals("HTML Form Elements",selenium.getTitle());

//check all the checkboxes
selenium.check("//input[@name='checkboxes[]' and @value='cb1']");
selenium.check("//input[@name='checkboxes[]' and @value='cb2']");
selenium.check("//input[@name='checkboxes[]' and @value='cb3']");

// submit the form
selenium.click("//input[@name='submitbutton' and @value='submit']");
selenium.waitForPageToLoad("30000");

//check the checkbox count
assertEquals(3,
  selenium.getXpathCount("//div[@id='_checkboxes']/ul/li").intValue());
}
```

19.2   getAttribute

Just as we can access the text of an element, we can also access the values of any of its attributes.

- getAttribute(String attributeLocator)

getAttribute takes a single argument, the locator to an attribute.

Selenium distinguishes between a "normal" locator and an "attribute" locator by having an attribute locator end with @attribute_name; e.g. @id to get the value of the id attribute.

So were I to get the name of one of the paragraphs under an identified div.

```
☐ <div id="_password">
    ⊞ <p name="_password">
```

Figure 19.8: div with an ID

I could use the following attribute locator to get the value of the name attribute:

- xpath=//div[@id='_password']/p@name

And use it in a test like this:

```
@Test
public void check_static_html_password_name(){
  selenium.type("username","eviltester");
  selenium.type("password","myPassword");
  selenium.click("//input[@name='submitbutton' and @value='submit']");
  selenium.waitForPageToLoad("30000");

  // check the name of the password display paragraph is _password
  assertEquals("_password",
    selenium.getAttribute("xpath=//div[@id='_password']/p@name"));
}
```

19.3   assignId

Because Selenium runs as JavaScript within the browser itself, we can actually amend the HTML in the browser. One command that Selenium provides for this is the `assignId` command.

- assignId(String locator, String identifier)

    – `locator` is a `String` to allow us to locate the element we want to add an `id` to
    – `identifier` is the `String` we want to add as the `id` on the element

We can use this to help us limit the number of complicated XPath statements we use and to enable us to go directly to specific page elements instead of long XPath statements.

As an example in the static HTML page we have been looking at the filename error message is in an element without an `id` or a `name` so we have to use an XPath to access the text. e.g.

```
assertEquals("No Value for filename", selenium.getText("xpath=//body/p[2]/
    strong"));
```

```
☐ <body>
      <p>Submitted Values</p>
   ☐ <div id="_username">
   ☐ <div id="_password">
   ☐ <div id="_comments">
   ☐ <p>
         <strong>No Value for filename</strong>
      </p>
```

Figure 19.9: No ID on the filename message

We could instead assign an `id` to the element and then use that `id` for any subsequent methods. e.g.

216

```
@Test
public void useAssignIDToCheckFilenameBlank(){
    selenium.type("username","eviltester");
    selenium.type("password","myPassword");
    selenium.click("//input[@name='submitbutton' and @value='submit']");
    selenium.waitForPageToLoad("30000");

    selenium.assignId("xpath=//body/p[2]/strong", "_filename");
    assertEquals("No Value for filename",selenium.getText("_filename"));
}
```

19.4   getBodyText and getHtmlSource

We may decide that we want to do a comprehensive set of actions on the static HTML and that doing it through lots of Selenium commands would slow our testing down, therefore we would rather process the HTML directly.

We can access the HTML using two commands:

- getBodyText - returns all the text on the page

- getHtmlSource - returns the HTML source of the page

Neither takes an argument and just return a string with all the details we require.

e.g. For the following code

```
@Test
public void getBodyText_getHtmlSource(){
    selenium.open("/selenium/basic_html_form.html");
    selenium.type("username","eviltester");
    selenium.type("password","myPassword");
    selenium.click("//input[@name='submitbutton' and @value='submit']");
    selenium.waitForPageToLoad("30000");

    System.out.println(selenium.getBodyText());
    System.out.println("-----");
    System.out.println(selenium.getHtmlSource());
}
```

getBodyText() returns all the text for all the elements:

```
Submitted Values
username
eviltester
password
myPassword
comments
Comments...
No Value for filename
hiddenField
Hidden Field Value
checkboxes
cb3
```

```
radioval
rd2
multipleselect
ms4
dropdown
dd3
submitbutton
submit
Go back to the main form
```

getHtmlSource() **returns the full HTML of the page**

```
<head>
<title>Processed Form Details</title>
</head><body>
<body>
<p>Submitted Values</p>

<div id="_username">
    <p name="_username">
        <strong>username</strong></p>
    <ul>
        <li id="_valueusername">eviltester</li>
    </ul>
</div>
<div id="_password">
    <p name="_password"><strong>password</strong></p>
    <ul>
        <li id="_valuepassword">myPassword</li>
    </ul>
</div>
<div id="_comments"><p name="_comments"><strong>comments</strong></p>
    <ul>
        <li id="_valuecomments">Comments
 <!-- some stuff removed -->
</body>
```

19.5   goBack

In one of the previous examples we used click to return to the form entry page. We could also have used the back button.

Selenium provides a mechanism for simulating this with the goBack command.

* goBack()

goBack **takes no arguments**

```
@Test
public void submit_form_with_values_and_go_back(){
  // check the title on the form page
  assertEquals("HTML Form Elements",selenium.getTitle());
  selenium.type("username","eviltester");
  selenium.type("password","myPassword");
  selenium.click("//input[@name='submitbutton' and @value='submit']");
```

218

```
        selenium.waitForPageToLoad("30000");

        // check the title on the detail page
        assertEquals("Processed Form Details",selenium.getTitle());

        selenium.goBack();

        //check title for the form page again
        assertEquals("HTML Form Elements",selenium.getTitle());
    }
```

19.6   highlight

Selenium's `highlight` command briefly highlights an element on the screen to help you debug your tests.

- `highlight(String locator)`

The single argument to `highlight` is the locator of the element you want to draw attention to. e.g.

```
        selenium.highlight("username");
        selenium.type("username","eviltester");
```

The above code would briefly highlight the username input field.

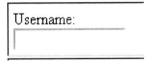

Figure 19.10: Highlighted username before typing

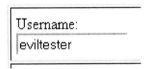

Figure 19.11: Not highlighted after typing

The brief flashes on screen may help you follow what Selenium is doing.

Chapter 20

Using JavaScript with Selenium

Selenium has commands for using JavaScript within Selenium.

These commands are a little more advanced than the commands we have used before but they allow us to expand Selenium functionality within our tests without relying on Selenium IDE User Extensions:

- `isAlertPresent` - returns true if an alert has been generated in JavaScript

- `getAlert` - returns the text of the last alert generated in JavaScript

- `fireEvent` - trigger an event on an element

- `getEval` - run some JavaScript and return the result

- `runScript` - inject some JavaScript into the page and run it without returning a result

20.1   A Basic JavaScript Enabled Page

To provide some context to understand these commands I have created a small page with some JavaScript elements:

http://unow.be/rc/basicajax[1]

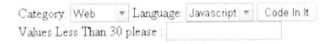

Figure 20.1: JavaScript enabled web page

This has two combo boxes wired together by JavaScript and a text input box with some JavaScript validation.

```
<form method="post" action="form_processor.php?ajax=1">
    <label for="combo1">Category:</label>
    <select name="id" id="combo1">
        <option value="1">Web</option>
        <option value="2">Desktop</option>
        <option value="3">Server</option>
    </select>
    <noscript>
        <input type="submit" name="submitbutton" value="Load Individuals"/>
    </noscript>
```

---

[1]http://www.compendiumdev.co.uk/selenium/basic_ajax.html

221

```
<label for="combo2">Language:</label>
<select name="language_id" id="combo2">
    <option value="1">Javascript</option>
    <option value="2">VBScript</option>
    <option value="3">Flash</option>
</select>

<input type="submit" name="submitbutton" value="Code In It"/>

</br>
Values Less Than 30 please : <input type="text" id="lteq30"
    onBlur="checkGT30(this.value)">
</form>
```

The code on the text input field `lteq30` is easy to spot in the code since you can see the call definition in the `onBlur` attribute.

```
onBlur="checkGT30(this.value)"
```

The code on the `combo1` select is far less visible as it is added dynamically when the page has loaded.

If a value greater than 30 is entered into the `lteq30` field then an error alert is displayed to the user.

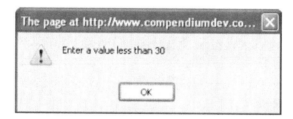

Figure 20.2: Alert Validation

20.2   The Class

As an example, I have created a new class `JavaScript_With_Selenium_Tests.java`, with the following basic setup and tear down code:

```java
package com.eviltester.seleniumtutorials.chap20;

import static org.junit.Assert.*;
import org.junit.AfterClass;
import org.junit.Before;
import org.junit.BeforeClass;
import org.junit.Test;
import com.thoughtworks.selenium.DefaultSelenium;
import com.thoughtworks.selenium.Selenium;

public class JavaScript_With_Selenium_Tests {

  private static Selenium selenium;
```

```
@BeforeClass
public static void setUpBeforeClass() throws Exception {
  selenium = new DefaultSelenium("localhost", 4444,
      "*firefox", "http://www.compendiumdev.co.uk");
  selenium.start();
}

@AfterClass
public static void tearDownAfterClass() throws Exception {
  selenium.close();
  selenium.stop();
}

@Before
public void setUp() throws Exception {
  selenium.open("/selenium/basic_ajax.html");
}
}
```

20.3   FireEvent, isAlertPresent, and getAlert

I once had to automate a particularly tricky HTML form. I was using Selenium's `type` and `typekeys` methods to add data into field values, but the application wasn't functioning as I expected.

After a bit of analysis I investigated the controls on the form and saw that they had events associated with them in JavaScript. Events on fields take the form `onX` where x is the name of the event. e.g.

```
Values Less Than 30 please : <input type="text" id="lteq30"
    onBlur="checkGT30(this.value)">
```

The above HTML snippet shows an input field with an `onBlur` event which, when triggered, calls a JavaScript function called `checkGT30` to validate this field.

If I create a test to automate this which types into this field. The `onBlur` event will not fire. If I try and select one of the other fields on the form, e.g. An item from a combo box, the event will not fire.

You can try it for yourself by visiting http://unow.be/rc/basicajax[2]

Manually type `45` into the input box, then try selecting a value from the first combo box, a dialog pops up with a validation warning.

If you use a Selenium test to do this. Then the dialog box does not appear.

```
@Test
public void enterAnInvalidValueInBlurInput(){
  selenium.type("xpath=//input[@id='lteq30']", "45");
  selenium.select("combo1", "Desktop");
  assertFalse(selenium.isAlertPresent());
}
```

---

[2]http://www.compendiumdev.co.uk/selenium/basic_ajax.html

`isAlertPresent` returns a boolean letting you know if you need to perform a `getAlert` function.

In the above example, `isAlertPresent` returns `false` because no JavaScript alert was created. And no JavaScript alert was created because the validation routine was not called.

In order to trigger the validation routine, we have to trigger the ''blur'' event on `lteq30` using the `fireEvent` command. As in the following test:

```
@Test
public void enterAnInvalidValueInBlurInputAndTriggerValidation(){
    selenium.type("xpath=//input[@id='lteq30']", "45");
    selenium.fireEvent("xpath=//input[@id='lteq30']", "blur");
    assertTrue(selenium.isAlertPresent());
    assertEquals("Enter a value less than 30", selenium.getAlert());
}
```

Here we know that the alert is generated because the `isAlertPresent` function returns true and so the `getAlert` function returns the text of the alert.

If you attempt to call `getAlert` without an alert having been triggered in JavaScript then an exception will be thrown.

Sometimes code of the following form might be used if the alert is irrelevant to our test and all we want to do is clear the alert:

```
if(selenium.isAlertPresent()){
    selenium.getAlert();
}
```

20.4   getEval

`getEval` takes a single String argument which it evaluates as JavaScript in the browser and returns the result of executing that JavaScript.

Complicated uses of this require JavaScript knowledge.

I have used this to get the actual HTML of elements on a page, and often use it in conjunction with `assignId` e.g.

```
@Test
public void showHTMLOfCombo1WithGetEval(){
    String javascript="";
    javascript = "window.document.getElementById('combo1').innerHTML;";
    String theInnerHTML = selenium.getEval(javascript);
    System.out.println(theInnerHTML);
}}
```

The above method would display on the console, the HTML contained between the `<select>` and `</select>` element tags in the HTML which have their `id` attribute assigned as `combo1`. i.e.

```
<option value="1">Web</option>
<option value="2">Desktop</option>
<option value="3">Server</option>
```

You can use `getEval` to evaluate any JavaScript that you can run in the browser.

NOTE:

You can use `getEval` as a way of augmenting Selenium or possibly working around Selenium bugs.

During the writing of this book I raised a defect against Selenium because I could not get the `assignId` command to work in Firefox 5.0.

http://unow.be/rc/bug2121[3]

As a workaround I used `getEval` to do the same job as `assignId`

e.g. assign an id to the form:

```
selenium.getEval("window.document.forms[0].setAttribute('id','form1');");
```

20.5   runScript

Runs a script in the context of the application but does not keep the script.

In the following example I use `runScript` to create a named JavaScript "object" (actually a function) called `EvilTester` with a method called `returnBob` (which returns the `String` "bob"). It also creates an Alert.

To demonstrate that the function created in the `RunScript` can not be used later in the test I try to call it. Since I know that trying to call an undefined function generates an exception, I trap the exception and assert that we got the expected assertion.

```
@Test
public void showValueOfInjectedJavaScriptFromRunScript(){
   // using runScript the function does not persist
   selenium.runScript("function EvilTester(){}; EvilTester.returnBob =
      function(){return 'bob';}; alert(EvilTester.returnBob());");
   // if dialog present then function ran
   assertTrue(selenium.isAlertPresent());
   assertEquals("bob",selenium.getAlert());

   // should not be able to call again so expect an exception
   try{
     selenium.getEval("EvilTester.returnBob();");
   }catch(Exception e){
     assertEquals(e.getMessage(),
       "ERROR: Threw an exception: EvilTester is not defined");
   }
 }
```

I could also have used the JUnit `expected` functionality. e.g.

---

[3]http://code.google.com/p/selenium/issues/detail?id=2121

```
@Test(expected=com.thoughtworks.selenium.SeleniumException.class)
public void showValueOfInjectedJavaScriptFromRunScriptExpectedException(){

    // using runScript the function does not persist
    selenium.runScript("function EvilTester(){}; EvilTester.returnBob =
        function(){return 'bob';}; alert(EvilTester.returnBob());");

    assertTrue(selenium.isAlertPresent());
    assertEquals("bob",selenium.getAlert());
    selenium.getEval("EvilTester.returnBob();");
}
```

This tells JUnit to expect the test to throw an exception. The test fails if the specific class of exception does not get thrown.

20.6   addScript and removeScript

Runs a script in the context of Selenium and keep it around for later use.

In the following script I use Selenium's `addScript` method to create a JavaScript function called `returnBob` which we can use elsewhere in the test. addScript takes two arguments, the JavaScript function and an optional id for the script. In the example below I have left the script id blank e.g. `""`. Use the id if you want to remove the script from the page with the `removeScript` command.

I use the JavaScript function created by the `addScript` command in the following `getEval` example.

```
@Test
public void showValueOfInjectedJavaScriptFromAddScript(){
    // using addScript the function persists for future use

  selenium.addScript(
    "function EvilTester(){}; EvilTester.returnBob = function(){return 'bob
        ';};",
    "");

  // use the function we created
  assertEquals("bob",selenium.getEval("EvilTester.returnBob();"));
}
```

Chapter 21

Starting Selenium From Code

The Selenium distribution's Selenium server .jar can also be called from code. So that instead of having to type `java -jar selenium-server-standalone-2.0.0.jar` at the command line, we can have our tests start up and close down a server when they run.

To do this we use the `startSeleniumServer()` command from the `SeleniumServer` Class.

21.1 Add Selenium Server to the project

You need to add the Selenium server `.jar` file to your class path. As before, amend the properties of your project to amend the Java Build Path, and choose the correct `.jar` as an external jar.

21.1.1 For Selenium 2.0.0 and above

For Selenium version 2.0.0 releases and above, we only need to add one `.jar` file. The Selenium Server Standalone `.jar`. If you have been using Selenium 2 for the previous sections then you do not need to add anything else to your project as the standalone `.jar` has everything you need.

21.1.2 For Selenium 1.0.3 and below

For Selenium RC we need to add the selenium server `.jar` file.

The examples below show Selenium server 1.0.1 but the principle is the same for all versions below Selenium 2.0.0. Add the `selenium-server.jar` file, from the selenium server directory, to your project.

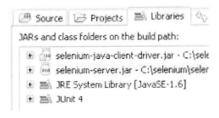

Figure 21.1: Properties Dialog with the Selenium server .jar added to build path

21.2 Start it in the code

You start Selenium Server by declaring a variable of type `SeleniumServer`, creating a new instance and then starting it. We wrap it with a try catch block because `SeleniumServer` will throw an exception if it can't start.

```
SeleniumServer seleniumServer=null;
try {
  seleniumServer = new SeleniumServer();
  seleniumServer.start();
} catch (Exception e) {
  e.printStackTrace();
}
```

Then connect to the server in the normal way. Your server has still started on your local machine using the same port.

```
Selenium selenium=null;
selenium = new DefaultSelenium("localhost", 4444,
    "*firefox", "http://www.compendiumdev.co.uk");
selenium.start();
```

Then do your normal test commands.

```
selenium.open("selenium/search.php");
selenium.type("xpath=//input[@name='q']", "Selenium-RC");
selenium.click("xpath=//input[@name='btnG' and @type='submit']");
selenium.waitForPageToLoad("10000");
```

And close selenium in the normal way.

Then close down the server.

```
if(seleniumServer!=null){
  seleniumServer.stop();
}
```

So a full individual test to do this would look like the following:

```
package com.eviltester.seleniumtutorials;

import org.junit.Test;
import org.openqa.selenium.server.SeleniumServer;
import com.thoughtworks.selenium.DefaultSelenium;
import com.thoughtworks.selenium.Selenium;

public class SeleniumServerInATest {

  @Test
  public void doASearch(){

    SeleniumServer seleniumServer=null;

    try {
      seleniumServer = new SeleniumServer();
      seleniumServer.start();
    } catch (Exception e) {
      e.printStackTrace();
    }
```

```
Selenium selenium=null;
selenium = new DefaultSelenium("localhost", 4444,
    "*firefox", "http://www.compendiumdev.co.uk");
selenium.start();

selenium.open("selenium/search.php");
selenium.type("xpath=//input[@name='q']", "Selenium-RC");
selenium.click("xpath=//input[@name='btnG' and @type='submit']");
selenium.waitForPageToLoad("10000");

selenium.close();
selenium.stop();

if(seleniumServer!=null){
  seleniumServer.stop();
}
  }
 }
}
```

Obviously we wouldn't start and stop the server in each test so we would refactor this to use the `@BeforeClass`, and `@AfterClass` annotations to start the server.

21.3   The Start Up routine explored

Typically the Selenium Server will not start because something else is already using the Port: e.g. another instance of Selenium.

21.3.1   BindException Handling

We can amend the code to check if the exception raised was a `BindException`. If this was the case then we could assume that a selenium server was already running and use the existing Selenium Server. e.g.

```
Try {
  seleniumServer = new SeleniumServer();
  seleniumServer.start();
} catch (java.net.BindException bE){
  // could not bind, assume that server is currently running
  // and carry on
  System.out.println("could not bind - carrying on");
}
catch (Exception e) {
  // any other exception stop
  throw new IllegalStateException("Can't start selenium server", e);
}
```

21.3.2   Stop Existing Server

We might choose to stop the running server and start a new one.

You would have to decide if this was a valid thing to do in your environment or not. If during the course of your testing you could not start a server then it might mean that your test setup was not closing down the server properly. And rather than working around this, you might find it more beneficial to work out how to stop the server automatically during your previous test run.

Since I think this is a useful technique to know, I include it here.

This will get a little more complicated so if you are new to Java I don't necessarily expect you to understand all of this yet.

Our main block doesn't change very much:

```
String stopSeleniumCommand =
  "http://localhost:4444/selenium-server/driver/?cmd=shutDownSeleniumServer";
try {
  seleniumServer = new SeleniumServer();
  seleniumServer.start();
} catch (java.net.BindException bE){
  // could not bind, assume that server is currently running
  // and carry on
  System.out.println("could not bind - carrying on");
  // try and stop it
  if( runHTTPCommand(stopSeleniumCommand)){
    try {
      seleniumServer = new SeleniumServer();
      seleniumServer.start();
    } catch (Exception e) {
      throw new IllegalStateException(
        "Could not stop existing server on blocked port 4444", e);
    }
  }
}
catch (Exception e) {
  // any other exception stop and start
  throw new IllegalStateException("Can't start selenium server", e);
}
```

This time, if we could not bind, we send an HTTP request to the server, and if it is a selenium server on that port, it will stop the server.

If that seemed to work then we try and start the server again.

The runHTTPCommand that does the magic to stop Selenium uses a little more complicated Java.

```
private boolean runHTTPCommand(String theCommand) throws IOException{
  URL url = new URL(theCommand);

  URLConnection seleniumConnection = url.openConnection();
  seleniumConnection.connect();

  InputStream inputStream = seleniumConnection.getInputStream();
  ByteArrayOutputStream outputSteam = new ByteArrayOutputStream();
  byte[] buffer = new byte[2048];
  int streamLength;
  while ((streamLength = inputStream.read(buffer)) != -1) {
        outputSteam.write(buffer, 0, streamLength);
  }
```

```
    inputStream.close();

    // give command some time to finish
    try {
      Thread.sleep(1000);
    } catch (InterruptedException e) {
      e.printStackTrace();
    }

    String stringifiedOutput = outputSteam.toString();
    if (stringifiedOutput.startsWith("OK"))
          return true;

    return false;
  }
```

This code, requires the addition of the following imports:

```
import java.io.ByteArrayOutputStream;
import java.io.IOException;
import java.io.InputStream;
import java.net.URL;
import java.net.URLConnection;
```

Basically it:

- creates a connection to run the command.

- issues the HTTP command

- retrieves the output result

- waits for the Selenium server to shutdown fully

- If the output result starts with ''OK'' then it returns true

- otherwise returns false

Try this code by adding it in a test and running it when a Selenium Server is already running from the command line. You should see the server shut down, and then the test run.

21.3.3   Custom Remote Control Configurations

Because we are now starting Selenium RC from code, we have the option to create custom configurations. At its most simple this might just mean choosing a different port to run the server against, but we can control any element of Selenium RC that is also configurable from the command line.

To do this we use the `RemoteControlConfiguration` class which is also contained in the Selenium server `.jar` file:

231

```
import org.openqa.selenium.server.RemoteControlConfiguration;
```

In the following test I create the server on a different port, using the `RemoteControlConfiguration`
object:

```
@Test
public void remoteControlConfigExample(){

    final int SELENIUM_PORT = 8888;
    final int SELENIUM_TIMEOUT = 45;

    RemoteControlConfiguration rcConfig = new RemoteControlConfiguration();
    rcConfig.setTimeoutInSeconds(SELENIUM_TIMEOUT);
    rcConfig.setPort(SELENIUM_PORT);
    SeleniumServer seleniumServer=null;
    try {
        seleniumServer = new SeleniumServer(rcConfig);
        seleniumServer.start();
    } catch (Exception e) {
        e.printStackTrace();
    }

    Selenium selenium=null;

    selenium = new DefaultSelenium("localhost", SELENIUM_PORT,
        "*firefox", "http://www.compendiumdev.co.uk");
    selenium.start();

    selenium.open("selenium/search.php");
    selenium.type("xpath=//input[@name='q']", "Selenium-RC");
    selenium.click("xpath=//input[@name='btnG' and @type='submit']");
    selenium.waitForPageToLoad("10000");

    selenium.close();
    selenium.stop();

    if(seleniumServer!=null){
        seleniumServer.stop();
    }
}
```

NOTE:

I also have to use the same port when I define the `DefaultSelenium` server.

I have declared `SELENIUM_PORT` and `SELENIUM_TIMEOUT` as final because they are constants
that will not change in the test.

Chapter 22

Running Tests Outside Eclipse

Thus far we have run all our tests from within Eclipse.

This has allowed us to get used to writing tests and debugging them, but has not prepared us for a production environment.

In a production environment, a robust test suite will run as part of a continuous integration build and on multiple browser configurations.

To support this we must have the ability to run our tests outside of the Eclipse environment.

Many tools exist to support this way of working and for simplicity I will demonstrate these principles using Ant , Hudson and Subversion.

22.1   What is Ant?

Ant is a build tool written in Java. This means that given a configuration file, written in XML, it will carry out a series of actions to compile the java application, run the tests, report the results, and package up the files we need for deployment.

http://unow.be/rc/ant[1]

Other build systems exist, but Ant is simple enough to get to grips with that it makes a suitable tool for beginners.

22.2   What is Hudson?

Hudson is a continuous integration server written in Java. This means that you can setup repeating jobs which will build your software and run your tests regularly.

http://unow.be/rc/hudsonwiki[2]

Again, other continuous integration systems exist, but Hudson has a very simple install routine and easy to use front end GUI, again making it suitable for beginners.

---

[1]http://ant.apache.org/
[2]http://wiki.hudson-ci.org/

22.3   What is Subversion?

Subversion is a version control system. We will store our code in the version control system and allow Hudson to check out the code as required to run the most recent version of the tests automatically.

http://unow.be/rc/svn[3]

---

[3]http://subversion.tigris.org/

Chapter 23

Using Ant to Run Selenium Tests

23.1 Prerequisite: Install Java JDK

To install Ant we need to have a Java JDK (Java Developer Kit) installed. Java comes in two editions:

- Java Runtime Edition, which we have installed to run Java applications.

- Java Development Kit, which we need to develop Java applications.

23.1.1 Install Java JDK

We are now moving into the territory of compiling java code to run outside of Eclipse. We need to install the JDK version of Java since it contains the java compiler.

Visit the Java JDK download page http://unow.be/rc/getjavase[1]

Choose to download the most recent JDK

Figure 23.1: Download the Standard Edition JDK

Accept the license agreement on the page.

Download the correct installer for your platform.

Run the executable that you download to install the JDK. By default it will install to a Java subdirectory of `Program Files` e.g. for version 6.0.26

---

[1]http://www.oracle.com/technetwork/java/javase/downloads

Windows x86	76.81 MB	jdk-6u26-windows-i586.exe
Windows Intel Itanium	63.32 MB	jdk-6u26-windows-ia64.exe
Windows x64	67.42 MB	jdk-6u26-windows-x64.exe

Figure 23.2: Installer for Windows x86 and x64

- `C:\Program Files\Java\jdk1.6.0_26\`

The default directory should work fine as `C:\Program Files\Java\` is the default directory for all versions of Java.

23.1.2   Update the Environment Variables and Path For Java

We need to add an environment variable to our windows configuration. On your `My Computer` icon, right click and select `properties` to access the `System Properties` dialog.

The environment variables are accessible by clicking the `[Environment Variables]` button on the `Advanced` tab.

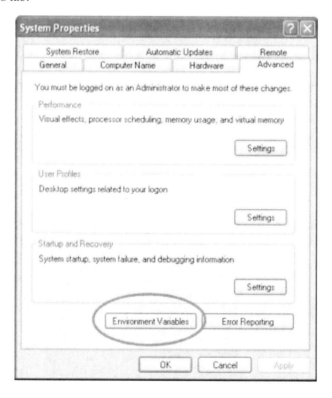

Figure 23.3: Environment Variables button on System Properties

Note: If you are going to use the winant installer you can skip this step as it will create a `JAVA_HOME` variable for you.

236

Click the [Environment Variables] button and use the Environment Variables dialog to add the following new User Variable.

- JAVA_HOME

The value of JAVA_HOME with the install directory of the Java JDK for 6.0.26 was:

- C:\Program Files\Java\jdk1.6.0_26

Figure 23.4: Set JAVA_HOME User variable

We also have to update the Path variable. Edit the existing Path variable (or create one if it does not exist) and append the path of Java. e.g. In my case, I had to add C:\Program Files\Java\jdk1.6.0_26\bin; Path entries are separated by ; (a semi-colon).

NOTE:
You may find that you have to add the variables as System Environment Variables, rather than User variables. This seems to be the case on Windows 7, particularly when installing Ant. If you encounter issues on your particular machine, experiment by adding the details as System and User variables.

23.1.3   Check that Java works

Type the command java -version. You should see a version string matching the JDK that you installed.

```
java version "1.6.0_26"
Java(TM) SE Runtime Environment (build 1.6.0_26-b03)
Java HotSpot(TM) Client VM (build 20.1-b02, mixed mode, sharing)
```

23.2   Install Ant

To Install Ant we are basically going to follow the instructions listed in the Ant manual

- For Windows machines

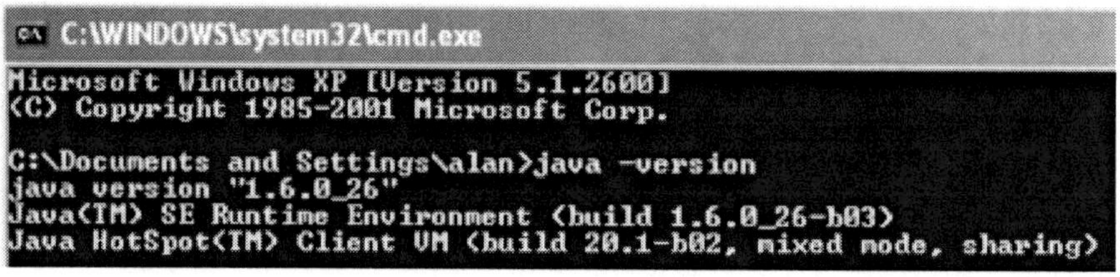

Figure 23.5: JDK version installed

  - Recommended: Use the automated installer
    * http://unow.be/rc/winant[2]
  - For a Manual Install we would following the instructions from:
    * http://unow.be/rc/antonwindows[3]

- For non-windows machines follow the instructions on the Apache site

  - http://unow.be/rc/antman[4]
  - specifically http://unow.be/rc/apinstall[5]

23.2.1   Install Ant Automatically

Download the installer.

- http://unow.be/rc/winant[6]

When you run the installer you will be asked to input the Directory of the JDK you installed, for me this was:

- `C:\Program Files\Java\jdk1.6.0_26`

23.2.2   Install Ant Manually

Skip this section if you installed Ant using the winAnt installer.

1. Download the current version of Ant from the binary downloads page http://unow.be/rc/antBin[7] (I downloaded the zipped version, at the time of writing this was `apache-ant-1.8.0-bin.zip`)

---

[2]http://code.google.com/p/winant
[3]http://wiki.apache.org/ant/AntOnWindows
[4]http://ant.apache.org/manual/index.html
[5]http://ant.apache.org/manual/install.html
[6]http://code.google.com/p/winant
[7]http://ant.apache.org/bindownload.cgi

2. Extract the contents of the archive to a folder on your drive. I unarchived the contents to `c:\apache-ant-1.8.0`

Update the Environment Variables and Path

We need to add the environment variables for Ant on our windows configuration. On your `My Computer` icon, right click and select `properties` to access the `System Properties` dialog.

The environment variables are accessible by clicking the `[Environment Variables]` button on the Advanced tab.

Click the `[Environment Variables]` button and use the `Environment Variables` dialog to add the following new System Variable.

- `ANT_HOME`

Click the `[New]` button on the `Environment Variables` dialog, in the `User variables` pane and enter `ANT_HOME` with the path that you installed Ant to, for me this was `c:\apache-ant-1.8.0`

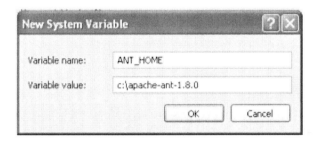

Figure 23.6: Set ANT_HOME system variable

We also have to update the `Path` variable, so edit the existing `Path` variable and append the path of Ant e.g. In my case, I had to add `c:\apache-ant-1.8.0\bin;` Remember: path entries are separated by `;`.

23.3   Check that Ant works

If you create a command line now and type the command `ant`.You should see the message

```
Buildfile: build.xml does not exist!
Build failed
```

While this may look as though Ant has failed to install correctly. It means that Ant has been found by the command line, has run, and is reporting the message that it could not find a `build.xml` file to run. That is what we expect, and we will create a build file for it in a later section.

23.4   Create a Lib Folder

Since we are going to be running under the command line. We are no longer going to rely on the Eclipse properties configuration to locate the library files that we need.

We will create a library folder in our Java project, and this will store the Selenium libraries and JUnit libraries. Then we will reference these libraries from Ant.

By moving the libraries into a folder associated with the project source code, it will also make it easier to integrate Ant with Hudson, and Hudson with Subversion.

In your source project folder, create a directory called `lib`.

For me this required creating `c:\selenium_tests\InitialSeleniumTests\lib`

Into this lib folder we will copy, from the Selenium installation, the jar files we need.

I have started creating folders in the lib folder for each version of selenium so that I can have multiple versions of selenium in the same project e.g. `lib\selenium_2.1.0`, `lib\selenium_2.0.0`

- For Selenium 2, add the selenium server standalone jar e.g. for version 2.1.0

    – `selenium-server-standalone-2.1.0.jar`

- For versions below Selenium 2 add the server and the client driver jar

    – `selenium-java-client-driver.jar`
    – `selenium-server.jar`

We also have to download and install JUnit because we want to use a `.jar` version from the lib directory rather than the version bundled with Eclipse.

To do this:

1. visit http://unow.be/rc/JUnit[8]

2. follow the link to `Download JUnit`

3. download the most recent JUnit jar file to your lib directory.

---

[8]http://JUnit.org/

240

23.5   Amend Eclipse Project Properties

We will now amend our Eclipse project properties to use these library files, so that when we develop within Eclipse, we use the same library files as Ant.

Amend the Java Build Path to use the libraries in the lib folder by removing the existing JUnit, and Selenium libraries and instead adding the libraries from the lib folder.

You will need to re-associate these with the source code, so you can either include the source jars in the lib folder, or point to the source jars in the folder where you installed Selenium.

23.6   Create an initial build.xml file

We have two different sets of tests in the book. Tests which rely on the server being started, in order to run. And tests which start the server themselves. This has made running all the tests from within Eclipse a little difficult and really we need to refactor all the tests to use the same mechanism. Which we will do in a later section.

Initially we can have both tests co-existing in the same `build.xml` file, with Ant starting and stopping the Selenium server as required.

We will start by creating a `build.xml` file with the tests which require the Selenium server, and then add the remaining tests in the next section.

NOTE:
This is stored as `build_server_tests.xml` in the supporting source code for the book.
You would run this from the command line as `ant -f build_server_tests.xml`
If you create the file in stages by following along with the book, you will be able to run it, just by typing `ant`

A `build.xml` file is an XML file which consists of:

- configuration elements, e.g. property, path etc.

- target elements - these do something

The target elements allow you to define a set of tasks, with dependencies between them. e.g.

- `<target name="target1"/>`

241

- `<target name="target2" depends="target1"/>`

- `<target name="target3" depends="target2"/>`

- `<target name="target4"/>`

- `<target name="target5" depends="target4"/>`

In the above example I could start Ant with:

- `ant target1` - only target1 would execute

- `ant target2` - Ant would execute target1 (because target2 depends on it) and if target1 completed successfully, then Ant would execute target2

- `ant target3` - Ant would execute, target1, target2 and target3

- `ant target4 target2` - Ant would execute target4, target1 and target2

- `ant target5 target3` - Ant would execute target4, target5, target1, target2, target3

So for each target which ''depends'' on other targets, Ant has to execute the ''depends on'' targets first to ensure they complete correctly before executing the targets which depend on them.

You can also see from the example command lines above that we can execute multiple targets from the command line, and subsets of the targets in the file.

The `build.xml` file explained:

```
<project name="Run Selenium Tests" default="all_selenium_tests" basedir=".">
```

- We start the Ant build file with a definition of the project. Naming it `Run Selenium Tests`. The default parameter is the name of the ''target'' that we are going to run.

- When we start Ant from the command line we can just run `ant`, which will look for a `build.xml` file, and if found will use that and will start execution with the target defined as default.

```
<property name="src" location="src" />
<property name="build" location="build" />
<property name="libs" location="lib" />
<property name="testresults" location="junit-results" />
<property name="testreport" location="junit-report" />
```

- Properties are ''variables'' that we can refer to later in the Ant file. This helps make the Ant file more maintainable because we can amend locations in a single place.

242

- To support multiple versions of Selenium in this text, I will create properties for the paths to Selenium Server and the client drivers. For Selenium 1.0.3 and below they would be.

```
<property name="seleniumclient"
    location="${libs}/selenium_1.0.3/selenium-java-client-driver.jar" />
<property name="seleniumserver"
    location="${libs}/selenium_1.0.3/selenium-server.jar" />
```

- For Selenium 2.0.0 and above they would be:

```
<property name="seleniumclient" location="" />
<property name="seleniumserver"
    location="${libs}/selenium_2.0.0/selenium-server-standalone-2.0.0.jar" />
```

For your purposes, the lines above are probably all you need.

You can amend the `seleniumclient` and `seleniumserver` properties when you want to swap between versions of Selenium.

For the purposes of the book. I will go further than this, to allow me to choose the version of Selenium I want to run from the command line. I will do this by adding `-DseleniumVersion=2.1.0` to the `ant` command I issue. To support this I need to create a set of conditional properties.

I create a default for the `seleniumVersion` property.

If I supply a version using `-DseleniumVersion` then the line below will have no effect because Ant properties can only be set once, so it acts as a default in the event that I do not set a value at the command line.

```
<property name="seleniumVersion" value="2.1.0" />
```

I set the directory based on the version name. So I use a naming convention for my Selenium lib directories.

```
<property name="seleniumLibsFolder" value="selenium_${seleniumVersion}" />
```

I could have saved myself some coding in the Ant file by renaming the `.jar` files when I add them to the libs folder, e.g renaming the `selenium-server-standalone-2.1.0.jar` to `selenium-server.jar`. I have chosen not to, so I need to use conditional tasks in ant to setup the correct names.

You can find information on conditional property setting in the Ant manual:

- http://unow.be/rc/antcondition[9]

- http://unow.be/rc/antconditions[10]

---

[9]http://ant.apache.org/manual/Tasks/condition.html
[10]http://ant.apache.org/manual/Tasks/conditions.html

To help you explain what I do below. I conditionally set a property value if the selenium version equals a particular value.

```
<condition property="seleniumServerJarName"
    value="selenium-server-standalone-${seleniumVersion}.jar">
    <or>
        <equals arg1="${seleniumVersion}" arg2="2.0.0" />
        <equals arg1="${seleniumVersion}" arg2="2.1.0" />
    </or>
</condition>
<condition property="seleniumServerJarName"
    value="selenium-server.jar">
    <or>
        <equals arg1="${seleniumVersion}" arg2="1.0.3" />
    </or>
</condition>

<property name="seleniumserverlocation"
    value="${libs}/${seleniumLibsFolder}/${seleniumServerJarName}" />

<condition property="seleniumclientlocation" value="">
    <or>
        <equals arg1="${seleniumVersion}" arg2="2.0.0" />
        <equals arg1="${seleniumVersion}" arg2="2.1.0" />
    </or>
</condition>
<condition property="seleniumclientlocation"
    value="${libs}/${seleniumLibsFolder}/selenium-java-client-driver.
        jar">
    <or>
        <equals arg1="${seleniumVersion}" arg2="1.0.3" />
    </or>
</condition>
```

Then I set the locations based on the property values above.

```
<property name="seleniumclient" location="${seleniumclientlocation}" />
<property name="seleniumserver" location="${seleniumserverlocation}" />
```

- Now we define the class path and the `.jar` files we want to use when running the test.

```
<path id="JUnit.class.path">
  <pathelement location="${libs}/junit-4.8.1.jar" />
  <pathelement location="${seleniumclient}" />
  <pathelement location="${seleniumserver}" />
  <pathelement location="${build}" />
</path>
```

- Using the `path` element I create a ''classpath'' which I will use to run JUnit. So here I define the set of folders and files that I want JUnit to search through when it runs the tests. Because the paths are defined as properties I simply change the `location` of the property rather than amending all the directory references in the build file.

244

- You can see that we refer to the properties that we set up at the start of the file using the notation:

```
${propertyname}
```

- I am defining the class path to point to the location of the JUnit and selenium jars stored in the /lib folder. And the compiled jar files which get placed into the /build directory.

```
<target name="clean">
  <delete dir="${build}" />
  <delete dir="${testresults}" />
  <delete dir="${testreport}" />
</target>
```

- The clean target will delete all the folders that are created during an Ant build. This uses the properties we setup earlier.

- We can use this build file to delete the /build, /junit-results and /junit-report folders by writing ant clean at the command line.

```
<target name="makedir">
  <mkdir dir="${build}" />
  <mkdir dir="${testresults}" />
  <mkdir dir="${testreport}" />
</target>
```

- The makedir target will create all the folders that are required for our Ant build.

- We can use this build file to make the /build, /junit-results and /junit-report folders by issuing ant make from the command line.

```
<target name="compile" depends="clean, makedir">
  <javac
    srcdir="${src}" destdir="${build}"
    debug="true" includeAntRuntime="false">
    <classpath refid="JUnit.class.path" />
  </javac>
</target>
```

- The compile target will create all the folders that are required for our Ant build.

- This target depends on clean and makedir so we know that before Ant compiles our code, it will delete, and then recreate, the folders defined by the properties build, testresults and testreport.

- This target uses an Ant command called `javac`, this compiles the java code that we have written (all our tests) and writes the jar file into the folder defined by the property `build`.

- You can see what this command does by issuing an `ant compile` command and looking in the `build` directory. You should see a folder structure that mirrors our package structure, and within the folders, `.class` files instead of `.java` files. The `.class` files are compiled versions of our source code.

```
<target name="run_JUnit_tests_requiring_server_started">
  <antcall target="start-selenium-server"/>
  <JUnit printsummary="yes" fork="yes" errorproperty="JUnit.error"
      failureproperty="JUnit.error">
    <classpath refid="JUnit.class.path" />
    <formatter type="xml" />
    <test todir="${testresults}"
        name="com.eviltester.seleniumtutorials.MyFirstSeleniumTests" />
    <test todir="${testresults}"
        name="com.eviltester.seleniumtutorials.MySecondSeleniumTests" />
    <test todir="${testresults}"
        name="com.eviltester.seleniumtutorials.chap18.HTML_form_tests" />
    <test todir="${testresults}"
        name="com.eviltester.seleniumtutorials.chap19.Static_HTML_tests" />
    <test todir="${testresults}"
        name="com.eviltester.seleniumtutorials.chap20.
            JavaScript_With_Selenium_Tests" />
  </JUnit>
  <antcall target="report-JUnit"/>
  <antcall target="stop-selenium-server"/>
  <fail if="JUnit.error" message="Selenium test(s) failed.  See reports!"/>
</target>
```

- The `run_JUnit_tests_requiring_server_started` is the target that does the most work for us.

- You can see that it does not have a `depends` statement, so it could be called from the command line, but we actually call it from within one of the other targets.

- Working through the target you can see an `antcall`. The `antcall` element allows us to treat Ant targets as though they were functions or subroutines in a program, effectively saying "run the target start-selenium-server".

```
<antcall target="start-selenium-server" />
```

- We then use the JUnit Ant command. This runs the JUnit tests which we just compiled and writes the test results to XML files.

  - This sets up a property `JUnit.error` which traps the JUnit values `errorproperty` and `failureproperty`, this causes JUnit to run all the tests, and if there is a failure it will set one of these properties and we can then use that to report a

246

failure. If we didn't do this we would have to use the `haltonerror` attribute, but this would stop the build on the first test failure - this might be desirable with unit tests, but with the functional tests we run, we want as many of those to run as we can.

- The `printsummary` attribute is currently set to "yes", which means that we get a one line summary for each test case. Another useful value is "withOutAndErr" which shows all the output that we might have written to System.out and System.err

- We set the classpath for JUnit to use so that it knows where to find our tests and the libraries that they use.

- Then the sequence of `<test></test>` elements, defines the classes we want to run as tests and the directory to write the XML results to.

- We call the `report-JUnit` target - this converts the output XML files to an HTML report

- We call the `stop-selenium-server` target which issues the http command to stop the selenium server.

- We then have a `<fail></fail>` element, which causes the build to fail, if the `JUnit.error` property was set when running the JUnit tests.

```
<target name="all_selenium_tests" depends="compile" description="The Main
    Target for running all tests">
    <antcall target="run_JUnit_tests_requiring_server_started"/>
</target>
```

- The `all_selenium_tests` target will ensure that the `compile` step has run.

- Then it runs the JUnit tests.

- This is the default target triggered when calling `ant`.

```
<target name="report-JUnit">
    <JUnitreport todir="${testreport}">
      <fileset dir="${testresults}">
        <include name="TEST-*.xml"/>
      </fileset>
      <report format="frames" todir="${testreport}"/>
    </JUnitreport>
</target>
```

- The `report-JUnit` target uses the `JUnitreport` task element which takes all the files in the `testresults` directory which match the naming convention `TEST-*.xml` and converts them into an HTML report which is written to the `testreport` directory.

247

```
<target name="start-selenium-server">
  <java jar="${seleniumserver}" fork="true" spawn="true" />
  <waitfor maxwait="2" maxwaitunit="minute" checkevery="100">
    <http url="http://localhost:4444/selenium-server/driver/?cmd=testComplete
      "/>
  </waitfor>
</target>
```

- The `start-selenium-server` target could be initiated from the command line with an `ant start-selenium-server` command.

- This build file uses an `antcall` during the `run_JUnit_tests_requiring_server_started` target.

- This makes a java call to run the Selenium server `.jar` file defined in the properties section.

- Then uses the `waitfor` task (http://unow.be/rc/antwaitfor[11]) to wait for 2 minutes, checking every 100 milliseconds if the http task has returned a 200 status (http://unow.be/rc/antconditions[12])

    - If at the end of 2 minutes Selenium had not started, then this task would fail and the build would fail

```
<target name="stop-selenium-server">
  <get taskname="selenium-shutdown"
    src="http://localhost:4444/selenium-server/driver/?cmd=
      shutDownSeleniumServer"
    dest="${testresults}\selenium-shutdown-output.txt" ignoreerrors="true" />
</target>
```

- The `stop-selenium-server` target could be initiated from the command line with `ant stop-selenium-server`.

- This uses the `get` task to call the URL which stops selenium, and write the results of the call to an output file in the `testresults` folder

```
</project>
```

- Finally we make the XML well formed by closing the `project` element

---

[11] http://ant.apache.org/manual/Tasks/waitfor.html
[12] http://ant.apache.org/manual/Tasks/conditions.html

23.7 Running the Ant file

This gives us an Ant file which, when run, will start up the selenium server, run the tests which require the server to be running, report the results and stop the server.

I run this by starting a command line in the source directory and issuing `ant` as a command.

The output from running this will show you the Ant targets run, and the error and success messages generated.

e.g.

```
Buildfile: C:\selenium_tests\InitialSeleniumTests\build.xml

clean:
    [delete] Deleting directory C:\selenium_tests\InitialSeleniumTests\build
    [delete] Deleting directory C:\selenium_tests\InitialSeleniumTests\junit-
        results
    [delete] Deleting directory C:\selenium_tests\InitialSeleniumTests\junit-
        report

makedir:
    [mkdir] Created dir: C:\selenium_tests\InitialSeleniumTests\build
    [mkdir] Created dir: C:\selenium_tests\InitialSeleniumTests\junit-results
    [mkdir] Created dir: C:\selenium_tests\InitialSeleniumTests\junit-report

compile:
    [javac] Compiling 18 source files to C:\selenium_tests\
        InitialSeleniumTests\build

all_selenium_tests:

run_JUnit_tests_requiring_server_started:

start-selenium-server:
    [JUnit] Running com.eviltester.seleniumtutorials.MyFirstSeleniumTests
    [JUnit] Tests run: 2, Failures: 0, Errors: 0, Time elapsed: 23.625 sec
    [JUnit] Running com.eviltester.seleniumtutorials.MySecondSeleniumTests
    [JUnit] Tests run: 10, Failures: 0, Errors: 0, Time elapsed: 161.297 sec
    [JUnit] Running com.eviltester.seleniumtutorials.chap18.HTML_form_tests
    [JUnit] Tests run: 14, Failures: 0, Errors: 0, Time elapsed: 43.203 sec
    [JUnit] Running com.eviltester.seleniumtutorials.chap19.Static_HTML_tests
    [JUnit] Tests run: 6, Failures: 0, Errors: 0, Time elapsed: 31.125 sec
    [JUnit] Running com.eviltester.seleniumtutorials.chap20.
        JavaScript_With_Selenium_Tests
    [JUnit] Tests run: 6, Failures: 0, Errors: 0, Time elapsed: 86.219 sec

report-JUnit:
[JUnitreport] Processing C:\selenium_tests\InitialSeleniumTests\junit-report\
    TESTS-TestSuites.xml to C:\DOCUME~1\Alan\LOCALS~1\Temp\null562923061
[JUnitreport] Loading stylesheet jar:file:/C:/apache-ant-1.8.0/lib/ant-JUnit.
    jar!/org/apache/tools/ant/taskdefs/optional/JUnit/xsl/junit-frames.xsl
[JUnitreport] Transform time: 10172ms
[JUnitreport] Deleting: C:\DOCUME~1\Alan\LOCALS~1\Temp\null562923061

stop-selenium-server:
[selenium-shutdown] Getting: http://localhost:4444/selenium-server/driver/?
    cmd=shutDownSeleniumServer
[selenium-shutdown] To: C:\selenium_tests\InitialSeleniumTests\junit-results\
    selenium-shutdown-output.txt
```

```
BUILD SUCCESSFUL
Total time: 6 minutes 13 seconds
```

From the above output you can see the following sequence:

- `clean` task ran and deleted the directories

- `makedir` task ran and created the directories

- the `compile` step compiled 18 source code files

- the `all_selenium_tests` step executed which started selenium and ran the tests

  - Note that if you run this with Selenium 1.0.3 or below you will see a warning about duplicate Ant. Previous versions of the selenium server had the ant.jar bundled within it. This did not give any issues, but was a cause for concern to some people when they saw it. This does not happen with Selenium 2.

- the JUnit report was created

- the selenium server was stopped

- the build was reported as successful

After running this build file, the `junit-report` directory contains a report of the tests run.

When we move the tests over to Hudson, the JUnit reports will be collated and stored with their build so that you have a historic record of the test runs for each build.

23.8   Add the Tests which require no server

Having created a build file which runs the tests requiring a selenium server to start. We now add the additional complexity of tests which require no server.

Given the way we have structured the build file, it is not hard to add this functionality.

In fact we only have to make two changes.

The addition of a new target to run those tests, and a call to run that target.

```
<target name="run_JUnit_tests_requiring_no_server">
  <JUnit printsummary="yes" fork="yes" errorproperty="JUnit.error"
      failureproperty="JUnit.error">
    <classpath refid="JUnit.class.path" />
    <formatter type="xml" />

    <test todir="${testresults}"
 name="com.eviltester.seleniumtutorials.chap21.
    Start_Selenium_Server_In_A_Test" />
    <test todir="${testresults}"
```

```
name="com.eviltester.seleniumtutorials.chap15.XpathExamplesAsTests" />
    <test todir="${testresults}"
name="com.eviltester.seleniumtutorials.chap16.CSSSelectorExamplesAsTests" />
  </JUnit>

  <antcall target="report-JUnit"/>

  <fail if="JUnit.error" message="Selenium test(s) failed.  See reports!"/>
</target>
```

- This JUnit test target does almost the same as the previous, the only differences being the omission of the `start-selenium-server` and `stop-selenium-server` antcalls

- This has led to a repetition of the antcall to `report-JUnit`, which means that the first time it is run it collates the results from running the tests with the server, and the second time it collates all the test runs.

```
<target name="all_selenium_tests" depends="compile" description="The Main
    Target for running all tests">
  <antcall target="run_JUnit_tests_requiring_server_started"/>
    <antcall target="run_JUnit_tests_requiring_no_server"/>
</target>
```

- The `all_selenium_tests` target now calls both JUnit test runs

23.9   Refactor The Build File

I will also refactor the build file. We have created the basics for running our tests in the above build file. I will want to have multiple build files to illustrate different setups and configurations - I could do this in a single build file but it will become complicated to read.

Instead I will take advantage of the fact that the Ant file is XML and use the standard XML Entity Inclusion mechanism to split my build file into components.

I will move the properties, `build`, `clean`, `makedir`, `compile` and `report-JUnit` targets into one file, and the `start` and `stop` selenium targets into another and include them as entities in my build file. This will result in a clean build file, and make it easy to see the core of what the build file does.

I create a file called `properties_build_clean_compile_report.xml` which has the Ant code we have discussed above.

I then create a second file called `start_stop_selenium.xml` into which I will add the targets that I need: `start-selenium-server` and `stop-selenium-server`.

- `properties_build_clean_compile_report.xml`

251

```xml
<!-- Sets variables which can later be used. -->
<!-- The value of a property is accessed via ${} -->
<property name="src" location="src" />
<property name="build" location="build" />
<property name="libs" location="lib" />
<property name="testresults" location="junit-results" />
<property name="testreport" location="junit-report" />

    <!--
        Make this conditional to support all versions of Selenium
        based on a property called seleniumVersion

        http://ant.apache.org/manual/Tasks/condition.html
        http://ant.apache.org/manual/Tasks/conditions.html

        value and location are synonymous so don't really need to distinguish
            between
        them, only did this to keep semantics of the attributes correct
    -->


    <!-- default Selenium version to use by build script, override from
        command line
        e.g. ant -f buildfile.xml -DseleniumVersion=2.1.0
        double check and adjust if necessary for each new version of Selenium
    -->
<property name="seleniumVersion" value="2.1.0" />

    <!-- use a regular naming convention for the folder to make things easy
        so all selenium versions go in lib/selenium_<versionnumber>
    -->
<property name="seleniumLibsFolder" value="selenium_${seleniumVersion}" />

    <!-- could have saved myself some pain by
        simply renaming the files when placed in
        appropriate libs subfolders -->
<condition property="seleniumServerJarName" value="selenium-server-
    standalone-${seleniumVersion}.jar">
    <or>
        <equals arg1="${seleniumVersion}" arg2="2.0.0" />
        <equals arg1="${seleniumVersion}" arg2="2.1.0" />
    </or>
</condition>
<condition property="seleniumServerJarName" value="selenium-server.jar">
    <or>
        <equals arg1="${seleniumVersion}" arg2="1.0.3" />
        <!-- 0.9.2 doesn't do everything we need for selenium simplified -->
        <!-- <equals arg1="${seleniumVersion}" arg2="0.9.2" /> -->
    </or>
</condition>

<property name="seleniumserverlocation" value="${libs}/${seleniumLibsFolder
    }/${seleniumServerJarName}" />

<condition property="seleniumclientlocation" value="">
    <or>
        <equals arg1="${seleniumVersion}" arg2="2.0.0" />
        <equals arg1="${seleniumVersion}" arg2="2.1.0" />
    </or>
</condition>
<condition property="seleniumclientlocation" value="${libs}/${
```

252

```
    seleniumLibsFolder}/selenium-java-client-driver.jar">
  <or>
    <equals arg1="${seleniumVersion}" arg2="1.0.3" />
    <!-- <equals arg1="${seleniumVersion}" arg2="0.9.2" />  -->
  </or>
</condition>


  <property name="seleniumclient" location="${seleniumclientlocation}" />
  <property name="seleniumserver" location="${seleniumserverlocation}" />

<!-- Define the classpath which includes the JUnit.jar and the classes after
    compiling-->
<path id="JUnit.class.path">
  <pathelement location="${libs}/junit-4.8.1.jar" />
  <pathelement location="${seleniumclient}" />
  <pathelement location="${seleniumserver}" />
  <pathelement location="${build}" />
</path>

<!-- Deletes the existing build and result directories-->
<target name="clean">
  <delete dir="${build}" />
  <delete dir="${testresults}" />
  <delete dir="${testreport}" />
</target>

<!-- Creates the  build, and test results directories-->
<target name="makedir">
  <mkdir dir="${build}" />
  <mkdir dir="${testresults}" />
  <mkdir dir="${testreport}" />
</target>

<!-- Compiles the java code -->
<target name="compile" depends="clean, makedir">
  <javac srcdir="${src}" destdir="${build}" debug="true"
    includeAntRuntime="false">
    <classpath refid="JUnit.class.path" />
  </javac>
</target>

<target name="report-JUnit">
  <JUnitreport todir="${testreport}">
  <fileset dir="${testresults}">
    <include name="TEST-*.xml"/>
  </fileset>
  <report format="frames" todir="${testreport}"/>
  </JUnitreport>
</target>


• start_stop_selenium.xml


 <target name="start-selenium-server">
  <java jar="${seleniumserver}"
           fork="true" spawn="true" />
        <waitfor maxwait="2" maxwaitunit="minute"
            checkevery="100">
```

253

```
                <http url="http://localhost:4444/selenium-server/driver/?cmd=
                    testComplete"/>
            </waitfor>
</target>

<target name="stop-selenium-server">
        <get taskname="selenium-shutdown"
            src="http://localhost:4444/selenium-server/driver/?cmd=
                shutDownSeleniumServer"
            dest="${testresults}\selenium-shutdown-output.txt" ignoreerrors="
                true" />
</target>
```

I then need to turn the build file into a ''proper'' XML file with the `doctype` to allow me to use entity notation. I do this by including the following at the top of the build file:

```
<?xml version="1.0"?>

<!DOCTYPE project [
        <!ENTITY start_stop_selenium SYSTEM "start_stop_selenium.xml">
        <!ENTITY properties_build_clean_compile_report SYSTEM
                "properties_build_clean_compile_report.xml">
]>
```

I include the XML files by referencing them in the build file by adding

```
&properties_build_clean_compile_report;
```

and

```
&start_stop_selenium;
```

at the point where I want to include the files.

So my build file would become:

```
<?xml version="1.0"?>

<!DOCTYPE project [
        <!ENTITY start_stop_selenium SYSTEM "start_stop_selenium.xml">
        <!ENTITY properties_build_clean_compile_report SYSTEM
                "properties_build_clean_compile_report.xml">
]>

<project name="Run Selenium Tests" default="all_selenium_tests">

    &properties_build_clean_compile_report;

    <target name="run_JUnit_tests_requiring_server_started">

        <antcall target="start-selenium-server"/>
        <JUnit printsummary="yes" fork="yes"
                errorproperty="JUnit.error" failureproperty="JUnit.error">
            <classpath refid="JUnit.class.path" />
            <formatter type="xml" />
            <test todir="${testresults}"
                    name="com.eviltester.seleniumtutorials.MyFirstSeleniumTests" /
                        >
            <test todir="${testresults}"
                    name="com.eviltester.seleniumtutorials.MySecondSeleniumTests"
                        />
```

```
            <test todir="${testresults}"
                    name="com.eviltester.seleniumtutorials.chap18.HTML_form_tests"
                        />
            <test todir="${testresults}"
                    name="com.eviltester.seleniumtutorials.chap19.
                        Static_HTML_tests" />
            <test todir="${testresults}"
             name="com.eviltester.seleniumtutorials.chap20.
                JavaScript_With_Selenium_Tests" />
        </JUnit>

        <antcall target="report-JUnit"/>
        <antcall target="stop-selenium-server"/>
        <fail if="JUnit.error" message="Selenium test(s) failed.  See reports!"
            />
    </target>

    <target name="run_JUnit_tests_requiring_no_server">
        <JUnit printsummary="yes" fork="yes" errorproperty="JUnit.error"
                failureproperty="JUnit.error">
            <classpath refid="JUnit.class.path" />
            <formatter type="xml" />

            <test todir="${testresults}"
         name="com.eviltester.seleniumtutorials.chap21.
            Start_Selenium_Server_In_A_Test" />
            <test todir="${testresults}"
                    name="com.eviltester.seleniumtutorials.chap15.
                        XpathExamplesAsTests" />
            <test todir="${testresults}"
                name="com.eviltester.seleniumtutorials.chap16.
                    CSSSelectorExamplesAsTests" />
        </JUnit>

        <antcall target="report-JUnit"/>
        <fail if="JUnit.error" message="Selenium test(s) failed.  See reports!"
            />
    </target>

    <target name="all_selenium_tests" depends="compile"
            description="The Main Target for running all tests">
        <antcall target="run_JUnit_tests_requiring_server_started"/>
        <antcall target="run_JUnit_tests_requiring_no_server"/>
    </target>

    &start_stop_selenium;

</project>
```

XML Entity Includes allow you to reuse parts of your Ant build files or cut back on the complexity of the build file to make it more readable.

23.10   Summary

Now that we have a `build.xml` file, all we have to do is open a command line and change directory to where the build file resides, then issue the command `ant` and all the tests that

NOTE:
In the source code download, this build file is `build_server_and_without.xml` which can be run with `ant -f build_server_and_without.xml`
Use `ant` if you have copy and pasted the code into `build.xml`

we have configured to run in the `build.xml` file will run.

A human readable report of the test run will be placed in the `/test-reports` folder.

23.11   Additional Reading

You can find details of all the task used in the Ant documentation (http://unow.be/rc/antdocs[13]):

- `property` http://unow.be/rc/antprop[14]

- `antcall` http://unow.be/rc/antcall[15]

- `delete` http://unow.be/rc/antdelete[16]

- `javac` http://unow.be/rc/antjavac[17]

- `get` http://unow.be/rc/antGet[18]

- `mkdir` http://unow.be/rc/mkdir[19]

- `JUnit` http://unow.be/rc/antJUnit[20]

- `JUnitreport` http://unow.be/rc/antJUnitreport[21]

- `fail` http://unow.be/rc/antfail[22]

- `waitfor` http://unow.be/rc/antwaitfor[23]

---

[13] http://ant.apache.org/manual/
[14] http://ant.apache.org/manual/Tasks/property.html
[15] http://ant.apache.org/manual/Tasks/antcall.html
[16] http://ant.apache.org/manual/Tasks/delete.html
[17] http://ant.apache.org/manual/Tasks/javac.html
[18] http://ant.apache.org/manual/Tasks/get.html
[19] http://ant.apache.org/manual/Tasks/mkdir.html
[20] http://ant.apache.org/manual/Tasks/junit.html
[21] http://ant.apache.org/manual/Tasks/junitreport.html
[22] http://ant.apache.org/manual/Tasks/fail.html
[23] http://ant.apache.org/manual/Tasks/waitfor.html

- `echo` http://unow.be/rc/antecho[24]

- `condition` http://unow.be/rc/antcondition[25]

- `or` http://unow.be/rc/antconditions[26]

I found the following references particularly useful while creating this chapter on Ant. You may like to read these as follow on reading to this chapter:

- http://unow.be/rc/antXMLentity[27]

- http://unow.be/rc/antHelloWorld[28]

- http://unow.be/rc/antwiki[29]

- http://unow.be/rc/vogellaant[30]

- http://unow.be/rc/rcci[31]

---

[24] http://ant.apache.org/manual/Tasks/echo.html

[25] http://ant.apache.org/manual/Tasks/condition.html

[26] http://ant.apache.org/manual/Tasks/conditions.html

[27] http://ant.apache.org/faq.html#xml-entity-include

[28] http://ant.apache.org/manual/tutorial-HelloWorldWithAnt.html

[29] http://en.wikibooks.org/wiki/Apache_Ant

[30] http://www.vogella.de/articles/ApacheAnt/ar01s04.html

[31] http://wiki.openqa.org/display/SRC/Selenium-RC+and+Continuous+Integration

Chapter 24

Using Hudson to Run Ant

24.1 Introducing Hudson

Hudson is a continuous integration server. This means that it can poll a source-code repository and rebuild an application, running all its tests, whenever the source code changes. Or, we can configure a test run to start at regular periods throughout the day. This is the approach that we will cover in this chapter.

NOTE:

Hudson has now split into two projects: Hudson, and Jenkins.

- Jenkins is available from

    - http://unow.be/rc/ciwiki[1]

Jenkins is a drop in replacement for hudson, so everything in this chapter applies to Jenkins.

24.2 Install Hudson

Hudson has a particularly simple install process.

Visit http://unow.be/rc/hudson[2]

Download the `hudson.war` to a directory of your choosing. I used `c:\hudson`

There should be link from the home page, or go direct to the downloads area of the site: http://unow.be/rc/gethudson[3]

A `.war` file is simply another java archive so we could run Hudson from the command line by typing:

```
java -jar hudson.war
```

---

[1] https://wiki.jenkins-ci.org/
[2] http://hudson-ci.org/
[3] http://hudson-ci.org/download

Figure 24.1: Visit hudson-ci.org to download hudson.war

To keep our Hudson configuration to a minimum we are going to control where Hudson saves its data. We will do this by setting the HUDSON_HOME environment variable when we start hudson.

```
java -DHUDSON_HOME="C:\hudson\home" -jar hudson.war
```

From the messages displayed in the console window you will see the port that the HTTP Listener has started on, by default this is `port=8080`. Visit http://localhost:8080/ to see the Hudson GUI.

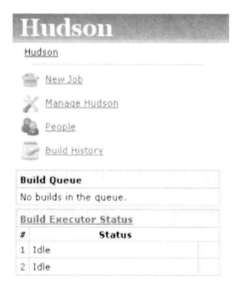

Figure 24.2: The Hudson GUI

260

We want to configure Hudson to use our Ant setup. Click the `Manage Hudson` link from the left hand menu. Then on the `Manage Hudson` screen, click on `Configure System`.

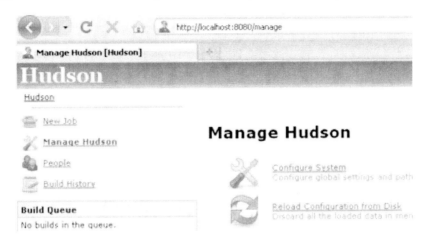

Figure 24.3: Manage Hudson

In the Hudson configuration we need to add an Ant configuration. So click the `[Add Ant]` button and type in a name e.g. "Ant 1.8" and set the `ANT_HOME` field to the directory that you have Ant installed in. You also need to check that the Shell executable is set to `cmd.exe` for Windows.

Click `Save` at the bottom of the page to save your configuration changes.

Now we want to create a Hudson Job to run our tests automatically. Click on `New Job` from the Menu, type in a job name and choose the `free-style` software project. Click the `[OK]` button.

I used the name `Automated Selenium Simplified Tests`.

24.3   Using Hudson without Version Control

In order to demonstrate the use of Hudson without imposing too many setup issues on you when you are learning the principles. I have chosen not to add the complexity of a version control system in to the examples.

In the next section I will provide an overview of using a version control system with Hudson, but I am not going to cover in this book how to setup a version control system. As that will increase the size of the book and increase the complexity of what we have to cover.

So we need to understand a little bit about how Hudson works and where it stores its files.

In Hudson select `Manage Hudson` then choose `Configure System`, at the top of the page, Hudson lists the home directory where it stores the projects.

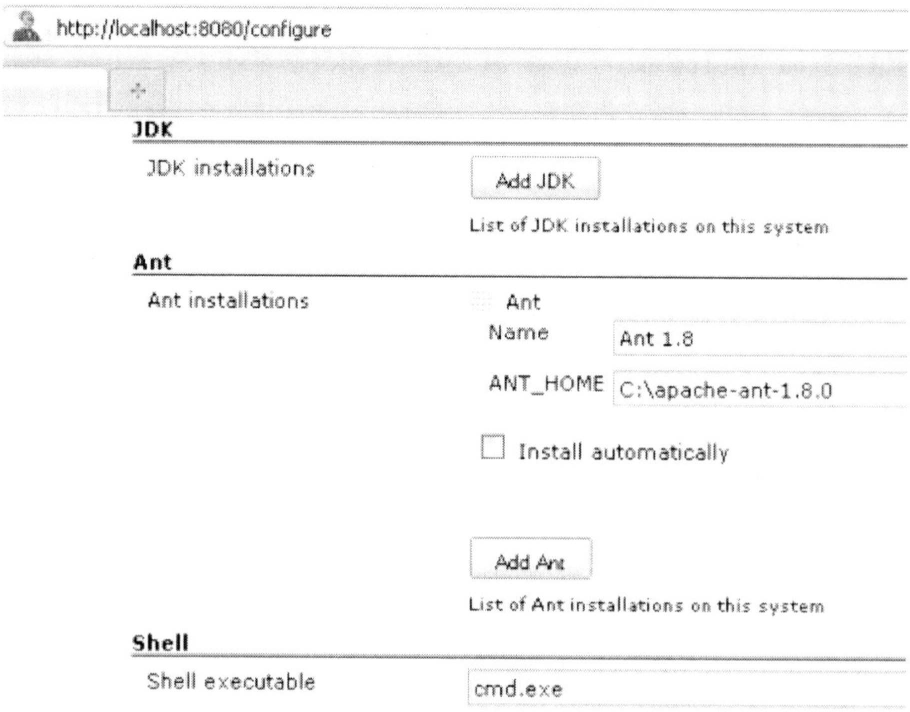

http://localhost:8080/configure

JDK

JDK installations   Add JDK

List of JDK installations on this system

Ant

Ant installations

   Ant
   Name   Ant 1.8

    ANT_HOME   C:\apache-ant-1.8.0

    ☐ Install automatically

    Add Ant

List of Ant installations on this system

Shell

Shell executable   cmd.exe

Figure 24.4: Configuration for our simple Hudson setup

NOTE:

Hudson uses the term Job and Project interchangeably, and inconsistently, between forms. So when you create a Hudson Job, it is also a Hudson Project.

If you started Hudson with -DHUDSON_HOME then this should show the directory you used.

Open a file explorer and look in your Hudson home directory.

In the jobs folder, Hudson creates a folder for each job that you configure. So we should now have a folder for Automated Selenium Simplified Tests.

Normally, we would have Hudson "checkout" our source-code from the version control system into a "workspace" folder of the Hudson job. Because we have not setup a version control system. We will simulate the "checkout" process with a .bat file which copies the files from our source-code folder to the Hudson workspace.

Once the files have been checked out, Hudson will run the Ant build file to build the project and run the tests.

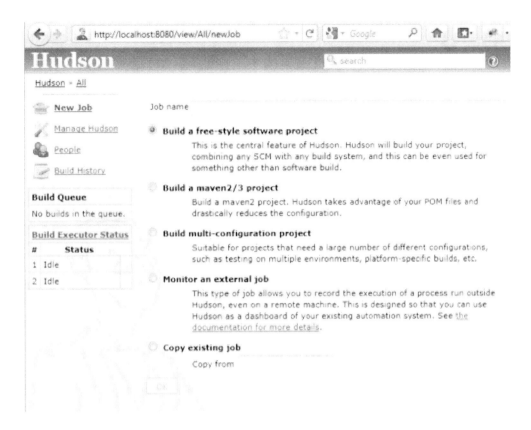

Figure 24.5: Create a new job

Figure 24.6: Hudson Home Directory

Then Hudson will take the JUnit test reports from the workspace and copy them into a "builds" folder that stores the details of all or builds to keep a historic record of the test runs.

I created a `nosvn.bat` file. If you use this concept remember to use the paths that you have setup on your system.

```
rmdir /s /q "C:\hudson\home\jobs\Automated Selenium Simplified Tests\
    workspace\"
mkdir "C:\hudson\home\jobs\Automated Selenium Simplified Tests\workspace\"
xcopy "C:\selenium_tests\InitialSeleniumTests" "C:\hudson\home\jobs\Automated
    Selenium Simplified Tests\workspace\" /e
```

263

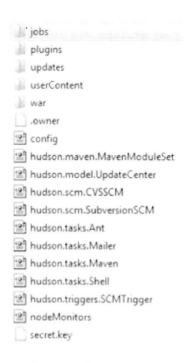

Figure 24.7: Hudson folder structure

All this file does is:

1. remove the workspace directory for the "Automated Selenium Simplified Tests" project

2. create the workspace directory for the "Automated Selenium Simplified Tests" project so we have a blank workspace

3. copy in the files from where I keep my source-code to the workspace we just created

This is exactly what the subversion job would do, but the subversion job, instead of copying files from a directory, would take the most recent versions from the version control repository and copy them to the workspace folder.

Having created your own `nosvn.bat` file, we can complete the configuration of the Hudson project.

24.4   Configure the Hudson Project

We need to add some `Build Steps` to the project.

Click the `[Add Build Step]` button, and select an `Execute Windows batch command` build step.

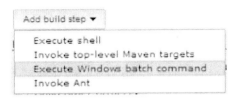

Figure 24.8: Add Execute Windows batch command

We will use this build step to run our `nosvn.bat` file to get all the files in the correct place for Hudson to execute and track the results. The command we want to run is our `nosvn.bat` file, so I just put the full path for that file in the command field.

Figure 24.9: Execute the nosvn.bat file

Next we want to run the Ant command so click `Add build step` and select `Invoke Ant` as the next build step to add.

Here you can leave the invoke Ant command as the default Ant Version as we only have one setup. If we had configured multiple Ant installs on the Hudson configuration we would have to choose the name of the Ant configuration from the drop down.

Figure 24.10: Use Default ''Invoke Ant'' configuration

The last thing we have to do before being able to run the test, is to gather the JUnit reports when the tests have finished.

We collate the JUnit reports in the `Post-build Actions` section.

Enable the `Publish JUnit test results report` and for the `Test report XMLs` we use:

`**/junit-results/*.xml`

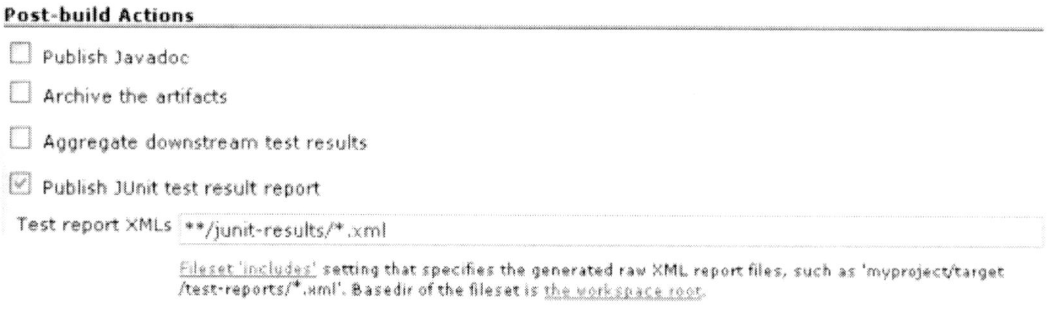

Post-build Actions

☐ Publish Javadoc

☐ Archive the artifacts

☐ Aggregate downstream test results

☑ Publish JUnit test result report

Test report XMLs `**/junit-results/*.xml`

Fileset 'includes' setting that specifies the generated raw XML report files, such as 'myproject/target /test-reports/.xml'. Basedir of the fileset is the workspace root.*

Figure 24.11: JUnit test result collation configuration

The `**/junit-results/*.xml` means, all the `.xml` files in the `junit-results` folder.

This will collate all the XML files and generate the HTML reports and store them in the Hudson builds for future use.

Save the configuration by pressing the `[Save]` button.

Now you should see the project GUI.

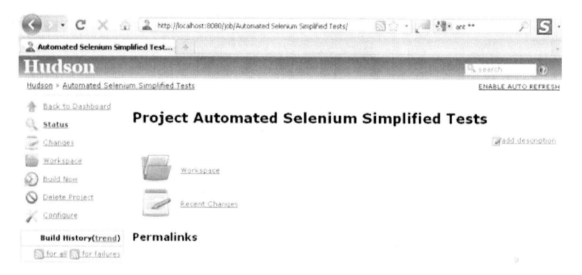

Figure 24.12: Initial view of the project GUI

Manually start a build by clicking `Build Now` and if you have everything setup correctly. Your tests should start running.

An item will show in the `Build History` with the date and time, follow the link for this build.

You monitor the progress of the build by clicking on the `Console Output`, and you see all the console messages written as the tests run.

You should then be able to view the test results by clicking on the `Latest Test Result` link from the project GUI.

24.5   Scheduling the build automatically

We can configure it to run automatically. Click on the `Configure` link from the Project GUI and amend the `Build Triggers` section to use the `Build Periodically`. Click on the `(?)` button to the right of the field to see the options that you can add to the schedule.

Figure 24.13: Build Triggers with Help expanded

By entering `0 * * * *` I have scheduled it for the 0th minute of every hour, of every day of every month no matter what day of the week it is.

The full options for the field are explained above, here are a few examples:

- 5 * * * 1-5 - 5 minutes after the hour on every working weekday (Monday - Friday)

- 0 */3 * * * - 0 minutes after the hour, every 3 hours of every day

Chapter 25

Adding Subversion to the mix

I use Subversion as my version control system.

If you want to install subversion locally then Visual SVN server seems like the easiest option:

- http://unow.be/rc/vsvn[1]

- http://unow.be/rc/vsvndocs[2]

You would also want to install TortoiseSVN

- http://unow.be/rc/tsvn[3]

TortoiseSVN provides right context menu integration in explorer to access your repositories.

After you have installed subversion, and imported your code into the repository, then check the code out so you can work on it. You can integrate subversion into Hudson by selecting the subversion option in the Source Code Management section. Adding in the URL to access your subversion repository and the folder you wish to checkout into the workspace.

You will be prompted to enter your authentication credentials, if the subversion repository you are using is not public.

You would also remove the Execute Windows batch command step from the Build section.

This should be all you have to do to amend your Hudson setup from the non-version controlled approach to a robust version control setup.

As an example, below I have listed the fields I have setup to pull down the source code from the public xp-dev subversion repository to run the tests under Hudson. The important configuration is in the Source Code Management \ Subversion section.

- Repository URL:

  – http://svn2.xp-dev.com/svn/seleniumsimplified/trunk/FinalSeleniumTests

---

[1]http://visualsvn.com/server/
[2]http://visualsvn.com/server/getting-started/
[3]http://tortoisesvn.tigris.org/

Figure 25.1: Subversion configuration in Hudson

- Local module directory:

    - .

- Check-out Strategy:

    - Always check out a fresh copy

- Repository browser

    - (Auto)

Chapter 26

Take Stock of Where we are

Before we move on, we should take a quick look at what we have managed to achieve, look at the weaknesses we have, and consider what to do next.

We have managed to:

- Write some tests using the IDE and run them from the command line

- Write some tests by converting from IDE tests into Eclipse

- Write tests which require the Selenium Server to be active:

    - `com.eviltester.seleniumtutorials.MyFirstSeleniumTests`

    - `com.eviltester.seleniumtutorials.MySecondSeleniumTests`

    - `com.eviltester.seleniumtutorials.chap18.HTML_form_tests`

    - `com.eviltester.seleniumtutorials.chap19.Static_HTML_tests`

    - `com.eviltester.seleniumtutorials.chap20.JavaScript_With_Selenium_Tests`

- Write tests which start the server themselves:

    - `com.eviltester.seleniumtutorials.chap21.Start_Selenium_Server_In_A_Test`

    - `com.eviltester.seleniumtutorials.chap15.XpathExamplesAsTests`

    - `com.eviltester.seleniumtutorials.chap16.CSSSelectorExamplesAsTests`

- Use Ant to run the tests

- Automatically run the tests from Hudson

- Integrating a version control system into Hudson

All of which means that you can start automating your tests.

Now we have to start making your automation ''Industrial Strength'':

1. Our tests should all use a common way of interacting with Selenium, so they should all start Selenium automatically.

2. We should run our tests across different browsers e.g. Internet Explorer and Firefox and Safari, and we should do this automatically.

3. We should start using Page Object Models and abstraction layers to make our tests more readable and more robust.

26.1 Plan Of Action

We will create a class to manage our connection to a Selenium Server. This will use an existing server if one exists, or start one if it doesn't. This way our tests don't have to keep containing code to manage the server.

We only really care about the tests in a few of the packages since many of our tests were "examples" of Selenium functionality:

- `MySecondSeleniumTests`

- `HTML_form_tests`

- `Static_HTML_tests`

- `JavaScript_With_Selenium_Tests`

We will refactor these tests after copying them into a new package. That way we can safely refactor and organise without disturbing the originals.

The first thing we will do is have all the tests use the `SeleniumManager` class.

Then we will start working through each test class and moving all references to Selenium into page objects.

Ideally we don't want our tests to use Selenium, we want our tests to be written in the language of the application, not the tool. So we want to create "Page Object Models" instead of writing tests using a "Tool Object Model".

Currently we have:

`test -> tool`

What we want is:

`test -> application page object model -> tool`

So instead of:

```
assertEquals("this page title",selenium.getTitle());
```

we would want to see:

```
assertEquals("this page title",resultsPage.getTitle());
```

This will make the tests more readable.

And instead of:

```
assertEquals(1,selenium.getXpathCount("//div[@id='_checkboxes']/ul/li").
    intValue());
```

we would want to see

```
assertEquals(1,resultsPage.getNumberOfCheckBoxes());
```

272

This makes the tests more readable and more maintainable. More maintainable because the XPath statements are contained in the page object model classes, rather than in all the tests. So they are localised into a single area. When the application changes, hopefully all we have to do is change the application page object model, and not the tests.

The tests should only have to change when the structure of the application fundamentally changes.

So we will build page object models for each of the pages that we have tested:

- http://compendiumdev.co.uk/selenium/basic_html_form.html

- http://compendiumdev.co.uk/selenium/search.php

- http://compendiumdev.co.uk/selenium/form_processor.php

We don't have to plan what the page object models will look like in advance. They will be supporting the tests, so we will take the approach of writing the test so that it looks the way we want it to. Then use Eclipse to create the objects and methods, and move the existing code from our tests into the objects.

We will be incrementally updating the tests so that at any point in time during the "refactoring", the tests remain functional and we will not break them. If anything, the tests will start to run faster and become more maintainable with minimal effort.

Once we have done this, we will see the inadequacies of the current test set and will be able to easily expand the tests so that they add more value.

We will also add some syntactic sugar to the page object models to increase the readability of the tests:

e.g.

- `.and()`

- `.then()`

- by passing back references to `this` from the above methods

We will also refactor the page object models themselves to create constants.

Then, we will set the tests to run on multiple browsers.

We will also see which tests can add value by making them data driven to increase the data coverage that can be achieved with a single test path.

Chapter 27

Evolving A Selenium Manager Class

We currently have two ways of starting and connecting to selenium:

- from the command line
- from the code

Both of these are valid options, and we are using very similar code for all the connection methods.

We will use a few guiding principles from this point forward:

- remove repeating code
- delegate responsibility to specific classes

Following these principles, we will create a single manager class which hides these implementation details for us so that we can have a common set of code to start and connect to the selenium server.

I want the basic code in the tests to look like the following:

```
@BeforeClass
static public void startServer(){
    sm = new SeleniumManager();
    sm.start("http://www.compendiumdev.co.uk");
    selenium = sm.getSelenium();
}

@AfterClass
static public void stopServer(){
  sm.stop();
}
```

This means that before a class of tests I will create a SeleniumManager object, start the server at the domain of my choice, and then retrieve a Selenium session from the manager to use in my tests.

After the tests have finished I just want to issue a single call to the SeleniumManager Object to close the browser, connection and the Selenium Server.

Also I want this to work regardless of whether the Selenium server is already running locally or not.

We will start by moving the source-code created in Chapter 21 ''Start Selenium Programmatically'' into a new class called SeleniumManager.

275

To do this, create a new test class called `Selenium_Manager_Tests`.

In a new package `com.eviltester.seleniumtutorials.refactored`

So that the code for this looks like the following:

```
package com.eviltester.seleniumtutorials.refactored;

import com.thoughtworks.selenium.Selenium;

public class Selenium_Manager_Tests {

  static SeleniumManager sm;
  static Selenium selenium;

  @BeforeClass
  static public void startServer(){
     sm = new SeleniumManager();
     sm.start("http://www.compendiumdev.co.uk");
     selenium = sm.getSelenium();
  }


  @AfterClass
  static public void stopServer(){
    sm.stop();
  }
}
```

This will look like it has a lot of errors in Eclipse.

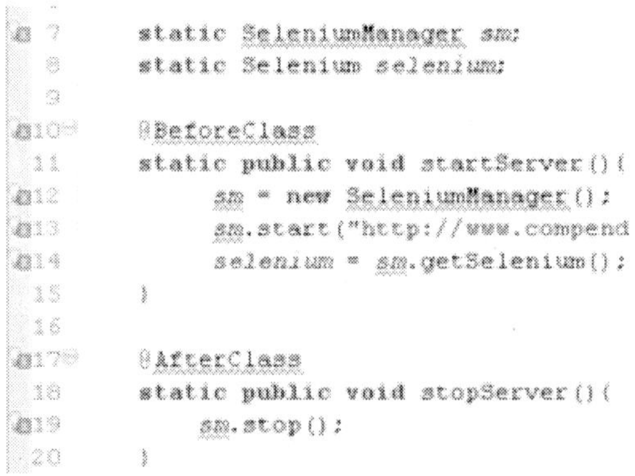

Figure 27.1: A Test Class using Selenium Manager with initial errors

Let me explain my reasoning for developing the class in this way.

We are about to start refactoring our existing test code into a page object model. This is a set of page object classes which will model our application and act as an abstraction layer which removes the implementation code of how to access a page. The page object model provides an interface which makes tests easier to read and easier to understand. I build the abstraction layer by writing tests which are readable.

276

I am doing the same here. The `SeleniumManager` abstracts away the details of how to start selenium and connect to the server. So create the interface by writing tests which are concise and readable.

Also by doing this, we can use the Eclipse automatic error-fixing code to help us write the class.

As an example, our first line with an error:

```
static SeleniumManager sm;
```

By clicking on the error marker on the left border, Eclipse will tell us that it cannot find the class because we have not created the `SeleniumManager` class yet.

```
SeleniumManager cannot be resolved to a type
```

Selecting the option `Create class 'SeleniumManager'` in the drop down, will cause Eclipse to create the basic class file for us and we can add the additional code we need.

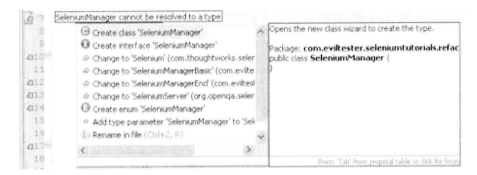

Figure 27.2: Click on error marker on left to see error and fixing options

This is all functionality you have seen before, but we can use it to very quickly build up the scaffolding code that we need to build our abstraction layers.

Select the option to `Create class 'SeleniumManager'`. I added it under a `seleniumutils` package to keep the ''helper'' classes separate from my page abstractions and tests.

This will create the `SeleniumManager.java` file

```
package com.eviltester.seleniumutils;

public class SeleniumManager {

}
```

Back to our `Selenium_Manager_Tests` class:

1. Fix the error on `@BeforeClass` by selecting the import option from the drop down menu: `Import 'BeforeClass' (org.junit)`

2. Fix the error on `@AfterClass` by selecting the drop down menu import option:

```
Import 'AfterClass' (org.junit)
```

Use the remaining errors to create the public methods that we want the `SeleniumManager` class to expose to our tests.

The line `sm.start("http://www.compendiumdev.co.uk");` shows an error marker. Click on the error marker and choose the option to `Create Method`. This will create a basic `start` method in `SeleniumManager` which we can amend to implement starting the server from the manager.

Follow this process for all the lines with error in the `Selenium_Manager_Tests` class.

You will end up with a `SeleniumManager` class like the following:

```
package com.eviltester.seleniumutils;

import com.thoughtworks.selenium.Selenium;

public class SeleniumManager {

  public void start(String string) {
    // TODO Auto-generated method stub
  }

  public Selenium getSelenium() {
    // TODO Auto-generated method stub
    return null;
  }

  public void stop() {
    // TODO Auto-generated method stub
  }
}
```

Clearly this class doesn't do anything. But it is good enough to remove all the errors in our test class.

Adding a test into the `Selenium_Manager_Tests` class and will force us to write the code to implement the `SeleniumManager`.

Add the following test into `Selenium_Manager_Tests.java`

```
@Test
public void openCompendiumDevHomePage(){
  selenium.open("/");
}
```

Remove the error on `@Test` by selecting the option to `Import 'Test' (org.junit)` from the drop down menu.

If you now run this test by right clicking on `Selenium_Manager_Tests.java` in Eclipse and selecting `Run as \ JUnit Test` then the test will run and fail because the selenium variable is `null`, because we haven't implemented any code in the `SeleniumManager`.

Fortunately we already have this code in one of our tests, so it will be easy to fill in the template provided by Eclipse.

278

We can reuse code from `Start_Selenium_Server_In_A_Test.java`.

Copy in code from the `checkForBindExceptionAndStopExistingServer` test.

Copy the following code into the `SeleniumManager start()` method.

```
SeleniumServer seleniumServer=null;
String stopSeleniumCommand =
  "http://localhost:4444/selenium-server/driver/?cmd=shutDownSeleniumServer";
try {
  seleniumServer = new SeleniumServer();
  seleniumServer.start();
} catch (java.net.BindException bE){
  // could not bind, assume that server is currently running
  // and carry on
  System.out.println("could not bind - carrying on");

  // try and stop it
  if( runHTTPCommand(stopSeleniumCommand)){
    try {
      seleniumServer = new SeleniumServer();
      seleniumServer.start();
    } catch (Exception e) {
      throw new IllegalStateException(
      "Could not stop existing server on blocked port 4444", e);
    }
  }
} catch (Exception e) {
  // any other exception stop and start
  throw new IllegalStateException("Can't start selenium server", e);
}

Selenium selenium=null;
selenium = new DefaultSelenium("localhost", 4444,
    "*firefox", "http://www.compendiumdev.co.uk");
selenium.start();
```

Eclipse will show an error on the following line:

```
if( runHTTPCommand(stopSeleniumCommand)){
```

The error occurs because we need to also copy in the private method `runHTTPCommand`. Copy the code, so `runHTTPCommand` becomes a private method of `SeleniumManager`.

There will still be an error on this line because of an unhandled `IOException`. Select the option to `Add throws declaration`.

Figure 27.3: Add throws declaration to start method

There should now be no errors in the `SeleniumManager` class. But we haven't finished implementing everything we need to have our test pass.

We have passed in a URL to our `start` method. We should amend the method definition signature to make it more descriptive. Change:

279

```
public void start(String string) throws IOException {
```

to

```
public void start(String baseURL) throws IOException {
```

Now, use the `baseURL` in the `start` method.

Amend:

```
selenium = new DefaultSelenium("localhost", 4444,
    "*firefox", "http://www.compendiumdev.co.uk");
```

to

```
selenium = new DefaultSelenium("localhost", 4444,"*firefox", baseURL);
```

Now fix the test we wrote in `Selenium_Manager_Tests`. To do that we need to return the selenium object which we instantiate with the `new DefaultSelenium...` command in `start()`, when we call the `getSelenium()` method.

To do that we have to change the selenium variable from being in scope of the `start()` method and instead be in scope to the class.

We can do this by moving the line `Selenium selenium=null;` out of the method and up to the top of the class declaration. When we move this we should also move the `SeleniumServer` declaration as this will be required in the stop method.

```
public class SeleniumManager {

  SeleniumServer seleniumServer=null;
  Selenium selenium=null;
  // code removed ...
```

So our `getSelenium` method can now be amended to read:

```
public Selenium getSelenium() {
    return selenium;
  }
```

We do have a reminder in our `SeleniumManager` code in the form of a TODO, even though our `Start_Selenium_Server` test would pass. We can write the code for the `stop()` method now too.

```
public void stop() {
  if(selenium!=null){
    selenium.close();
    selenium.stop();
  }

  if(seleniumServer!=null){
    seleniumServer.stop();
  }
}
```

In the `stop` method we check to see if the `selenium` object has been set, and if it has, we issue a close, followed by a stop.

Then if the `seleniumServer` object has been set (meaning that we created it programmatically) then we issue a `stop` command for the server.

We have one thing to do in our `Selenium_Manager_Tests` class because the `sm.start(...)` line is showing an error.

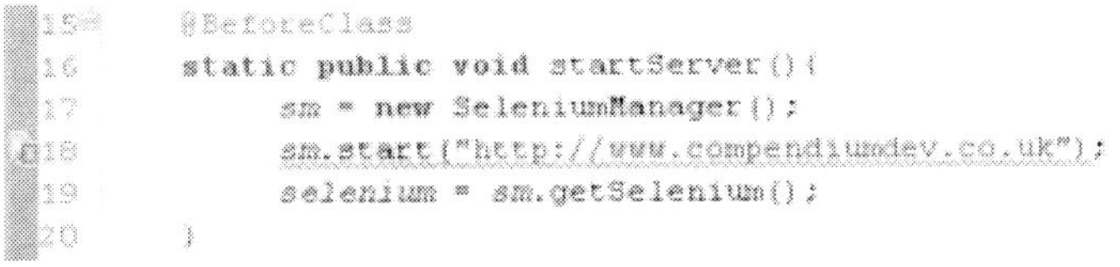

Figure 27.4: One last error to fix in the test

Use the right-click menu in Eclipse to `Add throws declaration` so that the `@BeforeClass` looks like the following:

```
@BeforeClass
static public void startServer() throws IOException{
    sm = new SeleniumManager();
    sm.start("http://www.compendiumdev.co.uk");
    selenium = sm.getSelenium();
}
```

And our `Start_Selenium_Server` test, should now pass and cleanly tidy up Selenium for us.

Perform the following actions and see:

1. Run the test and see that it creates the expected browser instances, the test passes, and the browser instances close

2. Check that selenium server is not running

   - opening http://localhost:4444/selenium-server/driver/?cmd should show an error message. e.g. IE will say `Internet Explorer cannot display the webpage`, Firefox will report `Problem loading page - Unable to connect`

3. Start up a selenium server, `java -jar selenium-server-standalone-2.0.0.jar` in the selenium server folder. And check that the server is running

   - opening http://localhost:4444/selenium-server/driver/?cmd in a browser should show an error message.

```
ERROR Server Exception: sessionId should not be null; has this session been
    started yet?
```

1. run the test

2. check that the selenium server has stopped by following step 2.1

NOTE:

You can find the finished Selenium Manager in the source code distribution as
`SeleniumManager02FirstEvolution.java` in `com.eviltester.seleniumutils`

We now have an abstraction layer to help remove the complexity of working with the Selenium Server. This will make the tests more consistent and easier to write.

But also:

- If we choose to amend our Selenium Server control behaviour and have it not stop a server if one is already running, we just have to amend SeleniumManager and not our test code.

- When we come to add multiple browsers in our Ant and Hudson builds we can do that by amending the `SeleniumManager` and not any of our tests.

- If we choose to move to WebDriver we just have to change `SeleniumManager` and not any of our tests.

We want our tests to remain stable, unless the conditions that they are testing change in the app. We don't want to have to amend our tests if the app structure or tool changes (where possible).

We achieve these aims through abstractions like the `SeleniumManager` and Page Object Models.

Chapter 28

Create Our First Page Objects

This chapter will provide the detail of how to convert a test using direct selenium commands into one using Page Objects. This will reinforce the basic techniques demonstrated in our previous chapter.

I will start by converting the Search page tests from `MySecondSeleniumTests.java`.

NOTE:

This was heavily refactored in Chapter 12, so I am starting with the refactored version with the `@BeforeClass` and `@AfterClass` methods in it.

This can be found in the `com.eviltester.seleniumtutorials.chap12` package from the downloadable source-code distribution, in the java class file `MySecondSeleniumTests_Refactored_BeforeClass_AfterClass.java`

I will initially go through the steps and refactoring in detail, but as we go through the chapter you will see that the basic steps are the same, so in later test refactorings I will only dwell on those steps which are different. As I step through I will explain the thought processes behind each step.

28.1 Create a SearchPageTests class

Since we are going to change these heavily. Rather than amending them in the java class file `MySecondSeleniumTests.java`, we will take the opportunity to rename the class to make it more representative of the area being tested and move it to a new package to keep it Separate from the previous tests.

So:

1. Create a copy of the class by right-clicking on the class in the package explorer and choosing "copy"

2. Right click on the `com.eviltester.seleniumtutorials.refactored` package and choose paste

This will copy the class into the package. The first thing we will do is rename it.

Right click on the `MySecondSeleniumTests.java` in the following package:

Select `refactor \ rename`. Then rename it as `SearchPageTests`

NOTE:

The only reason for doing a copy and paste here is to keep your old tests so that you can see the difference. Normally we would rely on a version control system to maintain versions and we would refactor or migrate to page object models directly. Learning to rely on copy and paste may mean that you do not learn to refactor as much as you need to, and risk tolerating repeated code across your tests.

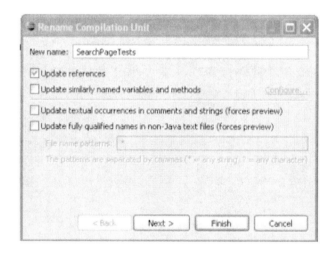

Figure 28.1: Rename to SearchPageTests

28.2   Add the SeleniumManager

The first thing we need to do, is bring in the `SeleniumManager` that we created.

Add the lines of code to use the Selenium Manager to the `SearchPageTests` class as illustrated below:

```java
public class SearchPageTests {
    static SeleniumManager sm;
    static Selenium selenium;

    @BeforeClass
    static public void automateTestSetup() throws IOException{
      sm = new SeleniumManager();
      sm.start("http://www.compendiumdev.co.uk");
      selenium = sm.getSelenium();
```

```
        startSeleniumAndSearchForSeleniumRC();
    }

    @AfterClass
    static public void stopSeleniumAndCloseBrowser() {
        sm.stop();
    }

    static void startSeleniumAndSearchForSeleniumRC() {
        selenium.open("/selenium/search.php");
        selenium.type("xpath=//input[@name='q']", "Selenium-RC");
        selenium.click("xpath=//input[@name='btnG' and @type='submit']");
        selenium.waitForPageToLoad("30000");
    }
```

To get to the above point I had to:

- Remove errors about the `SeleniumManager` not being recognised by importing the `SeleniumManager` class - you should be able to do this by right clicking on the error indicator and choosing the automated fix to `Import 'SeleniumManager'`

```
import com.eviltester.seleniumutils.SeleniumManager;
```

- Remove the error on the `sm.start(...)` line about an unhandled exception by right clicking on the error indicator and choosing the automated fix to create the exception declaration: `Add throws declaration`. This adds the `throws IOException` text to the `@BeforeClass` annotated method.

- Change the `startSeleniumAndSearchForSeleniumRC` method by deleting the instantiation of the selenium object, remove the return statement and change the method declaration to void. Remove the `selenium.start(...)` statement.

- I also took the opportunity to change the open statement from a fully qualified URL, to a URL relative to the base URL we entered in the `sm.start(...)` method.

Run the tests to make sure that they still pass.

Now we will illustrate the steps to move these tests over to page object models on a method by method basis.

28.3   Convert startSeleniumAndSearchForSeleniumRC

The first method we will look at is `startSeleniumAndSearchForSeleniumRC`:

```
static void startSeleniumAndSearchForSeleniumRC() {
    selenium.open("/selenium/search.php");
    selenium.type("xpath=//input[@name='q']", "Selenium-RC");
    selenium.click("xpath=//input[@name='btnG' and @type='submit']");
    selenium.waitForPageToLoad("30000");
}
```

285

Our basic approach will be to remove any of the statements using `selenium.` and move this functionality into a page object in a way that makes the test readable and maintainable.

We will use the following pattern initially in these tests to open pages with the page object model.

```
SearchPage searchPage = new SearchPage(selenium);
searchPage.open();
```

Add this code to your test and then we will look at it in more depth.

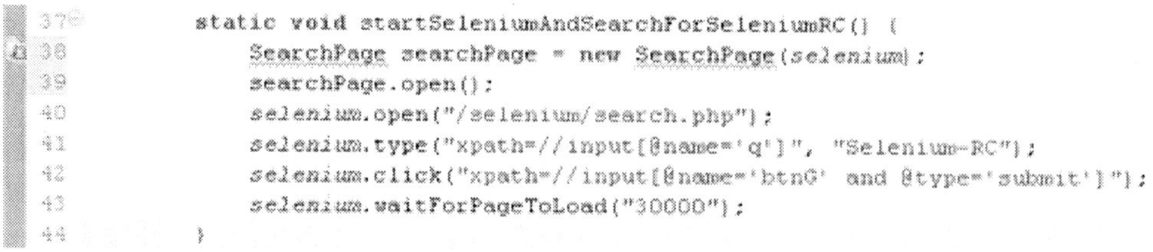

```
37   static void startSeleniumAndSearchForSeleniumRC() {
38       SearchPage searchPage = new SearchPage(selenium);
39       searchPage.open();
40       selenium.open("/selenium/search.php");
41       selenium.type("xpath=//input[@name='q']", "Selenium-RC");
42       selenium.click("xpath=//input[@name='btnG' and @type='submit']");
43       selenium.waitForPageToLoad("30000");
44   }
```

Figure 28.2: Adding initial SearchPage references to the test

I add the code to create and use the `SearchPage` object into the test before creating the `SearchPage` object and methods. I do this because I want to model what the interface will look like and how it will be used, and I want to take advantage of Eclipse's code fixing technology to make it easier for me to write the code, as we saw in the Chapter "Evolving A Selenium Manager Class".

I know that my `SearchPage` object will need to call selenium to implement the test, so I will pass the current selenium session to the `SearchPage` object when I create it. And I know that once I have the `searchPage` object, I want to call an `open()` method to open the page.

Now we can start implementing the page object using the Eclipse error fixing technology.

Left-click on the error in the left border and choose the option to create the class.

```
Create class 'SearchPage'
```

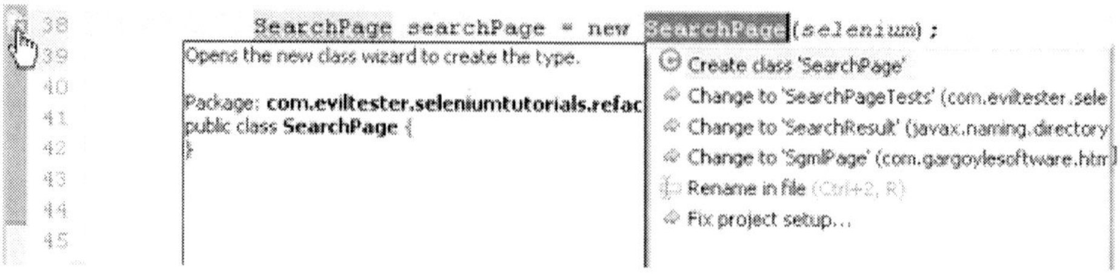

Figure 28.3: Create class 'SearchPage' automatically

In the New Java Class wizard, I will change the package location so that all the page objects are kept in the same package

```
com.eviltester.seleniumtutorials.refactored.pageObjectModel
```

By finishing the wizard, Eclipse will create a new class for us:

```
package com.eviltester.seleniumtutorials.refactored.pageObjectModel;

public class SearchPage {
}
```

We now have more errors to deal with in our test. First the undefined constructor:

```
The constructor SearchPage(Selenium) is undefined
```

Deal with this by choosing `Create constructor 'SearchPage(Selenium)'` from the drop down menu.

Save `SearchPage.java` to remove the error display in `SearchPageTests.java`. Do this after every move of code or creation of methods into `SearchPage.java`. This will force Eclipse to recompile the class and use the new version, which will fix the errors in our `SearchPageTests.java`.

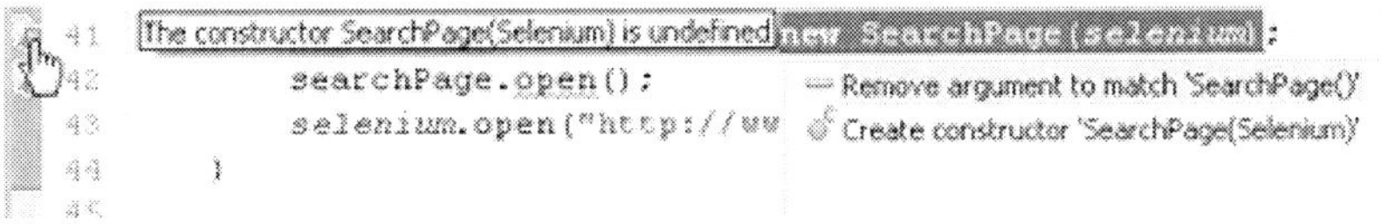

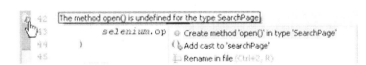

Figure 28.4: Left-click on error to use drop down to create constructor

Next we have to deal with the error on the `searchPage.open();` line. So choose to create the method:

```
Create method 'open()' in type 'SearchPage'
```

.

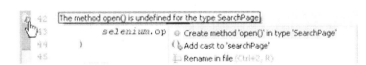

Figure 28.5: Left-click on error to user drop down to create open method

This will remove all the errors in our test, although we haven't implemented anything in our page object.

So now cut and paste the `selenium.open("/selenium/search.php")` line into the `SearchPage` object.

```
selenium.open("selenium/search.php");
```

We end up with a page object like this:

```
package com.eviltester.seleniumtutorials.refactored.pageObjectModel;

import com.thoughtworks.selenium.Selenium;

public class SearchPage {

  public SearchPage(Selenium selenium) {
    // TODO Auto-generated constructor stub
  }

  public void open() {
    selenium.open("/selenium/search.php");
  }

}
```

Now that our test has no errors we can turn our attention to the page object and fix the errors here.

Because we have references to a `selenium` object in the `open` method which we haven't declared or set, we are seeing the error `selenium cannot be resolved`.

We can fix this by amending the constructor as follows:

```
private Selenium selenium;

  public SearchPage(Selenium selenium) {
    this.selenium = selenium;
  }
```

Here we have declared a variable local to the class called `selenium`, of type `Selenium`, which will act as our reference to the current Selenium session.

In the constructor, we take the `selenium` value passed in as a parameter and assign it to our local class variable.

At this point we have the basics of our page object model for the search page. All it does is open the page, but it abstracts where that page is located from our tests, and all our test has to do is create the correct object and call the method to open the page.

If you run the `SearchPageTests` now you should find that they run without errors and do exactly the same thing.

Where possible I prefer to take the approach of refactoring to page object models incrementally from existing tests, and doing it in such a way that the existing tests do not break.

We still have lines in the test which use the `Selenium` object, so we need to move them into the `SearchPage` object.

Again, I start by writing what I want the test code to look like and I will initially do that with in line comments:

```
static void startSeleniumAndSearchForSeleniumRC() {
  SearchPage searchPage = new SearchPage(selenium);
  searchPage.open();
  //searchPage.typeSearchTerm("Selenium-RC");
```

288

```
    //searchPage.clickSearchButton();
    selenium.type("xpath=//input[@name='q']", "Selenium-RC");
    selenium.click("xpath=//input[@name='btnG' and @type='submit']");
    selenium.waitForPageToLoad("30000");
}
```

So remove comments from the line:

```
searchPage.typeSearchTerm("Selenium-RC");
```

This now has an error against it because the `typeSearchTerm` method does not exist.

By writing a call for a method that does not exist, I can quickly create it with a left-click on the error marker and choosing the option `Create method ...` from the pop-up menu.

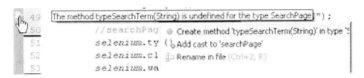

Figure 28.6: Create method typeSearchTerm

The method will be created in the page object, and all we have to do, is cut the code we are moving from the test.

```
    selenium.type("xpath=//input[@name='q']", "Selenium-RC");
```

And paste it into the page object method.

```
public void typeSearchTerm(String string) {
    selenium.type("xpath=//input[@name='q']", "Selenium-RC");
}
```

Then adjust the page object method to use the passed in parameters, and name the parameters appropriately.

```
public void typeSearchTerm(String searchTerm) {
    selenium.type("xpath=//input[@name='q']", searchTerm);
}
```

Now we will remove the comment marks from the code for:

```
searchPage.clickSearchButton();
```

Use the Eclipse pop-up menu to `Create Method 'clickSearchButton'`.

Cut and paste the code into the `clickSearchButton` method in `SearchPage`:

```
public void clickSearchButton() {
    selenium.click("xpath=//input[@name='btnG' and @type='submit']");
    selenium.waitForPageToLoad("30000");
}
```

We don't even have to amend any parameters this time.

Then we end up with the test that we wanted:

289

NOTE:

This is the basic pattern I use for refactoring from tests using Selenium directly into page object models:

- write the test as you want it to read

- make those statements comments until you are ready to implement them

- remove the comment marks and use Eclipse to create the method

- cut the code out of the test and paste it into the page object method

- amend the method to have sensible parameter names

- use the parameters in the body of the method

```
static void startSeleniumAndSearchForSeleniumRC() {
  SearchPage searchPage = new SearchPage(selenium);
  searchPage.open();
  searchPage.typeSearchTerm("Selenium-RC");
  searchPage.clickSearchButton();
}
```

28.4   typeInASearchTermAndAssertThatHomePageTextIsPresent

The next test to refactor is `typeInASearchTermAndAssertThatHomePageTextIsPresent`:

```
@Test
public void typeInASearchTermAndAssertThatHomePageTextIsPresent(){

  assertTrue(selenium.isTextPresent(
      "Selenium Remote-Control Selenium RC comes in two parts." +
      " A server which automatically"));
  assertTrue(selenium.isTextPresent(
      "launches and kills browsers, and acts as" +
      " a HTTP proxy for web requests from them."));
}
```

This time, I can see that I'm going to create an `isTextPresent` method on `searchPage`, so I will do that by amending the text directly, by changing `selenium` to `SearchPage`:

```
assertTrue(searchPage.isTextPresent(
    "Selenium Remote-Control Selenium RC comes in two parts." +
    " A server which automatically"));
```

Then use the same process as before to fix the error using Eclipse, amend the parameter and copy in the code to create the following method in `searchPage`:

```
public boolean isTextPresent(String textToSearchFor) {
  return selenium.isTextPresent(textToSearchFor);
}
```

All I do in the `isTextPresent` method is delegate the processing to the selenium method of the same name and return the result of doing this. The selenium method is named effectively enough that I don't see the need to change it in my test.

I make the same change on the other `assertTrue`.

One extra thing I will do here is refactor some of the code in the test.

I need the `searchPage` object created in `startSeleniumAndSearchForSeleniumRC` to be accessible in the tests. So I need to move the declaration for this object to the top of the code. e.g.

```
public class SearchPageTests {
  static SeleniumManager sm;
  static Selenium selenium;
  static SearchPage searchPage;
```

And in the `startSeleniumAndSearchForSeleniumRC` method:

```
static void startSeleniumAndSearchForSeleniumRC() {
    searchPage = new SearchPage(selenium);
```

Having done this, I run the tests again and make sure they still pass.

NOTE:

After a few refactoring steps, and amending the tests, run the tests and make sure that they still pass. If you run them from within Eclipse, hopefully you will find that they all run and continue to pass.

They should, as you haven't done anything to materially change the tests, all you have done is move the code which implements the tests into abstraction layers.

28.5   typeInASearchTermAndAssertThatHomePageURLExists

I rename `typeInASearchTermAndAssertThatHomePageURLExistsWithFewerXpath` to the shorter `typeInASearchTermAndAssertThatHomePageURLExists`.

```
@Test
public void typeInASearchTermAndAssertThatHomePageURLExists(){

    // create a new variable called matchingCountTotal to calculate
    // the total number of times our XPath matches, initially setting
    // it to 0
    int matchingCountTotal = 0;
```

291

```
// call getXpathCount with our XPath for the url and
// add the intValue version to the total
matchingCountTotal += selenium.getXpathCount(
    "//a[starts-with(@href,'http://selenium-rc.seleniumhq.org')]").intValue
        ();
matchingCountTotal += selenium.getXpathCount(
    "//a[starts-with(@href,'http://seleniumhq.org/projects/remote-control')
        ]").intValue();
assertTrue("No homepage URL found",matchingCountTotal>0);
}
```

NOTE:

There is a `rename` refactoring which renames all instances and references in the code.

The next step involves moving the XPath statements into the page object. It seems to me that a general statement of intent that I have for those lines is:

```
searchPage.numberOfURLsThatStartWith
```

Really, I want my test to look like this:

```
matchingCountTotal += searchPage.numberOfURLsThatStartWith(
                        "http://selenium-rc.seleniumhq.org");
matchingCountTotal += searchPage.numberOfURLsThatStartWith(
                        "http://seleniumhq.org/projects/remote-control");
```

So if I add that code into the test, I can use Eclipse to build the `numberOfURLsThatStartWith` method.

```
public int numberOfURLsThatStartWith(String aHREF) {
   return selenium.getXpathCount(
     "//a[starts-with(@href,'" + aHREF + "')]").intValue();
}
```

All I have done here is rename the parameter to be readable. Delegated the functionality to selenium's `getXPathCount` method. And replaced the URL which was hard coded into the XPath statement with the parameter we pass in.

One interesting side-effect is that I no longer need the comments that I added in to the test to explain what was going on, as the test is now more readable.

```
@Test
public void typeInASearchTermAndAssertThatHomePageURLExists(){

   int matchingCountTotal = 0;

   matchingCountTotal += searchPage.numberOfURLsThatStartWith(
          "http://selenium-rc.seleniumhq.org");
   matchingCountTotal += searchPage.numberOfURLsThatStartWith(
          "http://seleniumhq.org/projects/remote-control");

   assertTrue("No homepage URL found",matchingCountTotal>0);
}
```

28.6   typeInASearchTermAndCheckPageTitleHasSearchTermInIt

```
@Test
public void typeInASearchTermAndCheckPageTitleHasSearchTermInIt(){

  String pageTitle = selenium.getTitle();
  assertTrue("Page Title does not contain Selenium-RC search term: " +
      pageTitle,
        pageTitle.contains("Selenium-RC"));
}
```

All I have to do here is create a `searchPage.getTitle` method:

```
String pageTitle = searchPage.getTitle();
```

Which looks like the following when added to the SearchPage object and delegating to the `selenium.getTitle()` method:

```
public String getTitle() {
  return selenium.getTitle();
}
```

So our test becomes:

```
@Test
public void typeInASearchTermAndCheckPageTitleHasSearchTermInIt(){
  String pageTitle = searchPage.getTitle();
  assertTrue("Page Title does not contain Selenium-RC search term: " +
      pageTitle,
        pageTitle.contains("Selenium-RC"));
}
```

28.7   typeInASearchTermAndCheckSearchInputHasSearchTermInIt

```
@Test
public void typeInASearchTermAndCheckSearchInputHasSearchTermInIt(){

  String searchTerm = selenium.getValue(
      "xpath=//input[@name='q' and @title='Search']");

  assertTrue("Search Input does not contain Selenium-RC : " + searchTerm,
      searchTerm.equals("Selenium-RC"));
}
```

I think that this test should read:

```
String searchTerm = searchPage.getSearchTerm();
```

So I add that code to the test, then use Eclipse to create the `getSearchTerm` method.

Then move the code from my test into the `getSearchTerm` method in `SearchPage`:

```
public String getSearchTerm() {
  return selenium.getValue("xpath=//input[@name='q' and @title='Search']");
}
```

So the final test reads:

```
@Test
public void typeInASearchTermAndCheckSearchInputHasSearchTermInIt(){
  String searchTerm = searchPage.getSearchTerm();
  assertTrue("Search Input does not contain Selenium-RC : " + searchTerm,
      searchTerm.equals("Selenium-RC"));
}
```

28.8   After all that ...

28.8.1   SearchPageTests.java

```
package com.eviltester.seleniumtutorials.refactored;
import static org.junit.Assert.*;
import java.io.IOException;
import org.junit.*;
import com.eviltester.seleniumtutorials.refactored.pageObjectModel.SearchPage
   ;
import com.eviltester.seleniumutils.SeleniumManager;
import com.thoughtworks.selenium.*;

public class SearchPageTests {

  static SeleniumManager sm;
  static Selenium selenium;
  private SearchPage searchPage;

  @BeforeClass
  static public void startServer() throws IOException{
    sm = new SeleniumManager();
    sm.start("http://www.compendiumdev.co.uk");
    selenium = sm.getSelenium();
    startSeleniumAndSearchForSeleniumRC();
  }

  @AfterClass
  static public void stopServer(){
    sm.stop();
  }

  static void startSeleniumAndSearchForSeleniumRC() {
    searchPage = new SearchPage(selenium);
    searchPage.open();
    searchPage.typeSearchTerm("Selenium-RC");
    searchPage.clickSearchButton();
  }

  @Test
  public void typeInASearchTermAndAssertThatHomePageTextIsPresent(){
    assertTrue(searchPage.isTextPresent(
      "Selenium Remote-Control Selenium RC comes in two parts." +
      " A server which automatically"));
    assertTrue(searchPage.isTextPresent(
      "launches and kills browsers, and acts as" +
      " a HTTP proxy for web requests from them."));
  }

  @Test
  public void typeInASearchTermAndAssertThatHomePageURLExists(){
```

```
      int matchingCountTotal = 0;
      matchingCountTotal += searchPage.numberOfURLsThatStartWith(
            "http://selenium-rc.seleniumhq.org");
      matchingCountTotal += searchPage.numberOfURLsThatStartWith(
            "http://seleniumhq.org/projects/remote-control");
      assertTrue("No homepage URL found",matchingCountTotal>0);
   }

   @Test
   public void typeInASearchTermAndCheckPageTitleHasSearchTermInIt(){
      String pageTitle = searchPage.getTitle();
      assertTrue("Page Title does not contain Selenium-RC search term: "
         + pageTitle, pageTitle.contains("Selenium-RC"));
   }

   @Test
   public void typeInASearchTermAndCheckSearchInputHasSearchTermInIt(){
      String searchTerm = searchPage.getSearchTerm();
      assertTrue("Search Input does not contain Selenium-RC : " + searchTerm,
         searchTerm.equals("Selenium-RC"));
   }
}
```

28.8.2   SearchPage.java

And the page object abstraction looks as follows:

```
package com.eviltester.seleniumtutorials.refactored.pageObjectModel;
import com.thoughtworks.selenium.Selenium;

public class SearchPage {

   private Selenium selenium;

   public SearchPage(Selenium selenium) {
      this.selenium = selenium;
   }

   public void open() {
      selenium.open("/selenium/search.php");
   }

   public void typeSearchTerm(String searchTerm) {
      selenium.type("xpath=//input[@name='q']", searchTerm);
   }

   public void clickSearchButton() {
      selenium.click("xpath=//input[@name='btnG' and @type='submit']");
      selenium.waitForPageToLoad("30000");
   }

   public boolean isTextPresent(String textToSearchFor) {
      return selenium.isTextPresent(textToSearchFor);
   }

   public int numberOfURLsThatStartWith(String aHREF) {
      return selenium.getXpathCount(
            "//a[starts-with(@href,'" + aHREF + "')]").intValue();
   }

   public String getTitle() {
```

```
    return selenium.getTitle();
  }

  public String getSearchTerm() {
    return selenium.getValue("xpath=//input[@name='q' and @title='Search']");
  }
}
```

28.9 Final Notes

The tests and page object will evolve over time, as more tests get added, more methods will move into the `SearchPage` page object. If the application changes, hopefully all amendments can be made to the `SearchPage` object and not the test.

By removing the selenium command execution from the tests we can see the intent of those tests clearly and make them more readable.

Chapter 29

More Page Object Creation

All that remains now, is to take the other tests that we are interested in retaining, and refactor them to use page objects:

- `HTML_form_tests.java`

- `JavaScript_With_Selenium_Tests.java`

- `Static_HTML_tests.java`

The same basic principles apply for all of these.

29.1   The Tests

This chapter will go through the refactoring of these test files very quickly. Only covering the decisions that were made, or the points where we had to refactor differently.

You can find all the final code in the code distribution in the following package:

```
com.eviltester.seleniumtutorials.refactored
```

A useful exercise for you is to go through and do the refactorings yourself and create the page object model as outlined below. You have all the source-code to refer to if you make a mistake. Follow the same procedures as the previous chapter and the act of doing the refactoring will eventually make the thought processes and actions second nature for you.

29.1.1   HTML_form_tests.java

First I copy the `HTML_form_tests.java` from the chap18 package and paste it into the refactored package, i.e.

- from:

  - `com.eviltester.seleniumtutorials.chap18`

- to:

  - `com.eviltester.seleniumtutorials.refactored`

297

And then add the `SeleniumManager` code.

I change the `setUp` method to instantiate a `BasicHTMLForm` object, and call the open method on this object, instead of opening the page directly.

- Before

```
private static Selenium selenium;

@BeforeClass
public static void setUpBeforeClass()
      throws Exception {
  selenium = new DefaultSelenium(
        "localhost", 4444,
   "*firefox","http://www.compendiumdev.co.uk");
   selenium.start();
}

@AfterClass
public static void tearDownAfterClass() throws Exception {
   selenium.close();
   Selenium.stop();
}

@Before
public void setUp() throws Exception {
 selenium.open("/selenium/basic_html_form.html");
}
```

- After

```
static SeleniumManagerEnd sm;
static Selenium selenium;
BasicHTMLForm htmlForm;

@BeforeClass
static public void startServer() throws IOException{
  sm = new SeleniumManagerEnd();
  sm.start("http://www.compendiumdev.co.uk");
  selenium = sm.getSelenium();
}

@AfterClass
static public void stopServer(){
  sm.stop();
}

@Before
public void setUp() throws Exception {
  htmlForm = new BasicHTMLForm(selenium);
  htmlForm.open();
}
```

298

test_submit_form_with_default_values

```
@Test
public void test_submit_form_with_default_values(){
    selenium.click("//input[@name='submitbutton' and @value='submit']");
    selenium.waitForPageToLoad("30000");
}
```

Becomes:

```
@Test
public void test_submit_form_with_default_values(){
    htmlForm.clickSubmitButton();
}
```

Where all we did was move the method code into the page object `clickSubmitButton` method.

test_submit_form_without_clicking_submit

```
@Test
public void test_submit_form_without_clicking_submit(){
    selenium.submit("//form[@id='HTMLFormElements']");
    selenium.waitForPageToLoad("30000");
}
```

Becomes:

```
@Test
public void test_submit_form_without_clicking_submit(){
    htmlForm.submitForm();
}
```

Again, all we did was move the method code into the page object `submitForm` method.

test_submit_form_with_new_username

```
@Test
public void test_submit_form_with_new_username(){
    selenium.type("username","eviltester");
    selenium.click("//input[@name='submitbutton' and @value='submit']");
    selenium.waitForPageToLoad("30000");
}
```

Becomes:

```
@Test
public void test_submit_form_with_new_username(){
    htmlForm.typeUserName("eviltester");
    htmlForm.clickSubmitButton();
}
```

Here we reused the `clickSubmitButton`, which we refactored earlier, and we will re-use this throughout the tests. And added a more domain level `typeUserName`, this takes a parameter so that we can add any username we want. But hides away the information about how you type this, or where on the form it actually goes.

test_submit_form_with_new_password

```
@Test
public void test_submit_form_with_new_password(){
  selenium.type("password","myPassword");
  selenium.click("//input[@name='submitbutton' and @value='submit']");
  selenium.waitForPageToLoad("30000");
}
```

Becomes:

```
@Test
public void test_submit_form_with_new_password(){
  htmlForm.typePassword("myPassword");
  htmlForm.clickSubmitButton();
}
```

Here we keep the approach for `typePassword` consistent with `typeUserName`. It doesn't really matter what I call these methods because we can easily refactor them later. I am keeping this simple and using very similar language to the Selenium methods.

At the moment keeping it consistent will make the tests readable.

test_submit_form_with_new_password

```
@Test
public void test_submit_form_with_html_escaped_text(){
  selenium.type("comments", "\\\n\t\"I said, give me your pound sign\"\u00A3"
      );
  selenium.click("//input[@name='submitbutton' and @value='submit']");
  selenium.waitForPageToLoad("30000");
}
```

Becomes:

```
@Test
public void test_submit_form_with_html_escaped_text(){
  htmlForm.typeComments("\\\n\t\"I said, give me your pound sign\"\u00A3");
  htmlForm.clickSubmitButton();
}
```

Another very simple move of code into the page object, keeping the naming convention consistent.

test_submit_form_with_click_check_and_radio

```
@Test
public void test_submit_form_with_click_check_and_radio(){
  selenium.click("//input[@name='checkboxes[]' and @value='cb2']");
  selenium.click("//input[@name='checkboxes[]' and @value='cb3']");
  selenium.click("//input[@name='radioval' and @value='rd3']");
  selenium.click("//input[@name='submitbutton' and @value='submit']");
  selenium.waitForPageToLoad("30000");
}
```

Becomes:

```
@Test
public void test_submit_form_with_click_check_and_radio(){
  htmlForm.clickCheckBox("2");
  htmlForm.clickCheckBox("3");
  htmlForm.clickRadioButton("3");
  htmlForm.clickSubmitButton();
}
```

Here I made a decision to create a single `clickCheckBox` method, which would take as a parameter the "digit" of the checkbox value, since all checkbox values are very similar (`cb1`, `cb2`, `cb3`). This will work for the moment since the form is very simple. There is scope for the user to get the test wrong and choose a checkbox that doesn't exist e.g. `htmlForm.clickCheckBox("27");` But at the moment, refactoring quickly and keeping the abstraction layers simple seems to make sense.

I made the same decision for `clickRadioButton`.

test_submit_form_with_multiple_select_values

```
@Test
public void test_submit_form_with_multiple_select_values(){
  selenium.removeSelection("multipleselect[]", "label=Selection Item 3");
  selenium.addSelection("multipleselect[]", "label=Selection Item 4");
  selenium.addSelection("multipleselect[]", "label=Selection Item 1");
  selenium.removeSelection("multipleselect[]", "label=Selection Item 4");
  selenium.addSelection("multipleselect[]", "value=ms2");
  selenium.click("//input[@name='submitbutton' and @value='submit']");
  selenium.waitForPageToLoad("30000");
}
```

Becomes:

```
@Test
public void test_submit_form_with_multiple_select_values(){
  htmlForm.removeMultiSelection("3");
  htmlForm.selectMultiSelection("4");
  htmlForm.selectMultiSelection("1");
  htmlForm.removeMultiSelection("4");
  htmlForm.selectMultiSelection("2");
  htmlForm.clickSubmitButton();
}
```

One useful side-effect of using page object models is that it makes it very clear in the test that we are not actually "testing" anything. We are certainly "doing stuff" with the system. But we are not checking any results or conditions on the form. This is slightly less easy to see with the raw selenium access code because the test is not quite as readable.

test_submit_form_with_dropdown_values

```
@Test
public void test_submit_form_with_dropdown_values(){
  // by default 3 is selected, so select item 1
  selenium.select("dropdown", "label=Drop Down Item 1");
  selenium.click("//input[@name='submitbutton' and @value='submit']");
```

NOTE:
A useful exercise for the reader would be to add asserts into these tests.
e.g. After each of the removeMultiSelection or selectMultiSelection we should really
check that the values we expect to be selected are in fact selected.

```
    selenium.waitForPageToLoad("30000");
}
```

Becomes:

```
@Test
public void test_submit_form_with_dropdown_values(){
  htmlForm.selectDropDownItem("1");
  htmlForm.clickSubmitButton();
}
```

Create the abstraction layer (htmlForm) methods, and copy in the implementation code from
the test. I also removed the code comments because the method names are understandable
enough that the comments were no longer adding value.

test_submit_form_with_hidden_field

```
@Test
public void test_submit_form_with_hidden_field(){
  selenium.getEval(
  "this.browserbot.findElement(\"name=hiddenField\").value=\"amended value\""
      );
  selenium.click("//input[@name='submitbutton' and @value='submit']");
  selenium.waitForPageToLoad("30000");
}
```

Becomes:

```
@Test
public void test_submit_form_with_hidden_field(){
  htmlForm.setHiddenField("amended value");
  htmlForm.clickSubmitButton();
}
```

Move the code into htmlForm methods and reuse the form submit method. I took the
opportunity to make the hidden field's new value a parameter to the htmlform method. This
instantly makes the HtmlForm.setHiddenField method more reusable.

test_check_text_entered_values

```
@Test
public void test_check_text_entered_values(){
  selenium.type("username","eviltester");
  selenium.type("password","myPassword");
  selenium.type("comments", "simple text");
```

```
    assertEquals("username not as entered",
        "eviltester",selenium.getValue("username"));
    assertEquals("password not as entered",
        "myPassword",selenium.getValue("password"));
    assertEquals("comments not as entered",
        "simple text",selenium.getValue("comments"));
}
```

Becomes:

```
@Test
public void test_check_text_entered_values(){
  htmlForm.typeUserName("eviltester");
  htmlForm.typePassword("myPassword");
  htmlForm.typeComments("simple text");

  assertEquals("username not as entered", "eviltester",htmlForm.getUserName()
      );
  assertEquals("password not as entered", "myPassword",htmlForm.getPassword()
      );
  assertEquals("comments not as entered", "simple text",htmlForm.getComments
      ());
}
```

This test reuses some of the ''type'' methods created earlier, but introduces the ''accessor'' or ''get'' methods required in our test to have the ability to make assertions. I could have added the ''get'' methods at the same time as the ''type'' (or ''set'') methods. But I prefer to refactor the abstraction layer and therefore only add code into the abstraction layer when tests actually call for it. In this way I don't build methods which require maintenance but are never used.

test_check_checkbox_values

```
@Test
public void test_check_checkbox_values(){
  assertEquals("by default checkbox 1 is not selected", "off",
    selenium.getValue("//input[@name='checkboxes[]' and @value='cb1']"));
  assertEquals("by default checkbox 2 is not selected", "off",
    selenium.getValue("//input[@name='checkboxes[]' and @value='cb2']"));
  assertEquals("by default checkbox 3 is selected", "on",
    selenium.getValue("//input[@name='checkboxes[]' and @value='cb3']"));

  selenium.check("//input[@name='checkboxes[]' and @value='cb2']");
  selenium.uncheck("//input[@name='checkboxes[]' and @value='cb3']");

  assertFalse("checkbox 1 is still not selected",
    selenium.isChecked("//input[@name='checkboxes[]' and @value='cb1']"));
  assertTrue("checkbox 2 is now selected",
    selenium.isChecked("//input[@name='checkboxes[]' and @value='cb2']"));
  assertFalse("default checkbox 3 is no longer selected",
    selenium.isChecked("//input[@name='checkboxes[]' and @value='cb3']"));
}
```

Becomes:

```
@Test
public void test_check_checkbox_values(){
```

```
assertFalse("by default checkbox 1 is not selected",
    htmlForm.isCheckBoxSelected("1"));
assertFalse("by default checkbox 2 is not selected",
    htmlForm.isCheckBoxSelected("2"));
assertTrue("by default checkbox 3 is selected",
    htmlForm.isCheckBoxSelected("3"));

htmlForm.setChecked_CheckBox("2");
htmlForm.setUnChecked_CheckBox("3");

assertFalse("checkbox 1 is still not selected",
    htmlForm.isCheckBoxSelected("1"));
assertTrue("checkbox 2 is now selected",
    htmlForm.isCheckBoxSelected("2"));
assertFalse("default checkbox 3 is no longer selected",
    htmlForm.isCheckBoxSelected("3"));
}
```

I had a number of decision to make when refactoring the test. I already have some checkbox methods `clickCheckBox` but here I made the decision to add new methods to `setChecked` and `setUnchecked`. This is in keeping with the intent of the tests, and if it proves confusing later on then I can amend the methods. I also added accessors to check the state of the checkboxes, I did this by parameterising the `isCheckBoxSelected` method with a string representation of the numeric postfix value on the element id. This keeps the method consistent with previous usage.

test_check_radio_values

```
@Test
public void test_check_radio_values(){
  assertEquals("by default radio 1 is not selected", "off",
    selenium.getValue("//input[@name='radioval' and @value='rd1']"));
  assertEquals("by default radio 2 is selected", "on",
    selenium.getValue("//input[@name='radioval' and @value='rd2']"));
  assertEquals("by default radio 3 is not selected", "off",
    selenium.getValue("//input[@name='radioval' and @value='rd3']"));

  selenium.check("//input[@name='radioval' and @value='rd1']");

  assertTrue("radio 1 is now selected",
    selenium.isChecked("//input[@name='radioval' and @value='rd1']"));
  assertFalse("radio 2 is no longer selected",
    selenium.isChecked("//input[@name='radioval' and @value='rd2']"));
  assertFalse("radio 3 is not selected",
    selenium.isChecked("//input[@name='radioval' and @value='rd3']"));
}
```

Becomes:

```
@Test
public void test_check_radio_values(){

  assertFalse("by default radio 1 is not selected",
    htmlForm.isRadioButtonSelected("1"));
  assertTrue("by default radio 2 is selected",
    htmlForm.isRadioButtonSelected("2"));
  assertFalse("by default radio 3 is not selected",
```

```
          htmlForm.isRadioButtonSelected("3"));

       htmlForm.setChecked_RadioButton("1");

       assertTrue("radio 1 is now selected",
          htmlForm.isRadioButtonSelected("1"));
       assertFalse("radio 2 is no longer selected",
          htmlForm.isRadioButtonSelected("2"));
       assertFalse("radio 3 is not selected",
          htmlForm.isRadioButtonSelected("3"));
    }
```

Here I took the same approach as used for the checkbox test. With the exception that I did not add a `setUnChecked` method. I did not add this because it was not called for in the test. At this point, I'm not amending the tests to make them better, I'm working with the test as written. After I convert the tests to use an abstraction layer I will review the tests to make them more robust and this may increase the methods in the abstraction layer.

test_randomly_select_value_from_dropdown

```
@Test
public void test_randomly_select_value_from_dropdown(){

    // get all options in the dropdown
    String dropDownOptions[] = selenium.getSelectOptions("dropdown");

    // get the index of the currently selected item in the dropdown
    String currentDropDownItem = selenium.getSelectedIndex("dropdown");
    int previouslySelectedIndex =Integer.valueOf(currentDropDownItem);

    // randomly choose an item in the dropdown
    Random generator = new Random(); // requires import java.util.Random to be
        added
    int dropDownIndex = generator.nextInt(dropDownOptions.length);

    // make sure it isn't the same as the current one
    if(dropDownIndex==previouslySelectedIndex){
      // it is the same, so add one
      dropDownIndex++;

      // but this might push it out of bounds so modulus it
      dropDownIndex = dropDownIndex % dropDownOptions.length;
    }

    // select this new one
    selenium.select("dropdown", "label=" + dropDownOptions[dropDownIndex]);

    // check that something is selected
    assertTrue(selenium.isSomethingSelected("dropdown"));

    // check that what we wanted is selected
    assertEquals(dropDownIndex,
      Integer.valueOf(selenium.getSelectedIndex("dropdown")).intValue());

    //double check we didn't select the same thing
    assertTrue(dropDownIndex!=previouslySelectedIndex);
}
```

Becomes:

```
@Test
public void test_randomly_select_value_from_dropdown(){

    String dropDownOptions[] = htmlForm.getAllDropDownValues();
    int previouslySelectedIndex = htmlForm.getCurrentDropDownSelectionIndex();

    // randomly choose an item in the dropdown
    Random generator = new Random(); // requires import java.util.Random to be
        added

    int dropDownIndex = generator.nextInt(dropDownOptions.length);

    // make sure it isn't the same as the current one
    if(dropDownIndex==previouslySelectedIndex){
      // it is the same, so add one
      dropDownIndex++;

      // but this might push it out of bounds so modulus it
      dropDownIndex = dropDownIndex % dropDownOptions.length;
    }

    htmlForm.selectDropDown(dropDownOptions[dropDownIndex]);

    assertTrue(htmlForm.isADropDownItemSelected());
    assertEquals(dropDownIndex,htmlForm.getCurrentDropDownSelectionIndex());

    //double check we didn't select the same thing
    assertTrue(dropDownIndex!=previouslySelectedIndex);
}
```

Most of this test is test code, so very little had to be moved into the abstraction layer. For those abstraction layer items that I did add, the refactoring was the simple approach: design method usage, create method, move implementation code from test.

29.1.2   Static_HTML_tests.java

Before refactoring `static_html_tests.java` into page objects, I first of all have a look at the code to see if there are any beneficial local refactorings first.

NOTE:

You can find the code for the local refactorings in the package `com.eviltester.seleniumtutorials.chap19` and the java source-code file, `Static_HTML_tests_refactored_prior_to_page_objects.java`

I can see that there is considerable reuse of the following chunk of code:

```
selenium.type("username","eviltester");
selenium.type("password","myPassword");
selenium.click("//input[@name='submitbutton' and @value='submit']");
selenium.waitForPageToLoad("30000");
```

So I first extract this into a method called submitFormWithUserNameAndPassword using the automated "refactor \ Extract Method"

```
private void submitFormWithUserNameAndPassword() {
  selenium.type("username","eviltester");
  selenium.type("password","myPassword");
  selenium.click("//input[@name='submitbutton' and @value='submit']");
  selenium.waitForPageToLoad("30000");
}
```

This then reduces the amount of work I have to do during the refactoring to page objects.

First I copy the `Static_HTML_tests.java` from the `chap19` package to the refactored package. i.e.

- from:

  - com.eviltester.seleniumtutorials.chap19

- to:

  - com.eviltester.seleniumtutorials.refactored

And then add the `SeleniumManager` code.

I change the `setUp` method to instantiate a `BasicHTMLForm` object, and call the `open` method on this object, instead of opening the page directly.

- Before

```
private static Selenium selenium;

@BeforeClass
public static void setUpBeforeClass()
                    throws Exception {
  selenium = new DefaultSelenium(
            "localhost", 4444, "*firefox",
            "http://www.compendiumdev.co.uk");
  selenium.start();
}

@AfterClass
public static void tearDownAfterClass()
                    throws Exception {
  selenium.close();
  selenium.stop();
}

@Before
public void setUp() throws Exception {
selenium.open("/selenium/basic_html_form.html");
}
```

- After

307

```
static SeleniumManagerEnd sm;
static Selenium selenium;
BasicHTMLForm htmlForm;

@BeforeClass
static public void startServer()
                throws IOException{
 sm = new SeleniumManagerEnd();
 sm.start("http://www.compendiumdev.co.uk");
 selenium = sm.getSelenium();
 }

@AfterClass
static public void stopServer(){
   sm.stop();
 }

@Before
public void setUp() throws Exception {
   htmlForm = new BasicHTMLForm(selenium);
   htmlForm.open();
 }
```

SubmitFormWithUserNameAndPassword

```
private void submitFormWithUserNameAndPassword() {
   selenium.type("username","eviltester");
   selenium.type("password","myPassword");
   selenium.click("//input[@name='submitbutton' and @value='submit']");
   selenium.waitForPageToLoad("30000");
 }
```

Becomes:

```
HTMLFormResultsPage resultsPage;

private void submitFormWithUserNameAndPassword() {
   htmlForm.typeUserName("eviltester");
   htmlForm.typePassword("myPassword");
   resultsPage = htmlForm.clickSubmitButton();
 }
```

One interesting point of this refactoring is that it re-uses methods we created in previous refactorings and because I now want to use the page that follows the submitting of the form, I amended the clickSubmitButton method to return a new page object for the ResultsPage.

So the clickSubmitButton method now looks like:

```
public HTMLFormResultsPage clickSubmitButton() {
   selenium.click("//input[@name='submitbutton' and @value='submit']");
   selenium.waitForPageToLoad("30000");
   return new HTMLFormResultsPage(selenium);
 }
```

Here you can see that my method does not check that after the waitforPageToLoad, the page loaded is a result page or not. It assumes a result page and returns an HTMLFormResultPage instantiated with the current Selenium session.

308

I do not add a check here because I assume that if the application fails to return a search results page that there will be assertions in at least one of the tests to check if this is the case.

If I did want to add checks then I would probably rename the method. At the moment the method doesn't mention a side-effect about checking the ''type'' of the new page. So I would perhaps say `clickSubmitButtonAndWaitForResultsPage`.

But I would rather let the tests fail on follow on actions than put checks and asserts in the abstraction layer - this is based on hard won experience of constructing and maintaining suboptimal abstraction layers.

I decided not to update the `submitForm` method to return an `HTMLFormResultsPage` object. Since the test did not require this.

NOTE:
This was probably a mistake and I should have returned an `HTMLFormResultsPage` object. I can easily fix this with a future refactoring step. Part of the reason for engaging in refactoring, is to review the code that we have produced and determine how to make it better.
The important lesson? It doesn't matter that I made the mistake:

- I can easily change the method to return an `HTMLFormResultsPage` object.

- At the point that I actually need the method to return an `HTMLFormResultsPage` object I can change the method.

- It is just code, if it works and is clumsy, it still works. Code is one of the most fungible objects known to mankind. I offer you this advice to try and loosen you up. You will take decisions in your refactoring and abstraction layer construction that are suboptimal. None of these decisions are irreparable, and they offer you the chance to learn not to do it again. I have made my share of mistakes. There is no shame in this. We call this learning. When we approach mistake making with an attitude of flexibility, and the thought that we did the best that we knew how to do at the time. Then we learn, and we change. Don't beat yourself up about it.

submit_form_with_values_and_check_static_html

```
@Test
public void submit_form_with_values_and_check_static_html(){
    submitFormWithUserNameAndPassword();
```

```
    // check the title on the page
    assertEquals("Processed Form Details",selenium.getTitle());

    // check the username entered
    assertEquals( "eviltester",selenium.getText("_valueusername"));

    // check the submitted values text is on the page
    assertTrue(selenium.isTextPresent("Submitted Values"));

    //isElementPresent to check comments and filename
    assertTrue(selenium.isElementPresent("_comments"));
    assertFalse(selenium.isElementPresent("_filename"));

    // use getXPathCount to check the number of checkboxes
    assertEquals(1,selenium.getXpathCount(
      "//div[@id='_checkboxes']/ul/li").intValue());

    // click to go back to the form
    selenium.click("back_to_form");
    selenium.waitForPageToLoad("30000");

    // check the page title with getTitle
    assertEquals("HTML Form Elements",selenium.getTitle());

    //check all the checkboxes
    selenium.check("//input[@name='checkboxes[]' and @value='cb1']");
    selenium.check("//input[@name='checkboxes[]' and @value='cb2']");
    selenium.check("//input[@name='checkboxes[]' and @value='cb3']");

    // submit the form
    selenium.click("//input[@name='submitbutton' and @value='submit']");
    selenium.waitForPageToLoad("30000");

    //check the checkbox count
    assertEquals(3, selenium.getXpathCount(
        "//div[@id='_checkboxes']/ul/li").intValue());
}
```

Becomes:

```
@Test
public void submit_form_with_values_and_check_static_html(){
  submitFormWithUserNameAndPassword();

  assertEquals("Processed Form Details",resultsPage.getTitle());
  assertEquals( "eviltester",resultsPage.getUserName());

  assertTrue(resultsPage.hasHeading());
  assertTrue(resultsPage.hasComments());
  assertFalse(resultsPage.hasFilename());
  assertEquals(1,resultsPage.getCheckboxCount());

  htmlForm = resultsPage.goBackToForm();

  assertEquals("HTML Form Elements",htmlForm.getTitle());

  htmlForm.setChecked_CheckBox("1");
  htmlForm.setChecked_CheckBox("2");
  htmlForm.setChecked_CheckBox("3");
  resultsPage = htmlForm.clickSubmitButton();
```

```
        assertEquals(3,resultsPage.getCheckboxCount());
    }
```

We had already created many of the methods we needed and those that we didn't have, were easily created by writing the appropriate method and using Eclipse to create the skeleton, then moving across the code from the test.

check_static_html_password_name

```
@Test
public void check_static_html_password_name(){
    submitFormWithUserNameAndPassword();

    // check the name of the password display paragraph is _password
    assertEquals("_password",
        selenium.getAttribute("xpath=//div[@id='_password']/p@name"));
}
```

Becomes:

```
@Test
public void check_password_field_exists(){
    submitFormWithUserNameAndPassword();
    assertTrue("Does not have a password field",resultsPage.hasPassword());
}
```

One thing this test conversion showed me was that the test added no value. I decided to keep it because I thought it might be useful to have a test that checks that the form has a password element. I could easily have deleted this test and felt no ill effects.

useAssignIDToCheckFilenameBlank

```
@Test
public void useAssignIDToCheckFilenameBlank(){
    submitFormWithUserNameAndPassword();

    selenium.assignId("xpath=//body/p[2]/strong", "_filename");
    assertEquals("No Value for filename",selenium.getText("_filename"));
}
```

Becomes:

```
@Test
public void useAssignIDToCheckFilenameBlank(){
    submitFormWithUserNameAndPassword();
    assertEquals("No Value for filename",resultsPage.getFilename());
}
```

Because this initial test was intended to illustrate the assignment of an `id`, it doesn't add much value in its current form as there are other ways of checking if the filename is present. And indeed, in the implementation of `getFilename` I choose a more generic way of implementing the check. The check itself is valuable, and the approach is useful to know, but I will always attempt to use the simplest mechanism to implement an abstraction layer function. I find ''simple'' easier to maintain and understand.

getText_equals_getTitle

```
@Test
public void getText_equals_getTitle(){
  assertEquals("HTML Form Elements",selenium.getTitle());
  assertEquals(selenium.getTitle(),selenium.getText("//head/title"));
}
```

Becomes:

```
@Test
public void checkPageTitleAsExpected(){
  assertEquals("HTML Form Elements",htmlForm.getTitle());
}
```

Since this test was again a demonstration of alternative approaches. The final test adopts an implementation using the simplest and cleanest of the approaches. In this case this means delegating through to the `selenium.getTitle` method.

While some of the tests above had little value, I was still able to refactor them into something that provided some coverage value. Some of them had no value as they were purely illustrative. I list these below by name, but have removed them from the final source-code.

- `getBodyText_getHtmlSource`

- `submit_form_with_values_and_go_back`

29.1.3 JavaScript_With_Selenium_Tests.java

First I copy `JavaScript_With_Selenium_Tests.java` from the chap20 package and paste it into the refactored package

- from:

  - `com.eviltester.seleniumtutorials.chap20`

- to:

  - `com.eviltester.seleniumtutorials.refactored`

And then add the `SeleniumManager` code.

I change the `setUp` method to instantiate a `BasicHTMLForm` object, and call the `open` method on this object, instead of opening the page directly.

- Before

```
private static Selenium selenium;

@BeforeClass
public static void setUpBeforeClass()
                    throws Exception {
  selenium = new DefaultSelenium(
            "localhost", 4444, "*firefox",
            "http://www.compendiumdev.co.uk");
  selenium.start();
}

@AfterClass
public static void tearDownAfterClass()
                        throws Exception {
  selenium.close();
  selenium.stop();
}

@Before
public void setUp() throws Exception {
  selenium.open("/selenium/basic_ajax.html");
}
```

- After

```
static SeleniumManagerEnd sm;
static Selenium selenium;
BasicAjaxPage basicAjax;

@BeforeClass
static public void startServer()
                    throws IOException{
  sm = new SeleniumManagerEnd();
  sm.start("http://www.compendiumdev.co.uk");
  selenium = sm.getSelenium();
}

@AfterClass
static public void stopServer(){
  sm.stop();
}

@Before
public void setUp() throws Exception {
  basicAjax = new BasicAjaxPage(selenium);
  basicAjax.open();
}
```

enterAnInvalidValueInBlurInput

```
@Test
public void enterAnInvalidValueInBlurInput(){
  selenium.type("xpath=//input[@id='lteq30']", "45");
  selenium.select("combo1", "Desktop");
  assertFalse(selenium.isAlertPresent());
}
```

Becomes:

```
@Test
public void enterAnInvalidValueInBlurInput(){
  basicAjax.typeInputValue("45");
  basicAjax.selectCategory("Desktop");

  assertFalse(basicAjax.hasShownValidationAlert());
}
```

This test is a simple matter of creating some ''setter'' methods in `basicAjax` and an ''accessor'' method to allow the test to assert values.

enterAnInvalidValueInBlurInputAndTriggerValidation

```
@Test
public void enterAnInvalidValueInBlurInputAndTriggerValidation(){
  selenium.type("xpath=//input[@id='lteq30']", "45");
  selenium.fireEvent("xpath=//input[@id='lteq30']", "blur");
  assertTrue(selenium.isAlertPresent());
  assertEquals("Enter a value less than 30", selenium.getAlert());
}
```

Becomes:

```
@Test
public void enterAnInvalidValueInBlurInputAndTriggerValidation(){
  basicAjax.typeInputValue("45");
  basicAjax.triggerInputValidation();

  assertTrue(basicAjax.hasShownValidationAlert());
  assertEquals("Enter a value less than 30",
                  basicAjax.getValidationAlertMessage());
}
```

Here I had to take a decision about where to trigger the validation. I could have triggered it in the `typeInputValue` method, but I decided, for this test, to keep the two methods separate.

This does not mean that I always have to do this and it will be a simple matter, later, if required, to create a method which does both: type the value, trigger the validation. Again, I will wait until a test needs the combined method before constructing it. And I won't spend any time wondering if this refactoring was the ''best'' I could do or not. It will become clear in later usage scenarios if this was a useful refactoring or not.

Deleted Tests

The following tests were deleted from the refactored test class as they added no value to the final set of tests, the were simply methods which illustrated how to incorporate JavaScript in the test cases:

* `showHTMLOfCombo1WithGetEval`

* `showValueOfInjectedJavaScriptFromRunScriptExpectedException`

314

- `showValueOfInjectedJavaScriptFromRunScript`

- `showValueOfInjectedJavaScriptFromAddScript`

29.2   The Page Objects

29.2.1   BasicHTMLForm.java

The page object created during the `HTML_form_tests.java` and `Static_HTML_tests.java` refactoring can be found below.

All of the methods were built initially by using Eclipse's ''create method X'' option when fixing errors on the test. Then the code was copied in from the test. I then changed the name of the parameters to make them more representative of their function. In some cases I had to change the return type from `Object` to the appropriate type required.

Read the following code and see if you identify any possible refactorings:

```
package com.eviltester.seleniumtutorials.refactored.pageObjectModel;

import com.thoughtworks.selenium.Selenium;

public class BasicHTMLForm {

  Selenium selenium;

  public BasicHTMLForm(Selenium selenium) {
    this.selenium = selenium;
  }

  public HTMLFormResultsPage clickSubmitButton() {
    selenium.click("//input[@name='submitbutton' and @value='submit']");
    selenium.waitForPageToLoad("30000");
    return new HTMLFormResultsPage(selenium);
  }

  public void submitForm() {
    selenium.submit("//form[@id='HTMLFormElements']");
    selenium.waitForPageToLoad("30000");
  }

  public void typeUserName(String userName) {
    selenium.type("username",userName);
  }

  public void typePassword(String password) {
    selenium.type("password",password);
  }

  public void typeComments(String comments) {
    selenium.type("comments", comments);
  }

  public void typeFilename(String fileName) {
    selenium.type("filename", fileName);
  }
```

```
public void clickCheckBox(String checkBoxNumber){
  selenium.click("//input[@name='checkboxes[]' and @value='cb" +
      checkBoxNumber +"']");
}

public void clickRadioButton(String radioButtonNumber) {
  selenium.click("//input[@name='radioval' and @value='rd" +
      radioButtonNumber + "']");
}

public void removeMultiSelection(String selectionID) {
  selenium.removeSelection("multipleselect[]", "label=Selection Item " +
      selectionID);
}

public void selectMultiSelection(String selectionID) {
  selenium.addSelection("multipleselect[]", "label=Selection Item " +
      selectionID);
}

public void open() {
  selenium.open("/selenium/basic_html_form.html");
}

public void selectDropDownItem(String itemID) {
  selectDropDown("Drop Down Item " + itemID);
}

public void selectDropDown(String itemLabel) {
  selenium.select("dropdown", "label=" + itemLabel);
}

public void setHiddenField(String newHiddenFieldValue) {
  selenium.getEval(
    "this.browserbot.findElement(\"name=hiddenField\").value=\"" +
    newHiddenFieldValue + "\"");
}

public String getUserName() {
  return selenium.getValue("username");
}

public String getPassword() {
  return selenium.getValue("password");
}

public String getFileName() {
  return selenium.getValue("filename");
}

public String getComments() {
  return selenium.getValue("comments");
}

public boolean isCheckBoxSelected(String checkBoxIDNumber ) {
  return selenium.isChecked("//input[@name='checkboxes[]' and @value='cb" +
    checkBoxIDNumber +"']");
}

public void setChecked_CheckBox(String checkBoxIDNumber) {
```

```
    selenium.check("//input[@name='checkboxes[]' and @value='cb" +
        checkBoxIDNumber + "']");
}

public void setUnChecked_CheckBox(String checkBoxIDNumber) {
    selenium.uncheck("//input[@name='checkboxes[]' and @value='cb" +
        checkBoxIDNumber + "']");
}

public boolean isRadioButtonSelected(String radioButtonIDNumber) {
    return selenium.isChecked("//input[@name='radioval' and @value='rd" +
        radioButtonIDNumber + "']");
}

public void setChecked_RadioButton(String radioButtonIDNumber) {
    selenium.check("//input[@name='radioval' and @value='rd" +
        radioButtonIDNumber + "']");
}

public String[] getAllDropDownValues() {
    return selenium.getSelectOptions("dropdown");
}

public int getCurrentDropDownSelectionIndex() {
    // get the index of the currently selected item in the dropdown
    String currentDropDownItem = selenium.getSelectedIndex("dropdown");
    return Integer.valueOf(currentDropDownItem);
}

public boolean isADropDownItemSelected() {
    return selenium.isSomethingSelected("dropdown");
}

public String getTitle() {
    return selenium.getTitle();
}
}
```

Possible refactorings

Most of the code is simple enough that it will work fine if left without refactoring, I note however that:

- My locators for checkbox, multi-select, radio buttons, username, password, etc. have all been repeated in the code. I try to avoid repeated code, so would refactor this.

- I would create a constant for each of the locator strings.

For the more complicated locators, such as checkbox and radio buttons, I would use a String.format, using a %s representing the location of the parameter to add to the locator.

e.g.

from the function

```
public void setUnChecked_CheckBox(String checkBoxIDNumber) {
    selenium.uncheck("//input[@name='checkboxes[]' and @value='cb" +
        checkBoxIDNumber + "']");
}
```

I will start by making it take the form I want:

```
public void setUnChecked_CheckBox(String checkBoxIDNumber) {
    selenium.uncheck(String.format("//input[@name='checkboxes[]' and @value='cb
        %s']",checkBoxIDNumber));
}
```

Select the string to refactor and use the Eclipse refactoring Extract Into Constant. This will create a constant with the string that I can use in the other methods that access checkboxes.

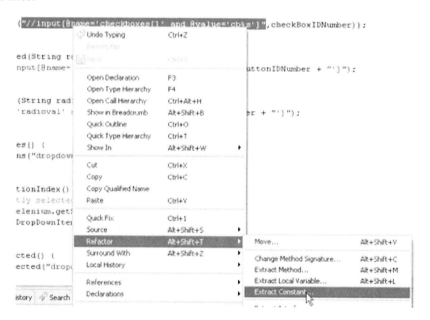

Figure 29.1: Refactor String into a constant

And in the wizard that follows I type in the name of the constant to create.

Figure 29.2: Enter a name for the constant

318

This refactoring gives us:

```
private static final String CHECKBOXES_LOCATOR = "//input[@name='checkboxes
    []' and @value='cb%s']";

public void setUnChecked_CheckBox(String checkBoxIDNumber) {
  selenium.uncheck(String.format(CHECKBOXES_LOCATOR,checkBoxIDNumber));
}
```

I then amend all the places which previously had the locator to instead use:

```
String.format(CHECKBOXES_LOCATOR,checkBoxIDNumber)
```

This has the advantage that should the locator to access the checkbox change, I only have a single place to remember to change the locator, which will have the knock on effect of fixing all methods that access the checkbox.

Based on the current needs of the tests, and given what we have currently learned, other than these changes I would probably keep this file as it is for just now.

NOTE:

You can see this refactoring fully completed in the `BasicHTMLForm.java` class in package:

```
com.eviltester.seleniumtutorials.refactored.pageObjectModel
```

The initial page object model, prior to this additional refactoring is in BasicHTML-Form.java in:

```
com.eviltester.seleniumtutorials.refactored.pageObjectModel.
    notFullyRefactored
```

29.2.2   HTMLFormResultsPage.java

This Java class was built using the exact method described above in `BasicHTMLForm.java`

One thing I did have to change was the `getFilename` method.

The `getFilename` method illustrates an interesting choice for me as an automator building an abstraction layer. I will discuss this method, after the source-code listing.

```
package com.eviltester.seleniumtutorials.refactored.pageObjectModel;

import com.thoughtworks.selenium.Selenium;

public class HTMLFormResultsPage {

  Selenium selenium;

  public HTMLFormResultsPage(Selenium selenium) {
    this.selenium = selenium;
  }
```

319

```
    public String getTitle() {
      return selenium.getTitle();
    }

    public String getUserName() {
      return selenium.getText("_valueusername");
    }

    public boolean hasHeading() {
      return selenium.isTextPresent("Submitted Values");
    }

    public boolean hasComments() {
      return selenium.isElementPresent("_comments");
    }

    public boolean hasFilename() {
      return selenium.isElementPresent("_filename");
    }

    public int getCheckboxCount() {
      return selenium.getXpathCount(
        "//div[@id='_checkboxes']/ul/li").intValue();
    }

    public BasicHTMLForm goBackToForm() {
      // click to go back to the form
      selenium.click("back_to_form");
      selenium.waitForPageToLoad("30000");
      return new BasicHTMLForm(selenium);
    }

    public String getFilename() {
      if(hasFilename()){
        return selenium.getText("_valuefilename");
      }else{
        return selenium.getText("xpath=//body/p[2]/strong");
      }
    }

    public boolean hasPassword() {
      return  selenium.isElementPresent("_password");
    }
  }
}
```

Discussion of getFilename

```
public String getFilename() {
  if(hasFilename()){
    return selenium.getText("_valuefilename");
  }else{
    return selenium.getText("xpath=//body/p[2]/strong");
  }
}
```

My abstraction layer methods are ''logical'' rather than ''physical'' in that they describe what will happen, but not how. So getFilename is to return the filename text, regardless

320

of the page structure. The test page to automate is structured differently depending on whether a filename was entered or not.

I could take the view that the application needs to be more testable by being made consistent. But in the short term I need to implement the method to support the test so I add a conditional into the method implementation so, regardless of the state of the page, the test can still get the information it needs.

I suspect that were I to expand the tests to have more tests with optional entries that I would have to take the above conditional method approach for many of the getX methods on the results page.

29.2.3   BasicAjaxPage.java

There was nothing new in the BasicAjaxPage.java refactoring. This was a simple cut and paste building exercise.

```java
package com.eviltester.seleniumtutorials.refactored.pageObjectModel;

import com.thoughtworks.selenium.Selenium;

public class BasicAjaxPage {

  Selenium selenium;

  public BasicAjaxPage(Selenium selenium) {
    this.selenium = selenium;
  }

  public void open() {
    selenium.open("/selenium/basic_ajax.html");
  }

  public void typeInputValue(String inputValue) {
    selenium.type("xpath=//input[@id='lteq30']", inputValue);
  }

  public void selectCategory(String string) {
    selenium.select("combo1", "Desktop");
  }

  public boolean hasShownValidationAlert() {
    return selenium.isAlertPresent();
  }

  public void triggerInputValidation() {
    selenium.fireEvent("xpath=//input[@id='lteq30']", "blur");
  }

  public String getValidationAlertMessage() {
    return selenium.getAlert();
  }
}
```

Chapter 30

Page Object Models Summary

Now that you have seen Page Object Models in action, we can cover a little theory and thoughts on the topic.

30.1 What is a Page Object Model?

I use the term Page Object Model because what we build is a collection of Objects, each of which models a Page or a Component on a page. The methods exposed by the Page Object are the interface that the user has with the page:

- accessors - get the values

    - `getTitle()`

    - `getDisplayedUsername()`

- setters - type and select values

    - `typeUserName("alan");`

- actions - e.g. clicking things

    - `clickLoginButton();`

    - `submitLoginForm();`

- answers - answers to questions we might ask about the page - like accessors but a slightly higher level of abstraction. In this way our tests can assert the truth or falsehood of the answer.

    - `isTitle("a title");`

    - this would use the getTitle method and return a boolean rather than asserting the value.

30.2 Grow an abstraction layer

I have had more success growing an abstraction layer, by creating a simple layer and refactoring it over time to meet the evolving needs of the test automation.

- Sometimes I create the selenium statements in the test, to get the test working and then refactor them out.

- Sometimes I start with what I want the test to look like, and grow the abstraction layer as I write the test. I prefer this method as it feels more like test driven development of tests.

30.3   Refactor the Page Objects internally

Treat all your test code as production quality code. So refactor all your code and have it as clean and waste free as possible. You do not initially need complicated mechanisms to move out your locators into text files, property files etc. Refactor your code into different levels of abstraction and move to higher levels of abstraction as you need to over time.

e.g.

- move literal strings into constants

- use `String.Format` to parametrize constants

- refactor into higher level methods

  - e.g. Example 1 below might lead to the creation of a `loginAs` method, which opens the page, types in the `username` and `password`, then clicks the `[login]` button. You might choose to make the `typeUsername` and other methods private. Or keep them public for use in more detailed tests. The construction of abstraction layers is a set of choices which are up to you.

```
ManageAccountPage loginAs(String username, String password)
```

30.4   Create Domain Level Abstractions

Once you have a collection of Page Objects, consider the use of a `User` class and refactor into a higher level abstraction. e.g.

Instead of:

```
// example 1
LoginPage loginPage = new LoginPage(selenium);
loginPage.open();
loginPage.typeUsername("alan");
loginPage.typePassword("mypass");
ManageAccountPage manageAccount = loginPage.clickLoginButton();
assertTrue(manageAccount.isTitle("Manage Account"));
```

consider refactoring the above into a method on a User class:

```
// example 2
User me = new User(selenium);
user.setUsername("alan");
user.setPassword("mypass");
user.logsIn();
```

Behind the scenes, the `User` object maintains its state and provides high level methods to access the system.

There are dangers with this approach as it can lead to a very large `User` class with lots of methods.

But I find that judicious use of this approach works well and helps makes the tests more readable.

So in addition to modelling the structure of your application. You create usage models which allow you to create more literate tests.

Build the abstraction layers appropriate to you which:

- help make the tests readable, and maintainable,

- model the application under tests

- model the use of the application

- model the style of testing you are doing

30.5   Lessons learned

Below are a few hints and tips relating to abstraction models:

- return other page objects from methods

- model state as different methods

    - `loginForm.clickLoginButton()`

    - `loginForm.clickLoginButtonExpectingFailedLogin()`

- return `this` for syntactic sugar methods

    - e.g. `and()`, `then()`

        * both of the methods would contain the code `{return this;}`

- grow the model organically through refactoring

- do not use asserts in the page object model

325

- collate page objects into a domain model (which can use asserts)

- refactor heavily within the page objects

  - split out components into new objects

Recommended Do Nots

- Do not try and create a whole abstraction layer at the start. Let it grow.

30.6   Related Study

- http://unow.be/rc/PageObjects[1] A short discussion on page objects with examples using WebDriver.

- http://unow.be/rc/gtacss[2] watch this video from GTAC 2007 by Simon Stewart on Web Driver. It provides a good overview of abstraction layers for testing and discusses web driver in detail, which is the important base technology for Selenium 2.x

- Growing Object Oriented Software Guided by Tests by Steve Friedman and Nat Pryce

  - An excellent book about evolving software with many important lessons for maintaining tests and abstractions.
  - http://unow.be/rc/goos[3]

---

[1]http://code.google.com/p/selenium/wiki/PageObjects
[2]http://www.youtube.com/watch?v=tGu1ud7hk5I
[3]http://www.growing-object-oriented-software.com/

Chapter 31

Data Driven Tests in JUnit

Data Driven testing is an important method of increasing data coverage without writing a lot of tests.

To support Data Driven testing we will look at JUnit's parameterized class runner.

31.1   Basic Data Driven Testing

I have created a small application to make the examples for the use of Data Driven testing simpler at http://www.compendiumdev.co.uk/selenium/calculate.php

Figure 31.1: A simple calculator example for data driven testing

In the code examples, you will see that I have already created a page object for the calculator and am using it in the test.

NOTE:

The code for this example is in `com.eviltester.seleniumtutorials.chap31.datadriven` as `CalculateTwoNumbersTests.java`

The page object CalculateForm.java, can be found in the package:

`com.eviltester.seleniumtutorials.chap31.datadriven.pageObjectModel`

This `calculate.php` form has two input fields for entering numbers, a central drop down for the calculation function to perform. A Calculate button which submits the form and displays the answer.

This has a very simple test path:

- type first number

- select function

- type second number

- press the [calculate] button

- check answer is correct

But we want to vary the data across this test path to choose different numbers, and different functions.

So I will show the important new code in snippets, explaining as I go, and then we can look at the whole code.

31.2   JUnit parameterized Class Runner And Constructor

At a high level, we will create a new test class which uses a parameterized runner. We will define a data provider for the test class which returns a collection of objects. For each object in the collection, the test runner will instantiate our test class, passing in the objects as parameters to the test class constructor, and then execute all the tests in the test class.

First, when I declare my class I annotate it with @RunWith(parameterized.class)

```
@RunWith(Parameterized.class)
public class CalculateTwoNumbersTests {
```

This is a different runner, which does a lot of magic under the covers to create our test class as many times as our data provider returns data, and runs all the tests in our test class with the parameters.

```
private String number1;
private String function;
private String number2;
private String answer;

public CalculateTwoNumbersTests(
        String num1, String function,
        String num2, String answer)
{
        this.number1 = num1;
        this.function = function;
        this.number2 = num2;
        this.answer = answer;
}
```

I need to pass the data for the tests as a set of parameters to a constructor. Then to access the data in the tests I need to store the parameters in class field variables.

And where does the data come from?

328

31.3　Data supplied by an @parameters annotated method

```
@Parameters
public static Collection data() {
    return Arrays.asList(
        new Object[][] {
            { "1", "plus", "1", "2" },
            { "2", "times", "2", "4" },
            { "5", "divide", "2", "2.5" },
            { "10", "minus", "4", "6" },
        }
    );
}
```

I create a method in the test class (here I called it `data()`). I annotate this method with the `@parameters` annotation from JUnit. This method returns a collection of Arrays. Each Array has the data that I will use as the parameters.

In the above example I create a multidimensional array of objects `new Object[][]` which I convert to a list of arrays. The test runner will call the method annotated by `@parameters` and for each array in the list, will pass the values through to the test constructor as parameters.

I have kept things simple in the example above by creating an array of data in the code. I could just as easily have had the `data()` method read a file and construct the data array from a file, e.g. A CSV file or XML file (you will see this in a few pages time).

31.4　A Data Driven Test

This is all the new magic. Thereafter our tests are as they have always been:

```
@BeforeClass
static public void startServer() throws IOException{
    sm = new SeleniumManager();
    sm.start("http://www.compendiumdev.co.uk");
    selenium = sm.getSelenium();
}

@Test
public void test_calculate_two_values(){
    calculate = new CalculateForm(selenium);
    calculate.open();

    calculate.setNumber1(this.number1);
    calculate.setFunction(this.function);
    calculate.setNumber2(this.number2);

    calculate = calculate.doCalculation();

    assertEquals(this.answer,calculate.getAnswer());
}

@AfterClass
static public void stopServer(){
    sm.stop();
}
```

Here you can see the `@Test` annotated method using the field variables that were instantiated by the constructor, so they have the values that were passed in from our data method.

31.5   Running a Data Driven Test

Running this test will show a slightly different JUnit test display:

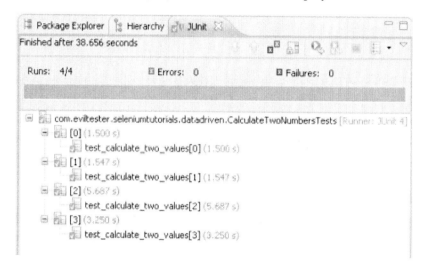

Figure 31.2: The Parameterized test results

Here you can see that the name of the test is displayed, with the index of the parameter object array used as parameters in the constructor.

`test_calculate_two_values[0]` is the first array of data in our `Object[][]`

i.e. `{ "1", "plus", "1", "2" }`

31.6   The full code for the test

```
package com.eviltester.seleniumtutorials.datadriven;
import static org.junit.Assert.assertEquals;
import java.io.IOException;
import java.util.Arrays;
import java.util.Collection;
import org.junit.AfterClass;
import org.junit.BeforeClass;
import org.junit.Test;
import org.junit.runner.RunWith;
import org.junit.runners.Parameterized;
import org.junit.runners.Parameterized.Parameters;
import com.eviltester.seleniumtutorials.datadriven.pageObjectModel.
    CalculateForm;
import com.eviltester.seleniumutils.SeleniumManager;
```

```
import com.thoughtworks.selenium.Selenium;

@RunWith(Parameterized.class)
public class CalculateTwoNumbersTests {

  static SeleniumManager sm;
  static Selenium selenium;
  static CalculateForm calculate;
  private String number1;
  private String function;
  private String number2;
  private String answer;

    public CalculateTwoNumbersTests(
      String num1, String function, String num2, String answer){
      this.number1 = num1;
      this.function = function;
      this.number2 = num2;
      this.answer = answer;
    }

    @Parameters
    public static Collection data() {
        return Arrays.asList( new Object[][] { { "1", "plus", "1", "2" },
                    { "2", "times", "2", "4" },
                    { "5", "divide", "2", "2.5" },
                    { "10", "minus", "4", "6" }, });}

  @BeforeClass
  static public void startServer() throws IOException{
     sm = new SeleniumManager();
     sm.start("http://www.compendiumdev.co.uk");
     selenium = sm.getSelenium();
  }

  @Test
  public void test_calculate_two_values(){
    calculate = new CalculateForm(selenium);
    calculate.open();
    calculate.setNumber1(this.number1);
    calculate.setFunction(this.function);
    calculate.setNumber2(this.number2);
    calculate = calculate.doCalculation();
    assertEquals(this.answer,calculate.getAnswer());
  }

  @AfterClass
  static public void stopServer(){
    sm.stop();
  }
}
```

You can see the new imports that I had to add for JUnit 4 parameterization functionality.

31.7 Multiple Tests

It is possible to have more than one @Test annotated method in the parameterized test class. e.g. I could add another (this test checks the calculation process by using the answer in the calculation):

```
@Test
public void test_reverse_calculate_two_values(){
  calculate = new CalculateForm(selenium);
  calculate.open();

  calculate.setNumber1(this.answer);

  if(this.function.compareTo("plus")==0)
    calculate.setFunction("minus");

  if(this.function.compareTo("minus")==0)
    calculate.setFunction("plus");

  if(this.function.compareTo("divide")==0)
    calculate.setFunction("times");

  if(this.function.compareTo("times")==0)
    calculate.setFunction("divide");

  calculate.setNumber2(this.number2);

  calculate = calculate.doCalculation();

  assertEquals(this.number1,calculate.getAnswer());
}
```

This would be run with the same parameters.

If you include an `@Test` method in a parameterized test class which does not use the parameters it will still be run as many times as there are items in the List.

31.8   Reading Data From Tab Delimited Files

To show the basic functioning of data driven tests our data was supplied from a hard coded collection.

For ease of maintenance some people prefer to keep the data separate from the code. In the next example we will see how to load in the data from a tab delimited file.

The benefit of a tab delimited file is that it is very easy to write a method to read and parse the file without worrying about adding additional libraries to our tests.

So I will need to create a `readTabDelimFile` method which, when given a file name, returns the data as a collection of String Arrays. A very quick google search revealed a simple example of reading a tab delimited file http://unow.be/rc/progzoo[1] so I simply customize their code to match our needs:

```
public static Collection<String[]> readTabDelimFile(String filename)
    throws NumberFormatException, IOException {

    ArrayList<String[]> lines = new ArrayList<String[]>();
  BufferedReader fh = new BufferedReader(new FileReader(filename));
  String s;
```

---

[1]http://progzoo.net/wiki/Read_a_Tab_Delimited_File

```
while ((s=fh.readLine())!=null){
  String f[] = s.split("\t");
  lines.add(f);
}
fh.close();
return lines;
}
```

Then we have to make the `@parameterized` method read the data from a tab Delimited file.

```
@Parameters
public static Collection data() throws NumberFormatException, IOException {
    return readTabDelimFile("resources\\datafiles\\calculate2numbers.tab");
}
```

Then I have to create the data file. Which I do by creating a folder called resources at the top level of my project, with a datafiles sub-folder beneath that.

Figure 31.3: Resources folder structure

I create the tab delimited file in a text editor with each line representing a full line of data, and with each value separated from the next with a [tab] character.

Figure 31.4: Using Notepad to edit a tab separated file

NOTE:

The data file is in the `resources\datafiles` folder, the code for data driven from a file is contained in the test class `CalculateTwoNumbersTestsTabFile.java` in package `com.eviltester.seleniumtutorials.chap31.datadriven`

31.9 General Hints

In the section above I tried to give an overview of the type of approach I use when trying to expand my tests.

1. I get the basics working (array provided by code)

2. Identify what I want to do next (use tab Separated files)

3. Find simple code on the internet (find simple code examples on the internet to reuse and build on)

4. Get the code working then customise to do what I need

If I were now to expand the test to use a spreadsheet, I would start looking for Java libraries to use for reading spreadsheets. Get those libraries working with simple examples using `System.out.println` to print the values from the spreadsheet and only once I was comfortable that I understood the library would I incorporate it into my test.

NOTE:

An alternative test framework called TestNG has much better support for data driven testing and in the results shows the actual parameters passed through to the test. While it is easy to move from JUnit to TestNG, this beginners guide will only cover JUnit. For more information on TestNG you can visit http://unow.be/rc/testng[2]

Related Reading:

- http://unow.be/rc/JUnit4excel[3] John Ferguson Smart has a good example of how to use Excel as the data source for the data driven tests.

- http://unow.be/rc/jparamrun[4] the official documentation of the parameterized class

- http://unow.be/rc/pJUnit[5] a good description from Daniel Meyer of how to understand the parameterized test class

---

[2] http://testng.org/doc/index.html
[3] http://weblogs.java.net/blog/johnsmart/archive/2009/11/28/data-driven-tests-junit-4-and-excel
[4] http://www.junit.org/apidocs/org/junit/runners/Parameterized.html
[5] http://ourcraft.wordpress.com/2008/08/27/writing-a-parameterized-junit-test/

Chapter 32

Screen Capture on Failure

I have left this chapter close to the end of the book because it contains the most complicated code that I will cover.

NOTE:
To follow this code you need an up to date version of JUnit 4.8.1 or above. If your version of Eclipse does not have a high enough version then you need to add a recent version of JUnit to your project.

- Download the JUnit jar from the JUnit website. http://unow.be/rc/getJUnit[1]

- Add this jar file to somewhere in your workspace e.g. a \lib or \libs folder

- Amend the `Java Build Path` in Eclipse from the `project properties` and on the `Libraries` tab click the `[Add External Jars]` button and select the JUnit jar you downloaded.

- Remove any other JUnit references from the build path.

This code also builds on the data driven test knowledge that we gained in the previous chapter.

Basically I will create a test, which uses all the browsers that support screen capture functionality under Selenium, do something that fails, and write the screenshots to a folder.

So before you see the complete listing I will go through the important details.

First, I have made this a data driven test

```
@Parameters
public static Collection testData(){
  return Arrays.asList(new Object[][]{  {"firefox"},
          {"chrome"},
          {"iexplore"},
          {"googlechrome"},
          {"iexploreproxy"}});
}
public ScreenCaptureOnFailureWithWatchmanTests(String currentBrowser){
  this.currentBrowser = currentBrowser;
}
```

---

[1] http://github.com/KentBeck/JUnit/downloads

In this case my data is the browser name. I have done this to demonstrate one way of making your tests run on multiple browsers. This is not the way I would recommend to you, but for the purposes of illustrating screenshot taking, this seemed like a convenient approach to take.

My constructor stores the browser name we want to use. I use this in the test when I start the server and open the browser to visit the specified home page, the test then checks for the wrong title to make the test fail.

```
@Test
public void captureScreenshots(){
    startServerAndOpenRoot(currentBrowser);
    assertEquals(WRONG_TITLE,selenium.getTitle());
}
```

We need to have a quick understanding of JUnit 4 rules.

JUnit 4 allows us to easily customize the behaviour of the test runner locally by the use of rules.

I can create a rule by adding the following into my test class:

```
@Rule
public MethodRule watchman= new TestWatchman() {

    @Override
    public void failed(Throwable e, FrameworkMethod method) {
        captureScreenShots( screenShotsFolder,
                currentBrowser,
            method.getName() + "_" + e.getClass().getSimpleName());
        stopSelenium();
    }

    @Override
    public void succeeded(FrameworkMethod method) {
        stopSelenium();
    }
};
```

I have created a custom rule, with a `TestWatchman` which allows me to augment the functionality of the test runner. In this case I am adding some additional functionality which runs when a test method has `failed` and when a test method has `succeeded`.

Here, if the test fails, our failed method above will override the JUnit test runner rule and will call our `captureScreenShots` method (which I will explain later). I pass to the `captureScreenShots` method the name of the `@Test` annotated method which failed:

```
method.getName()
```

I also pass in the name of the error which caused the test to fail:

```
e.getClass().getSimpleName()
```

I override the method called on a successful test ending, and in this case all I do is call the `stopSelenium` local method.

336

And that was it, that was all I had to do to trap the failure event on test running. Everything else in my test exists to support the taking of screenshots.

I also have to create a folder hierarchy to store the screenshots in. I have chosen to create a main `/screenshots` folder and beneath it, a date based folder so that every test run has a folder to store its tests in e.g.:

- `/screenshots/2010-05-10-13-22`

Then in the date based folder I store the screenshots and prefix each screenshot with the name of the browser in use.

So at the end of a test there would be a number of files:

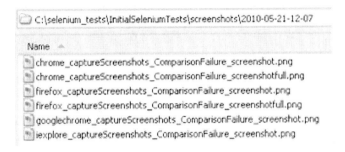

Figure 32.1: List of files generated by the test

I have a private method called in the `@BeforeClass` start up method to create the folder structure:

```
static private String createNowfolder() {
    String screenShotsFolder =
        System.getProperty("user.dir") +
        File.separator + "screenshots" + File.separator;
    SimpleDateFormat sdfmth = new SimpleDateFormat("yyyy-MM-dd-HH-mm");
    Calendar cal = Calendar.getInstance();
    screenShotsFolder = screenShotsFolder + sdfmth.format(cal.getTime());
    new File(screenShotsFolder).mkdirs();
    return screenShotsFolder + File.separator;
}
```

Then there is the important `captureScreenShots` method which captures the screenshot and saves it to a file.

There are two capture screenshot methods available from Selenium.

- `captureScreenshot`

  – captures the entire screen, browser agnostic

- `captureEntirePageScreenshot`

337

– captures the full page within the browser, only works on a subset of browsers: `iexploreproxy, firefox, chrome`

```
private void captureScreenShots(  String screenShotsFolder,
        String browser,
        String fileNameAppend) {
  selenium.windowMaximize();

  try{ Thread.sleep(1000);} catch (Exception e) {}

  String filename =   screenShotsFolder + browser + "_" +
      fileNameAppend + "_screenshot.png";
  selenium.captureScreenshot(filename);
  try{ selenium.captureEntirePageScreenshot(
      filename.replace(".png","full.png"),""); }catch(Exception e){}
}
```

In this method I first maximize the browser window so that it fills the screen. I do this because the `captureScreenshot` method captures the full screen, not just the browser details.

Because browsers might take a little time to maximize the screen and render it properly, I add a pause in the test using the `Thread.sleep(1000)` command. I wrap this in a try catch block to ignore the exception that `Thread.sleep` can throw.

I then build the filename path for the general screenshot.

For the `captureEntirePageScreenshot` I wrap it in a try catch block. This way, when an unsupported browser is used and an exception is thrown, it will be caught and ignored and no screenshot will be produced.

My complete test listing is:

```
package com.eviltester.seleniumtutorials.chap32.screenCapture;

import static org.junit.Assert.*;
import java.io.File;
import java.io.IOException;
import java.text.SimpleDateFormat;
import java.util.Arrays;
import java.util.Calendar;
import java.util.Collection;
import org.junit.AfterClass;
import org.junit.BeforeClass;
import org.junit.Test;
import org.openqa.selenium.server.SeleniumServer;
import com.thoughtworks.selenium.DefaultSelenium;
import com.thoughtworks.selenium.Selenium;

// for the @Rule annotation
import org.junit.rules.MethodRule;
import org.junit.Rule;
import org.junit.rules.TestWatchman;
import org.junit.runners.model.FrameworkMethod;

import org.junit.runner.RunWith;
import org.junit.runners.Parameterized;
import org.junit.runners.Parameterized.Parameters;
```

```java
@RunWith(Parameterized.class)
public class ScreenCaptureOnFailureWithWatchmanTests {

  static SeleniumServer server;
  static Selenium selenium;
  static String screenShotsFolder;
  String currentBrowser;

  final String WRONG_TITLE =
    "WRONG_TITLESoftware Testing Essays, Book Reviews and Information";

  @BeforeClass
  public static void startServer() throws Exception{
    server = new SeleniumServer();
    server.start();
    screenShotsFolder = createNowfolder();
  }

  @Rule
  public MethodRule watchman= new TestWatchman() {

    @Override
    public void failed(Throwable e, FrameworkMethod method) {
      captureScreenShots( screenShotsFolder,
            currentBrowser,
        method.getName() + "_" + e.getClass().getSimpleName());
      stopSelenium();
    }

    @Override
    public void succeeded(FrameworkMethod method) {
      stopSelenium();
    }
  };

  public ScreenCaptureOnFailureWithWatchmanTests(String currentBrowser){
    this.currentBrowser = currentBrowser;
  }

  @Parameters
  public static Collection testData(){
    return Arrays.asList(new Object[][]{{"firefox"},{"chrome"},
            {"iexplore"},{"googlechrome"}});
  }

  @Test
  public void captureScreenshots(){
      startServerAndOpenRoot(currentBrowser);
      assertEquals(WRONG_TITLE,selenium.getTitle());
  }

  private void captureScreenShots(String screenShotsFolder,
            String browser, String fileNameAppend) {
    selenium.windowMaximize();

    try { Thread.sleep(1000); } catch (Exception e) {}

    String filename = screenShotsFolder + browser + "_" +
            fileNameAppend + "_screenshot.png";
```

```
      selenium.captureScreenshot(filename);

    try{ selenium.captureEntirePageScreenshot(
      filename.replace(".png","full.png"),"");    }catch(Exception e){}
  }

  private void startServerAndOpenRoot(String browser) {
    selenium = new DefaultSelenium("localhost",
        server.getPort(), "*" + browser,
        "http://www.compendiumdev.co.uk");
    selenium.start();
    selenium.open("/");
  }

  static private String createNowfolder() {
    String screenShotsFolder = System.getProperty("user.dir") +
        File.separator + "screenshots" + File.separator;

    SimpleDateFormat sdfmth = new SimpleDateFormat("yyyy-MM-dd-HH-mm");
    Calendar cal = Calendar.getInstance();

    screenShotsFolder = screenShotsFolder + sdfmth.format(cal.getTime());

    new File(screenShotsFolder).mkdirs();
    return screenShotsFolder + File.separator;
  }

  public void stopSelenium(){
    selenium.close();
    selenium.stop();
  }

  @AfterClass
  public static void stopServer(){
    server.stop();
  }
}
```

Related Reading:

- http://unow.be/rc/TestWatchman[2] The official documentation for the TestWatch-man rules

- http://unow.be/rc/JUnitExt[3] A blog post by Mathieu Carbou describing how to use the `@Rule` annotation.

- http://unow.be/rc/plscreens[4] Patrick Lightbody describes the creation of an alternative JUnit 4 test runner to capture screenshots.

[2]http://kentbeck.github.com/junit/javadoc/latest/index.html?org/junit/rules/TestWatchman.html
[3]http://blog.mycila.com/2009/11/writing-your-own-junit-extensions-using.html
[4]http://www.sonatype.com/people/2009/10/selenium-part-4/

Chapter 33

Run the tests on multiple browsers

There are a lot of ways that I could setup the tests in order to run on multiple browsers, I have listed 3 below. This is not an exhaustive list, just the most obvious candidates:

- Method 1: Multiple browsers with data driven tests

- Method 2: Property Files

- Method 3: System Properties

We covered method 1 in the previous chapter "Chapter 32: Screen Capture on Failure".

33.1 Browser Codes

Selenium supports a number of browser codes which we can use when creating a selenium instance

```
selenium = new DefaultSelenium(
            "localhost", 4444, "*iexplore",
            "http://www.compendiumdev.co.uk");
```

Starting selenium with an incorrect browser code will force Selenium to give an error message, which also lists the supported browsers.

There are nuances associated with the different codes but we really don't need to understand very much about them.

If you want to use a browser then try the main code for it and see if the tests work:

i.e.

- `*firefox` - Mozilla Firefox

- `*iexplore` - Internet Explorer

- `*googlechrome` - Google Chrome

- `*konqueror` - Linux Konqueror

- `*safari` - Apple Safari

- `*opera` - Opera

If your tests fail to work then try a code which bypasses some of the browser security controls and gives Selenium more leeway with its security bypassing controls. Most of these codes have been retained for backwards compatibility, but sometimes a test that fails to run under the main code can run with one of the earlier codes. Even if you are using the most up to date version of Selenium. It really depends on your local desktop environment, the browser versions installed and the security protocols on your desktop machine:

For Firefox:

- `*firefoxproxy`

- `*pifirefox`

- `*chrome`

- `*firefoxchrome`

For Internet Explorer:

- `*iexploreproxy`

- `*piiexplore`

- `*iehta` - you should never really have to use `iehta` though

For Safari:

- `*safariproxy`

Custom is used for browsers that are not supported out of the box by Selenium. I have never needed to use this option. It is explained in the official documentation if you really need to use a custom browser.

- `*custom`

If you want to understand the reasons for the different codes then the official documentation is a useful place to start.

http://unow.be/rc/rcdocs[1]

I will not repeat the various explanations in here because they are well explained in the official documentation and, to be honest, you don't really need to know them in order to use Selenium.

---

[1] http://seleniumhq.org/docs/05_selenium_rc.html

33.2 Property Files

A property file is a simple text file. e.g.

```
# the browser to run tests on
browser = *iexplore
```

Any line beginning with # is a comment, any other line is a property. Where the name of the property is to the left of the = and the property value is to the right.

Java has a utility class for reading these property files which makes them a very simple method for controlling the configuration of a Java application without re-compiling the application.

One very common way that people have of setting up the Selenium configuration is through property files.

e.g. In our DefaultSelenium call we have a number of items which might be useful to have in a properties file

```
selenium = new DefaultSelenium(
                "localhost", 4444, "*iexplore",
                "http://www.compendiumdev.co.uk");
```

The host location, port and browser are all obvious candidates for reading from a properties file rather than hard coding into our code.

We might construct a property file like the following:

```
# the browser to run tests on
browser = *iexplore
host = localhost
port = 4444
```

We save the property file in our root directory for the project, in my case:

```
C:\selenium_tests\InitialSeleniumTests
```

Although we can name property files anything we want, the general convention is to call them "something".properties. I named it selenium.properties.

Now we just have to amend our SeleniumManager class to make use of a properties file.

I add the following code to SeleniumManager.java

```
String host;
String port;
String browser;

private void readProperties(){

  Properties props;
  props = new Properties();

  String filePath = "selenium.properties";

  try {
```

343

```
        props.load(new FileInputStream(filePath));
    } catch (FileNotFoundException e) {
        System.out.println("No Properties file found");
        e.printStackTrace();
    } catch (IOException e) {
        System.out.println("Error loading properties file");
        e.printStackTrace();
    }

    this.browser = props.getProperty("browser","*firefox");
    this.host = props.getProperty("host","localhost");
    this.port = props.getProperty("port","4444");
}
```

I added three variables to store the `host`, `port` and `browser`.

Then a new method to read in the values from the properties file.

I create a `Properties` object, which is the `java.utils` class for handling property files.

I use the `.load` method on the properties file to load the properties file.

Then I get the property with the `getProperty` method. The `getProperty` method takes two parameters, the first is the `key` of the property, the second is the `default value` if the property is not found.

We always have default values, even if the property file can't be read, or hasn't been created.

All I have to do then, is update the `.start` method in `SeleniumManager` to use these field variables.

```
public void start(String baseURL) throws IOException {

    String shutdownCommand =
        "http://%s:%s/selenium-server/driver/?cmd=shutDownSeleniumServer";

    readProperties();

    String stopSeleniumCommand = String.format(shutdownCommand,host,port);

    try {
        seleniumServer = new SeleniumServer();
        seleniumServer.start();
    } catch (java.net.BindException bE){
        System.out.println("could not bind - carrying on");
        if( runHTTPCommand(stopSeleniumCommand)){
            try {
                seleniumServer = new SeleniumServer();
                seleniumServer.start();
            } catch (Exception e) {
                throw new IllegalStateException(
                "Could not stop existing server on blocked port " + port, e);
            }
        }
    }
    catch (Exception e) {
        throw new IllegalStateException("Can't start selenium server", e);
    }
```

344

```
    selenium = new DefaultSelenium(host, new Integer(port), browser, baseURL);
    selenium.start();
}
```

Because we introduced the `SeleniumManager` class into our tests, we only have to make the changes once, and all the tests that use the `SeleniumManager` will now be configured by the properties file.

NOTE:

The code for this version of the `SeleniumManager` can be found in `com.eviltester.seleniumutils` as `SeleniumManager03PropertiesFile.java`

33.3 System Properties

An alternative properties mechanism is to use the system properties.

We can set these in our Ant file and in Hudson.

Reading these through Java is even easier than the properties file:

```
private static final String SELENIUM_PORT = "selenium.port";
private static final String SELENIUM_HOST = "selenium.host";
private static final String SELENIUM_BROWSER = "selenium.browser";

public void readSystemProperties() {
  Properties systemProperties = System.getProperties();

  if(systemProperties.containsKey(SELENIUM_BROWSER))
    this.browser = systemProperties.getProperty(SELENIUM_BROWSER);

  if(systemProperties.containsKey(SELENIUM_HOST))
    this.host = systemProperties.getProperty(SELENIUM_HOST);

  if(systemProperties.containsKey(SELENIUM_PORT))
    this.port = systemProperties.getProperty(SELENIUM_PORT);
}
```

Because I will allow system properties to override those set in the properties file I don't need to add any code to handle defaults, as the defaults are handled in `readProperties()`;

All that remains in `SeleniumManager` is to add a call to this method, as shown in this code extract:

```
public void start(String baseURL) throws IOException {
  String shutdownCommand =
    "http://%s:%s/selenium-server/driver/?cmd=shutDownSeleniumServer";
  readProperties();      // get the properties from a file
  readSystemProperties();    // system properties override the properties
  // code removed ...
```

I can set the system properties in the Ant file as the following extract shows:

```
<!-- setup a default browser property, overwrite with -DBROWSER=iexplore etc.
    -->
<property name="BROWSER" value="firefox" />

<target name="run_param_JUnit_tests">
  <JUnit printsummary="yes" fork="yes"
    errorproperty="JUnit.error" failureproperty="JUnit.error">

    <sysproperty key="selenium.browser" value="${BROWSER}"/>

    <classpath refid="JUnit.class.path" />
    <formatter type="xml" />

    <test todir="${testresults}"
    name="com.eviltester.seleniumtutorials.chap22.MultiBrowserExampleTest" />
  </JUnit>

  <antcall target="report-JUnit"/>
  <fail if="JUnit.error" message="Selenium test(s) failed.  See reports!"/>
</target>
```

In this extract I create a local property called BROWSER with a default value, and in the run_pm_JUnit_tests target to set the system property selenium.browser that will be picked up by the systemProperties.getProperty(SELENIUM_BROWSER); command.

This allows us to override the property in our Hudson build so that we can setup multiple Hudson builds, each of which run the tests on a different browser.

We add the properties in Hudson to the Advanced fields of the build section:

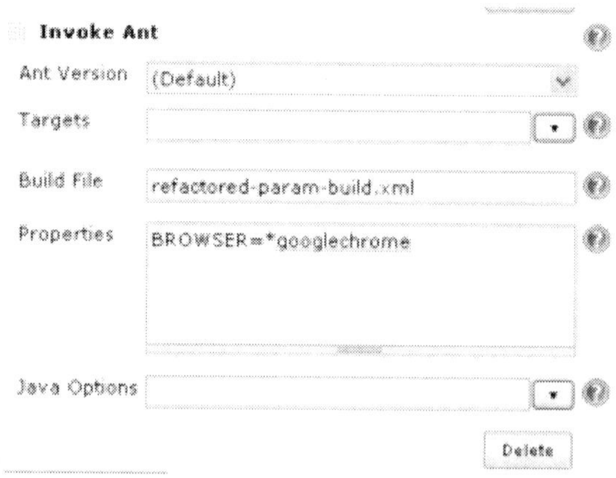

Figure 33.1: Override the system properties in Hudson

The properties field uses the same text format as our properties file. Note that the properties are case sensitive. In the Ant file I used:

```
<property name="BROWSER" value="firefox" />
```

Therefore I have to use BROWSER in the properties section to override that property.

346

```
BROWSER=*googlechrome
```

If I run this build setup then the tests will run under Google Chrome browser. If I remove the properties above then it will use the default setup in the Ant file `firefox`.

If I run the tests directly within Eclipse, the system properties will not be set so the `selenium.properties` file will be used to define the parameters.

NOTE:

See the `refactored-pm-build.xml` file for example usage.

The `SeleniumManager` class with this code added is in package `com.eviltester.seleniumutils` as `SeleniumManager04SystemProperties.java`

Chapter 34

JavaScript And Dynamic HTML Testing Redux

Or... a little more about JavaScript testing.

For some reason, testing Ajax enabled websites, or dynamic HTML websites can cause initial concern for testers learning automation.

I don't think that this is due to the complexity of using Selenium to test it, really you only have to learn one new command (`waitForCondition`).

The concern seems to stem from the investigation required to work out what the Ajax or dynamic HTML does and how to identify the requisite states for when the Ajax processing has finished.

34.1   Example Dynamic HTML Page

You saw in Chapter 20 "Using JavaScript with Selenium" the example dynamic HTML page. http://unow.be/rc/basicajax[1]

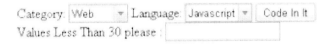

Figure 34.1: Dynamic HTML form

When the user selects one of the Category values, the `Language` dropdown is repopulated with a relevant set of languages by making a call to the server and then updating the dropdown with the results passed back from the Server. This client/server interaction is represented on screen by the display of an animated GIF to the left of the [Code in It] button.

Figure 34.2: Client/Server interaction animated GIF

If we write a test, which selects the `Category` entry and then checks for a particular language being displayed in the `Language` dropdown. The test will fail because the `Language` drop down will not have been changed.

---

[1]http://www.compendiumdev.co.uk/selenium/basic_ajax.html

```
@Test(expected=org.junit.ComparisonFailure.class)
public void chooseACategoryAndCheckTheLanguageThrowsExceptionDueToNoWait(){
  ajaxPage.selectCategory("Server");
  assertEquals("Cobol",ajaxPage.getLanguage());

  ajaxPage.selectCategory("Web");
  assertEquals("Javascript",ajaxPage.getLanguage());

  ajaxPage.selectCategory("Desktop");
  assertEquals("C++",ajaxPage.getLanguage());
}
```

We can't use a `WaitForPageToLoad` because the page does not reload, JavaScript is being used to refresh the entry.

We have to use the `WaitForCondition` method.

NOTE:

In the above test, note that I used the optional (`expected='...'`) notation. This allows me to write tests which ''fail'' but do not show as failures in the running of the test because I have told the test runner to expect the test to fail and throw an exception.

34.2   First Model the behaviour in the test

The first thing I will do is model the behaviour I expect in the test.

```
@Test
public void chooseACategoryAndCheckTheLanguage(){

  ajaxPage.selectCategory("Server");
  ajaxPage.waitForAjaxSymbolToGoAway();

  assertEquals("Cobol",ajaxPage.getLanguage());

  ajaxPage.selectCategory("Web");
  ajaxPage.waitForAjaxSymbolToGoAway();

  assertEquals("Javascript",ajaxPage.getLanguage());

  ajaxPage.selectCategory("Desktop");
  ajaxPage.waitForAjaxSymbolToGoAway();

  assertEquals("C++",ajaxPage.getLanguage());
}
```

All I have to do now, is write the `waitForAjaxSymbolToGoAway` in my page object model and my test should pass.

Easy.

350

34.3   Code the check in the page object model

The Selenium `WaitForCondition` method takes two parameters:

- A JavaScript statement to evaluate

- A Timeout for how long should we wait for the condition to return true

The `WaitForCondition` basically loops, evaluating the supplied JavaScript, until it returns true, or the timeout occurs.

The first hard part then, about `WaitForCondition`, is learning enough JavaScript to be able to make use of it.

The second is understanding the functioning of the page.

34.3.1   First understand the page

Before we try and figure out what JavaScript we need we have to have a look at the page and see what happens.

By examining the source-code for the `basic_ajax.html` page I can see the image in the page:

```
<span id="ajaxBusy" style="display: none;">
    <img src="ajax-loader.gif"/></span>
```

By default the image will not display, because of the CSS style values use `display: none;`.

I need to write a wait condition which checks the style value of the `ajaxBusy` item.

A quick google search later for ''javascript check if display none'' and I have the basic information that I need `style.display== 'none'`

- for more information visit http://unow.be/rc/7togglers[2]

We have already seen that to interact with the page with JavaScript in Selenium that I have to prefix the access commands with `window.document`.

So I can write a method in my `BasicAjaxPage.java` page object as follows:

```
public void waitForAjaxSymbolToGoAway() {
  selenium.waitForCondition(
    "window.document.getElementById('ajaxBusy').style.display=='none'",
    "4000");
}
```

---

[2]http://www.dustindiaz.com/seven-togglers/

This gets the element with the id `ajaxBusy` and checks that the display value in the CSS style is `none`.

The JavaScript that we need to use `waitForCondition` doesn't really need to go much beyond basic accessor styles and you can usually find examples via a quick search.

My test now passes.

34.4   Summary

It could be very easy to put yourself off testing at this level. Because you do have to know a bit of JavaScript. You do have to know a bit of CSS. You do have to be able to analyse the application page and work out what is happening.

But as you saw, you don't need much knowledge. You just need to be able to figure out what you want to do, have the skills to find the information, and then translate it into tests.

This will come with practice after you try to automate a few dynamic HTML or Ajax pages.

Your developers should be able to help write the conditions, and the easy way to learn is to work closely with the development team.

NOTE:
The tests and page object model for this chapter can be found as `BasicAjaxPage.java` and `MoreJavaScriptTests.java` in the package `com.eviltester.seleniumtutorials.chap34.javascript`.

Chapter 35

Cookie Handling

Cookies are small files which are stored on your computer which web sites use to store client specific information e.g. Session identifiers, or tracking information.

Chances are, any website which can remember who you are when you visit, without you telling it, has placed a cookie on your computer which it accesses when you next visit the site.

For more information on cookies, visit the Wikipedia entry for ''HTTP Cookie'' http://unow.be/rc/HTTPcookie[1]

35.1   Cookies in the example application

The search page http://www.compendiumdev.co.uk/selenium/search.php uses cookies to track:

- previous search terms

- time and date of the last visit

- number of times visited

It creates the following cookies via JavaScript:

- `seleniumSimplifiedSearchNumVisits` to count the number of visits to the page

- `seleniumSimplifiedSearchLastVisit` to store the time and date of the last visit

- `seleniumSimplifiedLastSearch` to store the value of the last search

35.2   How to see cookies on a web page?

If you visit the search page above then you can see the cookies for yourself using Firefox.

353

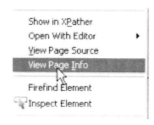

Figure 35.1: View Page Info

Figure 35.2: Page Info Dialog shows basic page information

35.2.1 Firefox by Default

Right click and choose `View Page Info` from the pop-up menu.

On the `Page Info` dialog, click the `[Details]` button.

On the `Page Info Details` dialog, click the `[View Cookies]` button.

You then see the `Cookies` management dialog. Here you can see the cookie details and remove them.

35.2.2 Firecookie - Firebug Plugin

To have more control over the cookies, you could use a Firebug plugin in Firefox called Firecookie by Jan Odvarko.

http://unow.be/rc/firecookie[2]

---

[1]http://en.wikipedia.org/wiki/HTTP_cookie
[2]https://addons.mozilla.org/en-US/firefox/addon/6683/

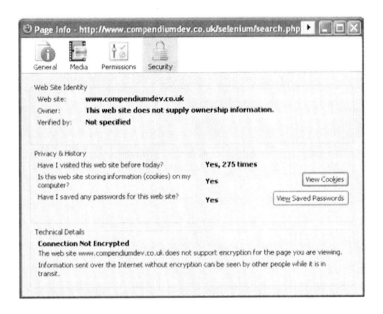

Figure 35.3: Page Info dialog showing details allows you to view the cookies

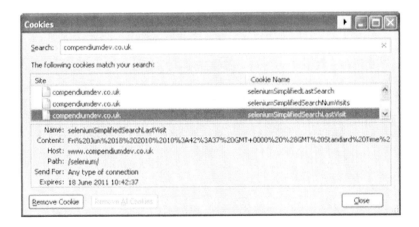

Figure 35.4: Cookies Management Dialog

This allows you to Edit the cookie as well as delete it. When we are testing with cookies, the ability to edit them comes in particularly handy. Editing them is less important for automation but I still tend to use the plugin than rely on the default cookie management.

Figure 35.5: Firecookie plugin for amending and viewing cookies

By right clicking on the cookie name you can choose to `Edit` cookie from the pop-up menu.

Figure 35.6: Edit cookie in firecookie

Here you can edit the details of the cookies.

35.3   Selenium Cookie Commands

Selenium provides the following commands for working with cookies:

- `deleteAllVisibleCookies();`

    – delete all the cookies for the current page

- `isCookiePresent("<cookie_name>");`

    – return true if a particular cookie name is present on the page

- `createCookie("<cookie_details>");`

    – create a cookie for the current page

- `getCookie();`

    – returns all the cookies for the current page

- `getCookieByName("<cookie_name>");`

    – return a cookie for a given name.

- `deleteCookie("<cookie_name>","<options>");`

  - delete a named cookie,
  - the options string takes a comma separated list of options:
    * `path` = the path under the specified domain which the cookie was created for
      · e.g. `path=/selenium/`
    * `domain` = the domain used to create the cookie
      · e.g. `domain=compendiumdev.co.uk`
    * `recurse=true` :try all sub-domains of the current domain
    * Note: I have found certain variations of using the `deleteCookie` method incompatible between browers. You will see these later in the chapter.

35.4 Example Code For Cookie Testing

35.4.1 Basic Class

I create a basic class to add the following tests in. This will reuse the `SeleniumManager` and the `SearchPage` object that we created in previous chapters.

```
package com.eviltester.seleniumtutorials.chap35.cookies;

import static org.junit.Assert.*;
import java.io.IOException;
import org.junit.AfterClass;
import org.junit.BeforeClass;
import org.junit.Test;
import com.eviltester.seleniumtutorials.refactored.pageObjectModel.SearchPage
    ;
import com.eviltester.seleniumutils.SeleniumManager;
import com.thoughtworks.selenium.Selenium;

public class CookieTests {
  static SeleniumManager sm;
  static Selenium selenium;
  SearchPage searchPage;

  @BeforeClass
  static public void startServer() throws IOException{
    sm = new SeleniumManager();
    sm.start("http://www.compendiumdev.co.uk");
    selenium = sm.getSelenium();
  }

  @AfterClass
  static public void stopServer(){
    sm.stop();
  }
}
```

35.4.2 Check Cookie Creation using deleteAllVisibleCookies and isCookiePresent

To the above class I will add a test that checks for cookie creation.

This test uses the `deleteAllVisibleCookies` and `isCookiePresent` methods to check that cookies get created.

I will first visit the page, and delete all the cookies. This way I know that I am starting from a clean position.

I will then open the page and check that two cookies get created on page visitation. Then I will do a search and check that the third cookie gets created.

```
@Test
public void checkCookiesGetCreated() {
  searchPage = new SearchPage(selenium);
  searchPage.open();

  selenium.deleteAllVisibleCookies();

  assertCookieDoesNotExist("seleniumSimplifiedSearchNumVisits");
  assertCookieDoesNotExist("seleniumSimplifiedSearchLastVisit");
  assertCookieDoesNotExist("seleniumSimplifiedLastSearch");

  searchPage.open();
  assertCookieExists("seleniumSimplifiedSearchNumVisits");
  assertCookieExists("seleniumSimplifiedSearchLastVisit");
  assertCookieDoesNotExist("seleniumSimplifiedLastSearch");

  searchPage.typeSearchTerm("selenium");
  searchPage.clickSearchButton();
  assertCookieExists("seleniumSimplifiedSearchNumVisits");
  assertCookieExists("seleniumSimplifiedSearchLastVisit");
  assertCookieExists("seleniumSimplifiedLastSearch");
}

private void assertCookieDoesNotExist(String cookieName) {
  String cookieMessage = "We deleted all cookies, %s should not exist";

  assertFalse(  String.format(cookieMessage,cookieName),
      selenium.isCookiePresent(cookieName));
}

private void assertCookieExists(String cookieName) {
  String cookieMessage = "We added cookie %s, it should exist";

  assertTrue( String.format(cookieMessage,cookieName),
      selenium.isCookiePresent(cookieName));
}
```

I created the private helper methods to remove repeated code in the test and help make the test itself more readable. If I find that I use methods like this across multiple tests then I would probably refactor them into a new class to make them available to all the tests, rather that creating them as private methods in each test class.

35.4.3 Get Cookie values using getCookie and getCookieByName

getCookie

The `getCookie` method returns a single string with all the cookies for the current page.

After running a `searchPage.open()` command the `getCookie()` method for the search page would return a string like the following:

```
seleniumSimplifiedSearchLastVisit=Fri%20Jun%2018%2012%3A10%3A04%20UTC%202010;
    seleniumSimplifiedSearchNumVisits=1
```

This string has all the cookies separated by ; (a semicolon).

You can see that each cookie has the format: `<cookie name>=<cookie value>` Cookie values are url-encoded (http://unow.be/rc/pcencoding[3])

`getCookie` is unlikely to be a method that you use very frequently as you can get the cookies directly using the `getCookieByName`, but it can prove useful when you check to see if any cookies you did not expect to be added are on the page.

The following example test shows one way of parsing the results of the `getCookie` string:

```java
@Test
public void parseResultsOfGetCookieExplored() throws
    UnsupportedEncodingException {
  searchPage = new SearchPage(selenium);
  searchPage.open();

  // split the cookie string so that each entry in the array
  // is a cookie name=value
  String []cookies = selenium.getCookie().split(";");

  for (int i = 0; i < cookies.length; i++) {
    // split the cookie=name value into name[0] and value[1] entries
    String []cookieNameValue = cookies[i].split("=");

    // remove extra spaces and encoding on the name and value
    String cookieName = cookieNameValue[0].trim();
    String cookieValue =
        URLDecoder.decode(cookieNameValue[1].trim(),"UTF-8");

    // compare against the 'byName' methods
    assertTrue("expected to find cookie by name " + cookieName,
      selenium.isCookiePresent(cookieName));
    assertEquals(cookieValue,
      URLDecoder.decode(selenium.getCookieByName(cookieName,"UTF-8")));
  }
}
```

In the above code we first split the returned value from `getCookie` so that the ; separated values become entries in a java array.

We loop over the array and split each cookie on the = character to give us an array where the first (`[0]`) value in the array is the cookie name and the second (`[1]`) is the cookie name.

---

[3]http://en.wikipedia.org/wiki/Percent-encoding

I have to .trim() the returned values to remove any header or trailing whitespace characters. I decode both values to ensure that the comparisons are consistent.

We use the java.net.URLDecoder:

```
import java.net.URLDecoder;
```

Again, you probably won't use getCookie very much but it is worth knowing for those occasions where the cookies require parsing or decoding.

getCookieByName

You have already seen getCookieByName in action in the previous example test but I will now show it in the context of an actual test on the page.

```
@Test
public void getCookieByNameExplored() {

    String lastSearchTerm="";

    // open page and set to no cookies
    searchPage = new SearchPage(selenium);
    searchPage.open();
    selenium.deleteAllVisibleCookies();

    /* open the page 10 times and check cookie increments */
    for (int i = 1; i < 11; i++) {

        lastSearchTerm = "Selenium " + i;
        searchPage.typeSearchTerm(lastSearchTerm);
        searchPage.clickSearchButton();

        assertEquals(i + "",
            selenium.getCookieByName("seleniumSimplifiedSearchNumVisits"));
        assertEquals(lastSearchTerm,
            selenium.getCookieByName("seleniumSimplifiedLastSearch"));

        assertCookieExists("seleniumSimplifiedSearchLastVisit");
    }
}
```

In this test we open the page and delete all the cookies to get it in a known state. Then we loop around ten times and perform a search. Then on the resulting page we check that the number of visits has been incremented and that the last search term was stored correctly.

deleteCookie

Most of the time you will be able to use deleteCookie without passing through any options e.g.

```
selenium.deleteCookie("seleniumSimplifiedSearchNumVisits","");
```

If you need to get more specific then the following test illustrates some of the variations around using deleteCookie:

NOTE:

I used a shorthand way of allowing an integer to be compared with a string in the `assertEquals` statement:

```
assertEquals(i + "",
    selenium.getCookieByName("seleniumSimplifiedSearchNumVisits"));
```

Here I converted the integer into a string by adding an empty string to it e.g.

`i + ""`

An old Visual Basic trick that I've carried through into other languages. It also helps avoid null pointer exceptions on string comparisons.

Domain	Size	Path
www.compendiumdev.co.uk	39 B	/selenium/

Figure 35.7: Cookie domain and path

```
@Test
public void deleteCookieExplored() {
  searchPage = new SearchPage(selenium);
  searchPage.open();

  // simple delete works fine
  selenium.deleteCookie("seleniumSimplifiedSearchNumVisits","");
  assertCookieDoesNotExist("seleniumSimplifiedSearchNumVisits");

  // full domain and path work fine - you can see these in firecookie
  // issues getting this working in firefox, but works fine in IE
  if(sm.getBrowser().contains("ie")){
    searchPage.open();
    selenium.deleteCookie("seleniumSimplifiedSearchNumVisits",
      "domain=www.compendiumdev.co.uk, path=/selenium/");
    assertCookieDoesNotExist("seleniumSimplifiedSearchNumVisits");
  }

  // delete example using just the domain
  if(sm.getBrowser().contains("ie")){
    searchPage.open();
    selenium.deleteCookie("seleniumSimplifiedSearchNumVisits",
      "domain=www.compendiumdev.co.uk");
    assertCookieDoesNotExist("seleniumSimplifiedSearchNumVisits");
  }

  searchPage.open();
  // missing domain and having path will delete the cookie
  selenium.deleteCookie("seleniumSimplifiedSearchNumVisits", "path=/selenium/
    ");
  assertCookieDoesNotExist("seleniumSimplifiedSearchNumVisits");

  // fail to delete when missing domain and getting path wrong
  searchPage.open();
```

```
selenium.deleteCookie("seleniumSimplifiedSearchNumVisits", "path=/wrongpath
    /");
assertCookieExists("seleniumSimplifiedSearchNumVisits");

searchPage.open();
// missing out the path and recurse succeed
selenium.deleteCookie("seleniumSimplifiedSearchNumVisits",
    "domain=www.compendiumdev.co.uk, recurse=true");
assertCookieDoesNotExist("seleniumSimplifiedSearchNumVisits");

// fail to delete when domain wrong even if path right
searchPage.open();
selenium.deleteCookie("seleniumSimplifiedSearchNumVisits",
    "domain=compendiumdev.co.uk, path=/selenium/");
assertCookieExists("seleniumSimplifiedSearchNumVisits");

searchPage.open();
// getting the domain wrong will pass if we recurse through subdomains
selenium.deleteCookie("seleniumSimplifiedSearchNumVisits",
    "domain=compendiumdev.co.uk, recurse=true");
assertCookieDoesNotExist("seleniumSimplifiedSearchNumVisits");

searchPage.open();
// getting the domain wrong can pass if we recurse through subdomains,
// path makes no difference
selenium.deleteCookie("seleniumSimplifiedSearchNumVisits",
    "domain=compendiumdev.co.uk, recurse=true, path=/selenium/");
assertCookieDoesNotExist("seleniumSimplifiedSearchNumVisits");

searchPage.open();
// getting the domain wrong can pass if we recurse through subdomains
// even if we get the path wrong
selenium.deleteCookie("seleniumSimplifiedSearchNumVisits",
    "domain=compendiumdev.co.uk, recurse=true, path=/sele/");
assertCookieDoesNotExist("seleniumSimplifiedSearchNumVisits");
}
```

In the above example you can see the incompatibilities I had when running `deleteCookie` on different browsers. The base `deleteCookie` call with just the cookie name was portable across all browsers. The combination of `domain`, without the `recurse` parameter failed on Firefox, but passed on Internet Explorer.

NOTE:

When your test code doesn't work, try it in different browsers, as you may have encountered a browser incompatibility problem.

Keep the checks and method usages as simple as possible to avoid browser incompatibility issues, but not so simple that you can result in false positives in the test (i.e. a check passing when it should not)

createCookie

If you need to create initial conditions for a test through cookies then you can use the `createCookie` command.

```
createCookie(<name value pair>,<options>);
```

- The name value pair, as we saw earlier from `getCookies()` has the format `name=value` where the value is URL encoded.

- Options, uses a comma separated list to have multiple options in a single string. If you choose not to use path and domain then the current page path and domain will be used.

  - `path`
    * the path under the domain for the cookie
    * e.g. `path=/selenium/`
  - `domain`
    * the domain the cookie relates to
  - `max_age`
    * a value in seconds for the cookie to be valid
    * e.g. `max_age = 6000`
      · 100 minutes
    * we can use `max_age` to create a session cookie by using a negative number
      · e.g. `max_age=-200`

`createCookie` does not URL encode the cookie values. To do this use the `URLEncode.encode` method from `java.net.URLEncoder`

```
import java.net.URLEncoder;
@Test
public void createCookieExplored() throws IOException {

    searchPage = new SearchPage(selenium);
    searchPage.open();
    selenium.deleteAllVisibleCookies();

    searchPage.open();
    assertCookieDoesNotExist("seleniumSimplifiedLastSearch");

    String lastSearch = "Search For This";
    String lastSearchAsCookieValue = URLEncoder.encode(lastSearch, "UTF-8");
    selenium.createCookie( "seleniumSimplifiedLastSearch=" +
        lastSearchAsCookieValue,
        "max_age=6000");

    searchPage.open();
    assertCookieExists("seleniumSimplifiedLastSearch");
    assertEquals(selenium.getCookieByName("seleniumSimplifiedLastSearch"),
      lastSearchAsCookieValue);
}
```

NOTE:

The code for this chapter can be found in class `CookieTests.java` in the package `com.eviltester.seleniumtutorials.chap35.cookies`

Chapter 36

The Future of Selenium

The Selenium tool suite is constantly being worked on. Having been embraced by Google and Mozilla, with many of the key figures in Selenium development working at both companies, the future for Selenium looks rosy.

It can often seem daunting choosing between the many open-source software testing tools to know which ones will be supported and maintained over the years. The fact is that Selenium has a talented set of programming and testing talent behind the tool and using it on a daily basis.

Selenium is also used in spin off tools like the load testing tool from BrowserMob.com, which uses the selenium API as its scripting language from JavaScript to write the automated tests.

The current direction for Selenium, which manifested as Selenium 2.0.0 merges the code bases for Selenium RC and WebDriver.

Selenium takes the automation approach of driving the website through JavaScript with the Selenium RC server using Selenium Core to automate the site. This has some issues with security and cross browser scripting which is why there are so many ways of instantiating a browser session for the supported browsers. e.g. `*iexplore`, `*firefox`, `*firefoxproxy`, `*iexploreproxy`

WebDriver takes a different approach. It calls the browsers directly through their respective automation interfaces. This means that all tests run in the browser and have no security issues as it is the raw browser that takes all the actions.

WebDriver has a different API than Selenium. It is a far more Object Oriented interface and can seem cleaner. WebDriver also supports the use of HTMLUnit which means you can test websites without creating a real browser so tests can run faster and more easily in a Continuous Integration environment.

Selenium 2 supports both APIs:

- the Selenium API (large set of commands on the Selenium interface)

- the WebDriver API (object oriented browser automation based interface)

This means that you should still be able to write tests using the Selenium API, but have the tool drive the browser directly. This should see an end to some of the JavaScript injection issues and make the tests faster to run.

It also means that the WebDriver API can be used with the Selenium JavaScript injection approach, allowing WebDriver access to browsers which it doesn't yet have a native automation driver for.

All of this basically means that:

- Selenium is still being developed

- The Selenium API you have started learning with this text will remain usable in future versions of Selenium

The time you have spent learning Selenium should be an investment in time and you can look forward to continuing to learn more in the future.

36.1   If you want to experiment with WebDriver

Since we have built the `SeleniumManager` abstraction class to remove the details of Selenium for us, we can easily start using WebDriver by making a few changes to this class.

You can find the official guide to emulating Selenium RC in WebDriver on the Selenium web site: http://unow.be/rc/wdemulate[1]

This small section is designed to help you take the first steps towards experimenting with WebDriver using the basic frameworks that we have explored in this book.

WebDriver is part of the selenium server standalone `.jar` that you have been using in this book.

You only have a few changes to make to the Selenium Manager to allow you to start using WebDriver instead of Selenium RC

- Add a new field in `SeleniumManager` called `useSeleniumTwo`

```
public class SeleniumManager {

  SeleniumServer seleniumServer=null;
  Selenium selenium=null;

  String host;
  String port;
  String browser;
  private boolean useWebDriver=true;
// code removed ...
```

- Manually change this from true to false depending on whether you want to use WebDriver or not.

    - You can easily expand the class to have some helper methods to do this. See the `SeleniumManager.java` for an example

---

[1]http://seleniumhq.org/docs/03_webdriver.html#emulating-selenium-rc

- Add code to return a `WebDriverBackedSelenium` instance instead of a Selenium Server instance

```
public void start(String baseURL) throws IOException {
  readProperties(); // get the properties from a file
  readSystemProperties(); // allow system properties to override properties
      file

  if(useWebDriver){
    WebDriver driver = new FirefoxDriver();
    selenium = new WebDriverBackedSelenium(driver, baseURL);
    return;
  }
// code removed ...
```

- Use Eclipse to fix the include errors

```
import org.openqa.selenium.WebDriver;
import org.openqa.selenium.WebDriverBackedSelenium;
import org.openqa.selenium.firefox.FirefoxDriver;
```

- The above includes should be added by Eclipse automatically as you fix the errors in the code, or you can add them manually.

The above is the minimum amount of code required to use the Firefox driver for WebDriver to have all tests which use the `SeleniumManager` running under WebDriver's Selenium RC Emulation.

So now if you run any of the tests that you have created which use the `SeleniumManager` then they should run using WebDriver instead of Selenium RC.

You will find that not all tests run because there will be some subtle differences required when using WebDriver, but the vast majority of the tests should run and pass successfully.

NOTE:
You can find more comprehensive code for using WebDriver in the `SeleniumManager.java` class.
It is commented out by default so as not to require everyone to amend the properties to reference WebDriver.

Chapter 37

Structuring the tests and code

I will use this chapter to tie up all the loose ends, to demonstrate what a production ready version of the previous chapters might look like.

In previous chapters we have created a disparate set of tests which mostly exist to demonstrate the capabilities of Selenium. In this chapter we will:

- throw away the ''tests'' which don't test anything,

- restructure the code as if in a production environment, to separate tests from page object models

- refactor code to have constants and manageable XPaths

- create a base class to derive our tests from

- tidy the Ant builds

- setup Hudson

This is the chapter you are most likely to refer to for creating the test suites that you use on your projects.

Throughout this chapter I will describe the decisions taken, explain the justification for the decisions and discuss alternatives that we could have pursued.

The decisions taken will be pragmatic, as you would take decisions in the real world. Which means that they are not abstract theoretical decisions. They are decisions which, while they work, involved some compromise, so as part of discussing the alternatives we will explore those compromises.

The code for this chapter is in a new project. You can download the project code, and add it to your own subversion repository from:

http://unow.be/rc/finalSource[1]

Note: You will need to copy in your Selenium server `.jar` file to the lib folder to get the same set of files as from the xp-dev server (this was removed from the zip file due to the size of the file).

Or use it directly from the open subversion server provided by XP-dev (http://unow.be/rc/xpdev[2])

http://svn2.xp-dev.com/svn/seleniumsimplified/trunk/FinalSeleniumTests/

I will use the above subversion link later when I setup Hudson to run the tests.

---

[1]http://www.compendiumdev.co.uk/selenium/finalChapterSource_2ndEdition.zip
[2]http://www.xp-dev.com/

37.1 Java project folder and package structures

In Java, we logically organise our source-code using packages, we physically organise our source-code using folders.

There are many different ways of organizing a Java program physically. I have chosen to adopt the standard directory layout as described by the Maven project.

http://unow.be/rc/mavenlayout[3]

Maven is a software project management tool which can help with organising project builds and dependencies, although we haven't used it in this book, more and more people are using Maven so using the standard directory layout has the advantages that:

- people are more likely to have familiarity with it

- moving to Maven later should be easier

- you don't really have to debate too much about a subjective decision and can adopt an approach based on lessons learned by previous experienced Java developers

The basic folder structure for our project using these maven guidelines is:

```
project name
    src
        main
            java
                ...package structure represented here...
        test
            java
                ...package structure represented here...
            resources
```

In addition, because we are not using maven, I need a folder to store those libraries which my project has a dependency upon, i.e. JUnit4.x and the selenium server. So I create a `lib` directory at the root level of the project. Lib is not mentioned in the maven documentation because maven itself manages these dependencies, so they are stored in a local repository outside of the direct file management of the project.

- `lib`

    - `/lib` is not mentioned in the maven structure but I have chosen to put it at the root level of the folder

I left all my properties files and build files at the root directory.

During the previous chapters, the physical layout was not a big issue because:

---

[3]http://maven.apache.org/guides/introduction/introduction-to-the-standard-directory-layout.html

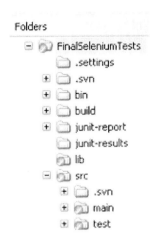

Figure 37.1: New Folder structure based on Maven guidelines

- we were learning and did not need a lot of rules and formalities getting in the way

- our Ant files individually selected the classes to run

- we didn't really make a distinction between "tests" and "test code"

- we were not trying to fit in with a production project so we could do what we wanted

- while we did run the tests through Ant and Hudson, our main method for running the tests was directly in Eclipse

Now though:

- we want to be able to fit in with production quality projects, and learn professional practices

- we do want to separate "tests" from "test code"

- we want to make the Ant files easier to maintain and not individually add test classes

It is very easy to discuss and argue about the proper structure to use for your tests. I made a simple decision to separate my "tests" from my "code" (code being all the java classes that abstract away the system). I think this makes it easier for me to make amendments because I know which folder branch to go into for the different parts of my code.

If I find myself doing a lot of maintenance work in the test branch then I need to rethink my abstraction strategy as I may have written my tests at the wrong level of abstraction. Ideally my tests should remain unchanged after a system change. If the test conditions are still valid, I want most of my changes to be in the abstraction layer. This is not a hard and fast rule as it may not be worth the time building up an abstraction layer which removes all rework.

Our ''tests'' are those classes which have `@Test` annotations within them. Our ''test code'' covers our `SeleniumManager`, and our Page Object Models. These are classes with code which theoretically we might choose to release as a separate `.jar` file for re-use on other projects. We actually want to maintain a separation in how we think about this code because, if we have built our abstraction layer correctly, when the application changes, only the abstraction layer changes - not the tests.

Also by separating out the ''tests'' from ''test code'', in the Ant files we can run all the classes in the `src\test` folder by using a fileset.

37.2 Changing what goes into Version Control

In previous chapters I was lazy about what went into version control and included the Eclipse property files:

- `\.settings`

- `.classpath`

- `.project`

This seemed a convenient ''poor practice'' to use, because it stopped you having to configure the project for your particular environment.

But really, we should not have these configuration elements under version control as they can be unique to everyone's machine.

37.2.1 Configuring Source-code Folders in Eclipse

By removing these, when you import the project into Eclipse, you need to add the following folders as `source folders` to allow you to run the tests from within Eclipse:

- `src\main\java`

- `src\test\java`

To do this:

1. select the source-code folder in the Package Explorer e.g. `src\main\java`

2. right-click the mouse and select `build path\ use as source folder`

3. the folder will then be shown as the root of a package hierarchy

You can see all the source folders listed in the `Java Build Path`.

Select the source folder, right-click and select `build path \ configure build path`.

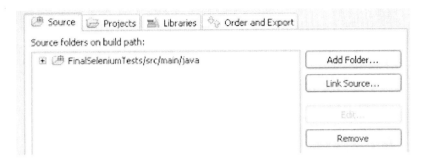

Figure 37.2: Manage the source folders in the project properties dialog

37.2.2   Add libraries

I also added the libraries in the `\lib` folder using the `Add External JARs` function. As we have done in previous chapters.

37.3   Re-organise the Classes and Packages

Because I built the tests in the previous chapters over time, they were organised in a very adhoc fashion.

I will move all the tests around, and into the appropriate source folders.

You can see that I have logically organised all my tests into classes in packages for the areas under test.

Even if the package only contains one class - as many of them do since we only have a very few tests. I still create packages to order them. I find that this:

- makes it easier to see coverage at a high level

- makes it easier to add new test classes

- makes it easier to find tests when I have to maintain them over time

You can also see that I have split the "test code" from the "tests". All tests are in `src/test/java` and all test code is in `src/main/java`.

373

Figure 37.3: Reorganised Package Structure

Figure 37.4: Test Code Packages

I have organised the "test code" so that all classes related to the `SeleniumManager` are in a `seleniumManager` package, base classes for tests are in their own package `testClasses` and all Page Object Models are in another package.

I will explain `SeleniumSimplifiedTest.java` and `TheSeleniumManager.java` in the next section.

374

37.4   Share the Server among tests and create a base test class

In the earlier chapters, our tests used the `SeleniumManager` class to make it easier to manage the `SeleniumServer`, and our test classes start and stop the server within the class.

I made some changes to the `SeleniumManager`:

- to allow me to reuse the same `SeleniumServer` between tests.

- to allow me to reuse the same `Selenium` session between test classes

Since all our tests work on the same domain, if I change the selenium manager to use the same server instance with all the tests, and use the same Selenium instance for all tests that work with the same base URL, there should be a considerable speed up in the test execution speed.

Since all of our tests share the same structure I will create a class for them all to inherit from.

37.4.1   Share the Server using a Singleton

To have all the tests use the same Selenium server I only allow access to `SeleniumManager` via a singleton. In this way only one instantiated object of `SeleniumManager` is in use.

To implement this, I introduce a `TheSeleniumManager` class:

```
public class TheSeleniumManager {

  private volatile static SeleniumManager instance = null;

  private TheSeleniumManager() {
  }

  public static SeleniumManager getSeleniumManager() {

    if(instance == null) {
      synchronized(SeleniumManager.class){
        if(instance == null) {
          instance = new SeleniumManager();
          instance.useSeleniumOne();
          instance.resetProperties();
        }
      }
    }
    return instance;
  }
// code removed ...
```

All of the above complicated code mans that to get access to `SeleniumManager`, you have to call the static method on `TheSeleniumManager` and if no selenium manager has been created, then create one, and once created, it will be reused.

This code was adapted from the Java Singleton code on Wikipedia where you can learn more about Singletons in general. (http://unow.be/rc/singleton[4])

So in my test I would use it as follows:

```
sm = TheSeleniumManager.getSeleniumManager().
    start("http://www.compendiumdev.co.uk");
```

I made further amendments in the `SeleniumManager` code so that calls to `.start()` reuse the same Selenium server and Selenium instance unless the base URL changes. We will look at this code later.

37.4.2   Create a Base Class

My justifications for introducing a base class now:

- having written a lot of tests I can see the commonalities between our tests

- I would like to have the screen shots being taken on error that we saw in one of our tests using the JUnit `TestWatchman`

- it will simplify my test classes

The Initial Base Class I created looked like this:

```
package com.eviltester.seleniumSimplified.testClasses;

import java.io.IOException;
import org.junit.AfterClass;
import org.junit.BeforeClass;
import org.junit.Rule;
import org.junit.rules.MethodRule;
import org.junit.rules.TestWatchman;
import org.junit.runners.model.FrameworkMethod;
import com.eviltester.seleniumutils.seleniumManager.SeleniumManager;
import com.eviltester.seleniumutils.seleniumManager.TheSeleniumManager;
import com.thoughtworks.selenium.Selenium;

public class SeleniumSimplifiedTest {

  protected static SeleniumManager sm;
  protected static Selenium selenium;
  protected static String screenShotsFolder;
  protected static String currentBrowser;

  @BeforeClass
  static public void startServer() throws IOException{
    sm = TheSeleniumManager.getSeleniumManager().
      start("http://www.compendiumdev.co.uk");
    selenium = sm.getSelenium();
    screenShotsFolder = null;
    currentBrowser = sm.getBrowser().replace("*", "");
```

---

[4]http://en.wikipedia.org/wiki/Singleton_pattern

```
      }

      @Rule
      public MethodRule watchman= new TestWatchman() {

         @Override
         public void failed(Throwable e, FrameworkMethod method) {
            captureScreenShots(screenShotsFolder,
               currentBrowser,method.getName() + "_" +
               e.getClass().getSimpleName());
         }

         @Override
         public void succeeded(FrameworkMethod method) {
         }
      };

      private void captureScreenShots(String screenShotsFolder,
            String browser, String fileNameAppend) {
         // since captureScreenshot takes the screen, we should maximise the
         // browser before we take the screenshot
         selenium.windowMaximize();
         selenium.windowFocus();

         if(screenShotsFolder==null){
            screenShotsFolder = TheSeleniumManager.getScreenshotsFolder();
         }

         // give the browser a chance to maximise properly
         try { Thread.sleep(1000); } catch (Exception e) {}

         String filename =   screenShotsFolder + browser + "_" +
               fileNameAppend + "_screenshot.png";

         try{ selenium.captureScreenshot(filename);   }catch(Exception e){}
         try{ selenium.captureEntirePageScreenshot(
            filename.replace(".png","full.png"),"");    }
         catch(Exception e){}
      }

      @AfterClass
      static public void closeItDown(){
         sm.stopSelenium();
      }
   }
```

Most of this code should be completely familiar to you since we used it all in a previous test and all I have done is move the code into this base class.

I moved responsibility for managing the screenshot folder to the `SeleniumManager` singleton. This way I have one screenshot folder per `SeleniumManager` instantiation.

This is the screenshot folder management code from `TheSeleniumManager`:

```
private static String screenshotsFolder = null;

public static String getScreenshotsFolder() {
   // only create the folder when needed
   if(screenshotsFolder==null){
      screenshotsFolder = createNewfolder();
   }
```

```
        return screenshotsFolder;
    }

    static private String createNowfolder() {
        // setup the directory structure to create screenshots into
        String screenShotsFolder = System.getProperty("user.dir") +
                File.separator +
                "screenshots" +
                File.separator;
        SimpleDateFormat sdfmth = new SimpleDateFormat("yyyy-MM-dd-HH-mm-ss");
        Calendar cal = Calendar.getInstance();
        screenShotsFolder = screenShotsFolder + sdfmth.format(cal.getTime());
        new File(screenShotsFolder).mkdirs();
        return screenShotsFolder + File.separator;
    }
```

When the path for the screen shots folder is requested by a call to `getScreenshotsFolder`, if the folder has not been created then it creates the folder (as we saw in previous chapters), and then returns the path to the test.

Because of the `@AfterClass` method stopping the selenium session after every test class, the tests can run quite slowly. We will look at a method for preventing this happening and taking advantage of the `SeleniumManager` to reuse the Selenium session when we look at Test Suites.

To use this base class, our tests have to extend it. And this means we don't have to include any `@BeforeClass` or `@AfterClass` annotated methods in the test as the setup code from `SeleniumSimplifiedTest.java` will be used.

It is worth pointing out here that you can use the `@BeforeClass` annotation in tests which extend the `SeleniumSimplifiedTest.java`, as illustrated in `SearchPageTests.java`

e.g.

```
    public class SearchPageTests extends SeleniumSimplifiedTest{

        static SearchPage searchPage;

        @BeforeClass
        static public void automateTestSetup() throws IOException{
            startSeleniumAndSearchForSeleniumRC();
        }

        static void startSeleniumAndSearchForSeleniumRC() {
            searchPage = new SearchPage(selenium);
            searchPage.open();
            searchPage.typeSearchTerm("Selenium-RC");
            searchPage.clickSearchButton();
        }

        @Test
        public void typeInASearchTermAndAssertThatHomePageTextIsPresent(){
            assertTrue(searchPage.isTextPresent(
                "Selenium Remote-Control Selenium RC comes in two parts." +
                " A server which automatically"));
            assertTrue(searchPage.isTextPresent(
                "launches and kills browsers, and acts as" +
```

```
            " a HTTP proxy for web requests from them."));
    }
    // code removed ...
```

Here, we extend `SeleniumSimplifiedTest` so the `@BeforeClass` annotated method within `SeleniumSimplifiedTest` will be executed, then the `@BeforeClass` annotated method within `SearchPageTests` will be executed.

37.5   Get Ant Working

The main Ant file that I have created for this cut down project looks much the same as our previous Ant file:

```
<?xml version="1.0"?>

<!DOCTYPE project [
    <!ENTITY properties_build_clean_compile_report SYSTEM
      "properties_build_clean_compile_report.xml">
]>

<project name="Run Selenium Tests" default="all_selenium_tests">

  &properties_build_clean_compile_report;

  <!-- setup a default browser property, can be overwritten
    with -DBROWSER=iexplore etc.-->
    <property name="BROWSER" value="*firefox" />

  <target name="run_param_JUnit_tests">
    <JUnit printsummary="yes" fork="yes" errorproperty="JUnit.error"
      failureproperty="JUnit.error">
      <sysproperty key="selenium.browser" value="${BROWSER}"/>

      <classpath refid="JUnit.class.path" />
      <formatter type="xml" />

      <batchtest todir="${testresults}" >
            <fileset dir="${testDir}" includes="**/*.java" />
      </batchtest>
    </JUnit>

    <antcall target="report-JUnit"/>

    <fail if="JUnit.error" message="Selenium test(s) failed.  See reports!"/>
  </target>

  <target name="all_selenium_tests" depends="compile"
    description="The Main Target for running all tests">
    <antcall target="run_param_JUnit_tests"/>
  </target>
</project>
```

I removed the calls to start and stop the server.

I also removed the include for `start_stop_selenium.xml` as all our tests use the Selenium Manager.

I kept the `all_selenium_tests` target, simply to make it easy to add other targets in the Ant file, should I need to later. But I could just have easily put all the code inside the `run_pm_JUnit_tests` target, into `all_selenium_tests`, instead of calling it with an `antcall` element.

I have however amended this file to make it ''future proof'' so that it will run all the tests that I add into the `src/test/java` folder structure:

```
<batchtest todir="${testresults}" >
        <fileset dir="${testDir}" includes="**/*.java" />
</batchtest>
```

Instead of having a series of `<test.../>` entries, where each test was listed as a separate item:

```
<test todir="${testresults}"
  name="com.eviltester.seleniumtutorials.refactored.HTML_form_tests" />
```

The `batchtest` defines a group of tests to run where the set of files to use is defined by the `fileset` element. This `fileset` element is defined as including all `*.java` files no matter where in the `testDir` folder they occur.

The `${testDir}` folder is defined in the `properties_build_clean_compile_report.xml` file:

```
<property name="testDir" location="src/test/java" />
```

You can find more information on `fileset` and `batchtest` in the official Ant documentation:

- `batchtest` - http://unow.be/rc/antJUnit[5]

- `fileset` - http://unow.be/rc/antdir[6]

By adding the tests as a `batchtest` it means that I can add more tests into the folder structure without having to amend the Ant files which execute the tests.

37.6   Make sure all tests are valid tests

A lot of the early tests were designed to illustrate different commands in Selenium. What we really want are tests which do something and then assert that the application has done it. So I reworked the tests to remove any tests which don't add any value to the test coverage. e.g. Setting the text in a field without submitting the form or checking the results.

---

[5]http://ant.apache.org/manual/Tasks/junit.html
[6]http://ant.apache.org/manual/dirtasks.html

37.6.1 Create end to end tests where we assert after executing functionality

You can see the results of all my edits in the source code, but I took the view that all tests had to be functional end to end:

- We don't just enter text in a form field, and assert it. We have to submit the form we enter the text into and check the result.

- For Ajax, it was acceptable to test within the page itself as that was the functional boundary for the Ajax code.

37.6.2 Have all tests pass on multiple browsers

When I ran the tests under multiple browsers I started to see some tests failing. I took a pragmatic quick view of fixing this, as you can see in the `HTML_form_tests.java` for submitting a filename in a form.

NOTE:
I include the filename test as an example of an approach building suites, but I have had to @Ignore this in the downloadable source code because File element handling has grown unreliable when using the Selenium RC API.

```
@Test
public void test_submit_form_with_filename(){

    // skip this test if it is not chrome or firefox
    if(!"|chrome|".contains("|" + currentBrowser))
        return;

    htmlForm.typeFilename("c:\\selenium\\readme.txt");
    HTMLFormResultsPage results = htmlForm.clickSubmitButton();
    assertTrue(results.hasFilename());
    assertEquals("readme.txt",results.getFilename());
}
```

This means that only when the `chrome` or `firefox` browser is in use, will the test be run. This means that when running the test under `iexplore`, no test failures are reported, but it is also misleading because it suggests that we have tested this functionality under `iexplore`, when we haven't.

This may be a practical solution for a short period of time in a production system, but clearly if left for too long could make people think we are regularly testing things that we are not.

I suppose I could change the name of this test to make it a bit more obvious, e.g.

But this still is not a very good solution to the problem.

JUnit does not provide a simple method to categorise tests, but the best solution would be to only include the test if the browser is valid.

Later in the chapter, after I have explained Suites, I will show how to group tests into suites to run them on different browsers.

37.6.3   Locators as constants or methods

In order to make tests maintainable we want to avoid repeated code, or make it possible to make a change in a single place.

Locators as constants

To help with this, I very often refactor locators and other string literals into constants in my Page Object Models.

e.g. Using the `refactor \ extract constant...` I can easily convert string literals in my code to constants at the head of my code. In `BasicAjaxPage.java` I could refactor the string `"combo2"` to become a constant called `COMBO2_LOCATOR`.

Figure 37.5: Refactoring a string to a constant

This refactoring has the effect of generating the following code:

382

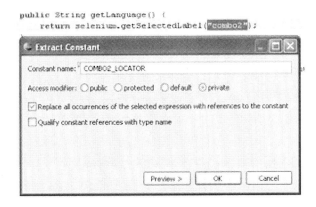

Figure 37.6: provide a name for the extracted constant

```
private static final String COMBO2_LOCATOR = "combo2";
// code removed ...
public String getLanguage() {
   return selenium.getSelectedLabel(COMBO2_LOCATOR);
}
```

This means that I can easily amend the locator if the application changes, and I can easily switch between using XPath or CSS locators, simply by amending the text in the constant.

I prefer to initially add the constants in the Page Object source code itself, although some people seem to like creating property files.

My preference would be to add it into the code, unless that proved difficult for some reason. If I ever had to have one XPath for IE and one for Firefox then I might choose to move the strings into a property file so I could more easily configure the tests.

But I try to keep my coding approach simple. And the simplest thing to start with was a constant in my code.

Locators as methods

I often find that I write methods to generate locators. I find this useful because web applications often generate HTML code on the fly, so id's might be generated automatically with consistent formats. This is the case for the HTMLFormResultsPage.java class.

I initially started refactoring my string literals into the form:

```
private static final String FILENAME_VALUE_ID = "_valuefilename";
private static final String FILENAME_ID = "_filename";
```

But since the results had a common pattern I took a dynamic approach to XPath and ID creation.

In this case I created a method to return the valueID and one for the normal ID:

383

```
private String getValueID(String fieldName) {
  return ID_PREFIX + VALUE_PREFIX + fieldName;
}

private String getID(String fieldName) {
  return ID_PREFIX + fieldName;
}
```

To make this work I have two common constants:

```
private static final String ID_PREFIX = "_";
private static final String VALUE_PREFIX = "value";
```

And then I create a constant for each field name I am interested in:

```
private static final String FN_FILENAME = "filename";
```

I then use these methods and constants in my main methods:

```
public boolean hasFilename() {
  return selenium.isElementPresent(getID(FN_FILENAME));
}
```

This is a more dynamic way of refactoring literals out of code. You can see it in action in `HTMLFormResultsPage.java`. I do this frequently when the page I'm testing has an algorithm for using id's, this allows me to refactor the page even further. It does mean that if the form changes I may have more work to do to put in exceptions to the algorithm, but when it works it means I can build the abstraction layer quickly.

37.7 Get Hudson Working

Since all my code is in subversion, I will be using Hudson to checkout the most up to date version of the tests and run it. I will setup multiple Hudson builds so that the tests run on multiple browsers by passing in the browser as a parameter to the build. I will also have each build trigger the next build.

The fields I have to fill in the build config are:

- Project Name

    – xp-dev Final Selenium Simplified IExplore

- Description

    – Runs the most up to date final tests from xp-dev svn on iexplore

- Subversion

    – Yes

- Repository URL

- http://svn2.xp-dev.com/svn/seleniumsimplified/trunk/FinalSeleniumTests/

- Build- Ant Version

  - (Default)

- Build - Properties

  - Publish JUnit test result report: Yes

- Test report XMLs

  - `**/junit-results/*.xml`

To create another build to run the tests under `firefox`, I copy the project name to the clipboard.

Then from the main Hudson dashboard I create a `New Job`, selecting the `Copy existing job` option, pasting in the project name I want to copy into this field.

After I press the `[OK]` button in the configuration edit for this new job. I have to amend the Build Properties by pressing the `[Advanced...]` button in the Build section.

Amend the properties to read `BROWSER = *firefox`

Then I need to make this build dependent upon the previous one. I do this by editing the Build Triggers. Selecting to `Build after other projects are built` and pasting in the name of the previous IExplore project.

Save this project config by clicking on the `[save]` button at the bottom.

Then go back to the main dashboard and edit the `xp-dev Final Selenium Simplified Iexplore` project.

Scroll down to the `Post-build Actions` section, and you will see that the `Build other projects` field has been selected.

You will also see that the `Trigger even if the build is unstable` checkbox has not been selected by default.

Because we want to check for cross browser, even if tests fail in the previous browser, we should check this box, and save the project.

If you run the IExplore project now, by selecting `Build Now` from the left hand menu. You should find that the tests run under Internet Explorer and under Firefox.

Note also that each time the tests run the browser closes between tests.

We will fix this in the next section to make the test execution share the same Selenium session and make the tests run much faster.

Because we are downloading from an external subversion server and the Selenium server .jar file is quite a large file the builds may take some time to start to get all the files checked out.

385

Figure 37.7: Hudson config to run tests from svn in Internet Explorer

You can speed up subsequent builds by amending the build configurations to `Use Update` under the `Source Code Management` options.

Figure 37.8: Copy from existing job

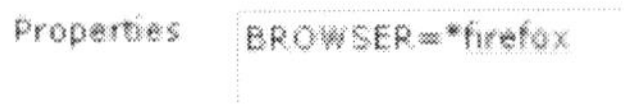

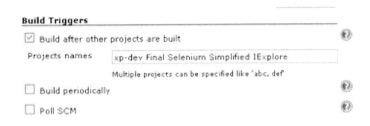

Figure 37.9: Change browser in the properties

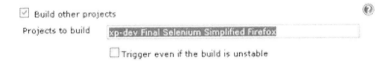

Figure 37.10: Build after IExplore

Figure 37.11: Build other projects by default only runs if previous build is stable

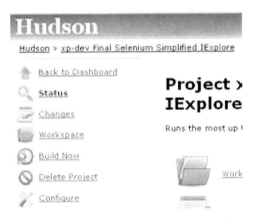

Figure 37.12: Manually trigger a build by clicking on Build Now

37.8 Speed up the test execution with a suite

With the setup currently explained, when we run the tests, the following happens:

- Test Class One:
  - start server,
  - start selenium session,
  - open browser,
  - run tests,
  - close browser,
  - stop session
- Test Class Two:
  - ... don't start server, but do all the same stuff as Test Class One
- Test Class Three:
  - ... don't start server, do all the same stuff as Test Class Two
  - stop server

This is quite slow because we don't reuse the browser instances or selenium sessions. Ideally what we want is:

- Start server

- Test Class One:
  - start selenium session,
  - open browser
  - run tests
- Test Class Two:
  - if I am using the same settings as Test Class One then reuse the session and browser
  - run tests
- Test Class Three
  - if I am using the same settings as Test Class One then reuse the session and browser
  - run tests
- close browser
- stop session

- stop server

We can achieve this if we introduce the notion of a test suite.

Very often when people use JUnit they refer to a suite of tests and the `<batchtest />` construct in Ant as meaning the same thing. But unfortunately they are not. `<batchtest />` is a convenient way of defining the tests to run but each test is run as a separate java program so a new `SeleniumManager` is started for each test, so in Ant we don't even get reuse of the SeleniumManager singleton.

If we run the tests from within Eclipse, by right clicking on a test folder and choosing to run as JUnit test, then a "true" suite is created and a single `SeleniumManager` is shared for all tests.

At this point we will introduce JUnit suites.

You can find the suite (`TestSuite.java`) below in the `src/test/java` source-code folder.

```
package com.eviltester.seleniumSimplified.testSuites;

import org.junit.AfterClass;
import org.junit.BeforeClass;
import org.junit.runner.RunWith;
import org.junit.runners.Suite;

import com.eviltester.seleniumSimplified.calculate.
    CalculateTwoNumbersMultipleTests;
import com.eviltester.seleniumSimplified.calculate.
    CalculateTwoNumbersTestsTabFile;
import com.eviltester.seleniumSimplified.cookies.CookieTests;
import com.eviltester.seleniumSimplified.htmlform.HTML_form_tests;
import com.eviltester.seleniumSimplified.javascript.AjaxPageTests;
import com.eviltester.seleniumSimplified.search.SearchPageTests;
import com.eviltester.seleniumutils.seleniumManager.TheSeleniumManager;

@RunWith(Suite.class)
@Suite.SuiteClasses({
  CalculateTwoNumbersMultipleTests.class,
  CalculateTwoNumbersTestsTabFile.class,
  CookieTests.class,
  HTML_form_tests.class,
  SearchPageTests.class,
  AjaxPageTests.class
})

public class TestSuite {
}
```

A JUnit suite, using the JUnit 4 annotations does not need to have any code in the body of the `TestSuite` class, and acts as a way of grouping the tests together to run as a single block.

If I right click on this class in Eclipse and run it, then it will run all the tests in all the classes imported via the `@Suite` annotation.

Since this suite of tests is a class in the src/test/java folder it would be run by our existing Ant scripts so I need to amend our Ant script to exclude this Suite from our list of files to execute as a batch:

```
<batchtest todir="${testresults}" >
        <fileset dir="${testDir}" includes="**/*.java" excludes="**/
            testSuites/*.java"/>
</batchtest>
```

Here I have added an exclusion for all java files in the testSuites folder, so if I adopt the convention of having all my suite related files in this folder then they will not run.

Then I can create multiple suite files, but not have to worry about the tests running multiple times by the refactored-pm-build.xml build file.

I will create a separate build file to run the suite.

You can find this as suite-build.xml in the code distribution for this chapter. This build file has a few minor differences to the <JUnit.../> section in the file:

```
<JUnit printsummary="yes" fork="yes" errorproperty="JUnit.error"
    failureproperty="JUnit.error">
 <sysproperty key="selenium.browser" value="${BROWSER}"/>
 <sysproperty key="selenium.stopAfterSuite" value="TRUE"/>

  <classpath refid="JUnit.class.path" />
  <formatter type="xml" />

  <test todir="${testresults}"
      name="com.eviltester.seleniumSimplified.TestSuite" />
</JUnit>
```

You can see that I have added a new property selenium.stopAfterSuite and I have changed the list of tests to run to run the individual test Suite.

Now we have to amend the rest of the code to take advantage of this system property.

I first of all amend the test suite class to have code.

```
public class TestSuite {
  @BeforeClass
  public static void run_before_suite(){
    // If I want to run the suite from within Eclipse (and not use ant)
    // and I want to have the tests run quickly I can set the
    // system property to control the Selenium Manager interaction here
    //System.setProperty("selenium.stopAfterSuite", "TRUE");
  }

  @AfterClass
  public static void run_after_suite(){
    TheSeleniumManager.getSeleniumManager().stopSelenium();
  }
}
```

Here I have create an @AfterClass annotated method called run_after_suite. We have already seen that we can nest @BeforeClass and @AfterClass annotations, so this annotation runs at the end of the TestSuite class which means that it runs at the end of the suite. So if we stopSelenium here then we don't have to stop it at the end of each test.

I have to amend the @AfterClass in SeleniumSimplifiedTest to only stop the test if the property selenium.stopAfterSuite is not set to TRUE

```
@AfterClass
static public void closeItDown(){

    // default to closing after test
    boolean closeAfterTest = true;

    // unless we set the system property selenium.stopAfterSuite=TRUE
    if(System.getProperties().containsKey("selenium.stopAfterSuite")){
      if(System.getProperty("selenium.stopAfterSuite").
            equalsIgnoreCase("TRUE")){
        closeAfterTest = false;
      }
    }

    if(closeAfterTest)
      sm.stopSelenium();
}
```

Here you can see that I have amended the closeItDown method in SeleniumSimplifiedTest to check for the presence of the property, if it is present and set to TRUE then we do not stopSelenium at the end of each test.

We can take advantage of this within Eclipse, by amending the Suite class so that the run_before_suite method sets the property.

```
@BeforeClass
  public static void run_before_suite(){
      // If I want to run the suite from within Eclipse (and not use ant)
      // and I want to have the tests run quickly I can set the
      // system property to control the Selenium Manager interaction here
      System.setProperty("selenium.stopAfterSuite", "TRUE");
  }
```

If I enable this line and right click and run the testSuite.java within Eclipse then all the tests will run and they will share the same Selenium session and browser.

I can take advantage of this in my Hudson build by amending the Build File option in the Advanced section of Invoke Ant under the Build section and having it use the suite-build.xml file instead of the default one.

Build

Invoke Ant

Ant Version	(Default)
Targets	
Build File	suite-build.xml

Figure 37.13: Use suite-build.xml instead of default build file

I amend all the Hudson projects in this way so that they all use the suite instead of the individual files.

The test run now takes advantage of all the features we have built into the `SeleniumManager`:

- the `SeleniumManager` is being shared across all tests,

- all screenshot errors will be saved into the same folder

- the Selenium server is shared for all tests

- the Selenium session is shared for all tests

- the same browser is shared for all tests

You can also see that because we abstracted away all of the details of managing Selenium into the `SeleniumSimplifiedTest.java` base class, and the `SeleniumManager` set of classes. None of our tests had to change when we changed the architecture behind the test execution.

37.9   Running Different Suites for Different Browsers

If JUnit supported groups of tests then we could simply create a group of tests for all browsers, sub groups for specific browsers and then in a suite say, run all the tests for these groups.

JUnit does not support a group notation.

But we can use the Suite notation to build groups by nesting suites.

37.9.1   Nested Suites

We saw that a basic Suite in JUnit does not have any code in the class:

```
@RunWith(Suite.class)
@Suite.SuiteClasses({
  CalculateTwoNumbersMultipleTests.class,
  CalculateTwoNumbersTestsTabFile.class,
  CookieTests.class,
  HTML_form_tests.class,
  SearchPageTests.class,
  AjaxPageTests.class
})

public class TestSuite {
}
```

I am going to start viewing suites with no code as a group, and Suites with an `@BeforeClass` and `@AfterClass` as Suites.

With this view I can create a suite around the above ''group'' as follows:

392

```
@RunWith(Suite.class)
@Suite.SuiteClasses({
  TestSuite.class,
})

public class AWrapperTestSuite {
  @AfterClass
  public static void run_after_suite(){
    TheSeleniumManager.getSeleniumManager().stopSelenium();
  }
}
```

Here I have nested one suite within another. It is perfectly possible for me to have @BeforeClass and @AfterClass within the ''group'' suites as well and have sub level setup and tear down processes. But in our current model I only want one level to issue the .stopSelenium() command so I am creating these wrapper Suites.

So, how do we use this to run tests for specific browsers only on those browsers?

Figure 37.14: Browser Specific Groups

37.9.2   Browser Specific Groups

I create suites with no method stopping Selenium as groups in the testSuite package e.g.

- AnyBrowserTestGroup.java

- ChromeOrFirefoxBrowserTestsGroup.java

Both of these are suites with empty class code e.g.

AnyBrowserTestGroup.java:

```
@RunWith(Suite.class)
@Suite.SuiteClasses({
  CalculateTwoNumbersMultipleTests.class,
  CalculateTwoNumbersTestsTabFile.class,
  CookieTests.class,
  HTML_form_tests.class,
  SearchPageTests.class,
  AjaxPageTests.class
})

public class AnyBrowserTestsGroup {
}
```

393

```
ChromeOrFirefoxBrowserTestsGroup.java:
    @RunWith(Suite.class)
    @Suite.SuiteClasses({
      Chrome_only_form_tests.class
    })

    public class ChromeOrFirefoxBrowserTestsGroup {
    }
```

To support this I moved the `test_submit_form_with_filename` test into its own class, which I named `Chrome_only_form_tests`.

Then I created suites which nest the above group suites. e.g.

```
    package com.eviltester.seleniumSimplified.testSuites;

    import org.junit.AfterClass;
    import org.junit.runner.RunWith;
    import org.junit.runners.Suite;
    import com.eviltester.seleniumutils.seleniumManager.TheSeleniumManager;

    @RunWith(Suite.class)
    @Suite.SuiteClasses({
      AnyBrowserTestsGroup.class,
      ChromeOrFirefoxBrowserTestsGroup.class
    })
    public class AllTestsChromeOrFirefoxBrowserTestSuite {

      @AfterClass
      public static void run_after_suite(){
        TheSeleniumManager.getSeleniumManager().stopSelenium();
      }
    }
```

This `AllTestsChromeOrFirefoxBrowserTestSuite` nests both Group suites as it will run all the tests.

To create a suite that excludes the Chrome test I just remove the class from the list of `SuiteClasses`.

```
    ChromeOrFirefoxBrowserTestGroup.class
```

37.9.3   Create a conditional Ant File

One last thing left to do; support this in Ant.

I create a `conditional-suite-build.xml` as a separate file. I am creating a separate file because you can then compare it with `suite-build.xml`

The changes are illustrated by the listing below:

```
    <target name="run_param_JUnit_tests">

      <condition property="selenium.suitename"
      value="com.eviltester.seleniumSimplified.testSuites.
        AllTestsChromeOrFirefoxBrowserTestSuite"
```

394

```
        else="com.eviltester.seleniumSimplified.testSuites.
            AllTestsAnyBrowserTestSuite">

    <or>
      <equals arg1="${BROWSER}" arg2="*chrome"/>
      <contains string="${BROWSER}" substring="firefox"/>
    </or>
     </condition>

    <JUnit printsummary="yes" fork="yes" errorproperty="JUnit.error"
        failureproperty="JUnit.error">

      <sysproperty key="selenium.browser" value="${BROWSER}"/>
      <sysproperty key="selenium.stopAfterSuite" value="TRUE"/>

      <classpath refid="JUnit.class.path" />
      <formatter type="xml" />

      <test todir="${testresults}" name="${selenium.suitename}" />

    </JUnit>

    <antcall target="report-JUnit"/>
    <fail if="JUnit.error" message="Selenium test(s) failed.  See reports!"/>
   </target>
```

I have added a `<condition ... />` block before the `<JUnit .../>` block.

This sets property `selenium.suitename` to the value the package path of the suite to run.

`com.eviltester.seleniumSimplified.testSuites.AllTestsChromeOrFirefoxBrowserTestSuite`

I only do this if the conditions within the `<or .../>` block are true.

If the `<or .../>` block is not true (e.g. if `*iexplore`) then it sets the property to the path of the `AllTestsAnyBrowserTestSuite`.

In the `<or .../>` block I check if the `BROWSER` property equals `*chrome`, or if it contains the string ''firefox''. If either of these are true, then it is valid to use the Chrome or Firefox test suite.

The other change was to use the property in the `<test .../>` element:

```
    <test todir="${testresults}" name="${selenium.suitename}" />
```

By using this type of structure in the Ant file I can have a single Ant file which conditionally chooses which suite to run, based on the browser I am using.

To call this from the command line I would use:

```
    ant -DBROWSER=*chrome -f conditional-suite-build.xml
```

And simply replace the browser with the name of the browser I want.

You already know how to amend the Hudson build to use this, just amend the advanced build properties to use a specific build file and pass in the Browser property.

In this way, we don't have to have misleading tests listed in our test run, and we only run the tests which are valid for that browser.

Related Reading:

- The Ant Condition task - http://unow.be/rc/antcondition[7]

- The Conditions available - http://unow.be/rc/antconditions[8]

37.10   Get WebDriver working

In the previous chapter I described the high level changes required to `SeleniumManager` to start moving over to WebDriver in Selenium 2

In the updated version for this chapter, you can switch over to a `SeleniumBacked` driver by amending `TheSeleniumManager.java` to `useSeleniumTwo` instead of `useSeleniumOne` in the `getSeleniumManager` method.

You will undoubtedly find some tests failing when you switch to WebDriver in Selenium 2 But by having this switch in your abstraction layer you can continue to monitor the progress of the backward compatibility of WebDriver implementation of the Selenium RC API before making a decision to move over to WebDriver.

37.11   Ways of using what we have built

In this final project we have a number of ways of working with our tests.

From Eclipse I can:

- amend `selenium.properties` to control the browser used to run the tests

- run an entire suite of tests quickly by amending the `TestSuite` class to set the system property which causes session reuse

- run individual tests, which use the `selenium.properties` browser, but also close the browser and session when they are finished

From the command line:

- run the tests using Ant and the default browser in the Ant file by typing `ant`

- by using `ant -DBROWSER=*googlechrome` I can run the tests with a browser of my choosing

---

[7]http://ant.apache.org/manual/Tasks/condition.html
[8]http://ant.apache.org/manual/Tasks/conditions.html

- by using `ant -f suite-build.xml` I can run the suite of tests quickly with the browser defined in the Ant file

- by using `ant -f suite-build.xml -DBROWSER=*googlechrome` I can run the suite of tests quickly with the browser defined in the command line

From Hudson:

- trigger builds in sequence to run the suite of tests against multiple browsers and track all the test results over time in Hudson itself.

This supports different ways of working.

I use the Eclipse method when I am writing and debugging tests. I initially test for cross browser compatibility when writing the tests by amending the properties file and rerunning the tests by right clicking from Eclipse.

Before doing a commit to subversion of any changes I made to the tests, I run the tests from the command line with Ant directly. I may choose to run the test for cross browser compatibility.

After checking the changes made to subversion, an automated build in Hudson will kick in to checkout the tests and run them on the test server to make sure that the tests run on a machine other than my own.

When you can do this, you have a production ready test setup.

37.12   Exercises For the reader:

- Refactor the `BasicHTMLForm.java` Page Object class so that instead of repeated code, the code instead calls a method e.g. instead of:

```
String.format(CHECKBOXES_LOCATOR,checkBoxIDNumber)
```

Use something like:

```
getCheckBoxLocator(checkBoxIDNumber)
```

If you look at the code in `HTMLFormResultsPage.java` where methods are used to generate locator values rather than constants. There is still a lot of code following the same pattern, e.g.

```
public String getDropDownValue() {
 if(hasDropDown()){
 return selenium.getText(getValueID(FN_DROPDOWN));
 }else{
 return selenium.getText(getNoValueLocator(FN_DROPDOWN));
 }
}
```

Can you refactor the code so that this code pattern only appears once in the code? Hint. One way to do this would involve the above code looking like:

```
public String getDropDownValue() {
 return getFieldNameValue(hasDropDown(),FN_DROPDOWN);
}
```

Does this make the code easier to read and maintain?

- Create a new Hudson build so that the tests run in Google's Chrome browser after the Firefox run.

- Create a new Hudson build so that the tests run in Firefox Chrome mode browser after the Google Chrome run.

- Change all your Hudson builds to use the `conditional-suite-build.xml`

  - Can you see the number of tests changing between browers?
  - 1 more test should be run for `*chrome`, and `*firefox`

- Change the code so that you can switch between Selenium 1.x and Selenium 2.x by changing a system property in the `selenium.properties` file and in the Ant files.

Chapter 38

In Closing

If you have worked your way through the book to this section then you should now have a good grasp on the basics creating production ready tests in Java using Selenium RC.

I know that readers have approached this book with very different levels of experience with programming, automated testing in general, and Selenium.

While I have tried to explain everything as well as I can, I still value feedback from readers to help me improve future versions of this text.

There is still a lot to learn, but you should have enough knowledge that you don't get phased by the prospect of learning more on your own.

This chapter will suggest some avenues for additional learning, but the key way of learning Selenium is to use it.

So:

- write lots of tests,

- refactor your tests,

- keep learning java,

- keep an eye on new updates to selenium,

- read the Selenium source code

38.1   Additional Reading

For Selenium:

- read the official documentation on the Selenium website http://unow.be/rc/officialdocs[1]

- subscribe to the email feed for the official Selenium Users group http://unow.be/rc/usersgroup[2]

For Java:

- Books:

---

[1]http://seleniumhq.org/docs
[2]http://groups.google.com/group/selenium-users

- Agile Java: Crafting Code with Test-Driven Development by Jeff Langr
  * An excellent learning guide to Java which teaches Java using Test Driven development.
- Implementation Patterns by Kent Beck
  * An overview of effective Java coding which is a tremendous confidence boost to beginners to Java that keeping your code simple is a perfectly valid coding style used by very experienced developers.
- Effective Java by Joshua Bloch
  * An overview of effective Java practices which speeds up your learning tremendously.
- Growing Object-oriented Software - guided by tests by Steve Freeman and Nat Pryce
  * An excellent overview of abstraction, refactoring and automated unit testing.

Videos:

- Watch the Eclipse and Java tutorials http://unow.be/rc/eclipsetutorial[3]

- Watch Google Tech Talks on Java and Selenium

- Watch the videos from previous Google Test Automation Conference

Web Searches:

- I use Google all the time to search for answers to my queries typically of the form ''thing I don't know java example''

Subscribe to the following blogs:

- http://unow.be/rc/e34[4]

  - Adam Goucher's Selenium blog

- http://unow.be/rc/sblog[5]

  - The Official Selenium Blog

- http://eviltester.com

---

[3]http://eclipsetutorial.sourceforge.net/
[4]http://element34.ca/
[5]http://seleniumhq.wordpress.com/

- The author's testing blog which contains Selenium posts

- http://unow.be/rc/autotester[6]

  - David Burns' testing blog. Author of ''Selenium 1.0 Testing Tools: Beginner's Guide''

- http://unow.be/rc/egblog[7]

  - Examples and tips for selenium

- http://unow.be/rc/reflections[8]

  - A Testing blogs aggregator where you will find many posts on testing and Selenium.

Download and study the source-code for this book:

- Follow the instructions in Chapter ''Play along at home'' and download the source-code:

  - http://unow.be/rc/initialSource[9]

- Install a subversion client and checkout the refactored source-code from:

  - http://unow.be/rc/svnFinalSeleniumTests[10]

---

[6] http://www.theautomatedtester.co.uk/

[7] http://seleniumexamples.com/blog/

[8] http://testingreflections.com/

[9] http://www.compendiumdev.co.uk/selenium/InitialSeleniumTests_JUNIT_2ndEdition.zip

[10] http://svn2.xp-dev.com/svn/seleniumsimplified/trunk/FinalSeleniumTests

Appendix A

Playing along at home

A.1 Prerequisites

You will need to have installed:

- Java

- Eclipse

Please see the early introductory sections in the book for instructions on how to install these.

A.2 Get The Code

A.2.1 From A Zip Archive

You can download all the source code for the examples in the book in two zip archives:

- http://unow.be/rc/initialSource[1]

- http://unow.be/rc/finalSource[2]

The first archive covers the code in the book prior to Chapter 36.

The second archive covers the code in the book from the refactoring section in chapter 37.

The following instructions apply to either of the zip archives once downloaded to your computer.

You will need to have installed:

- A zip archive utility

- Selenium server .jar files

Unarchive this zip file to your Eclipse workspace or a folder on your computer.

---

[1]http://www.compendiumdev.co.uk/selenium/InitialSeleniumTests_JUNIT_2ndEdition.zip
[2]http://www.compendiumdev.co.uk/selenium/finalChapterSource_2ndEdition.zip

A.2.2 From the Subversion Repositories

To use the subversion repositories you will need to install a subversion client and have followed the instructions for the client so that you know how to checkout a subversion repository.

There are 2 subversion repositories:

- http://unow.be/rc/svnInitialSeleniumTests[3]
- http://unow.be/rc/svnFinalSeleniumTests[4]

If the above URLs are shortened unow.be form, then unless your svn client follows redirects, you should checkout the code using the url in the footnote, or in the browser after redirection when you follow the url.

Checkout the required repository from the url above to a local folder.

A.3 Create a Project

Create a New Java Project by selecting `File \ New \ Java Project` from the main drop down menus.

In the `New Java Project` Wizard. Uncheck the `Use default location` checkbox. Then use the `[Browse...]` button to select the folder where you unarchived (or checked out) the files.

e.g. if I unarchive the zip contents into `c:\playAtHome\initialSeleniumTestsDownload` then the location text would read `c:\playAtHome\initialSeleniumTestsDownload`

Give the project a name e.g. `InitialTestsDownloaded`, then click the `[Finish]` button.

You will then need to right click on the project in the Package Explorer, and select `Build Path \ Configure Build Path`.

Either use the `[Add Library...]` button and select JUnit 4, or use the `[Add External JARs...]` button and select a local JUnit .jar file.

You also have to configure the project to use the Selenium libraries as described in Chapter 6. By adding the Selenium Server .jar as an external jar.

If you checkout the subversion repository then the JUnit .jar and the Selenium Server .jar are contained in the `lib` folder. These libraries are not in the zip file to save on download size.

This was initially described in "Chapter 6: Create a JUnit test Using the JUnit export from Selenium IDE" in the Section "Resolve Import Errors"

---

[3]http://svn2.xp-dev.com/svn/seleniumsimplified/trunk/InitialSeleniumTests
[4]http://svn2.xp-dev.com/svn/seleniumsimplified/trunk/FinalSeleniumTests

Appendix B

The SeleneseTestCase Class

B.1   What is SeleneseTestCase

The `SeleneseTestCase` class was deprecated in Selenium 2.0

It was a helper class provided in the Selenium RC distributions to make it a little easier to start coding with Selenium in Java.

Since it has been deprecated I don't expect you to use it, and we do not use it in Selenium Simplified, but I have moved all previous information in Selenium Simplified for the `SeleneseTestCase` into this section.

The fact that it has been deprecated means that it could be removed from future versions of Selenium without warning, so do not rely on it.

B.2   Details

Automatically generated IDE tests, use the `SeleneseTestCase` which hides a lot of complexity from us that we need to understand to get the best from Selenium.

Without using the `SeleneseTestCase` class you will take complete control of your Selenium test cases.

To use this particular class we `extend SeleneseTestCase`. Object Oriented Programming has a concept of "inheritance" where a class can inherit methods and variables from other classes. This allows reuse of code. So by extending the `SeleneseTestCase` distributed as part of Selenium, we get access to various source code to help us write our tests.

```
public class MyFirstSeleniumTests extends SeleneseTestCase{
```

- Inheritance (extends) in Java http://unow.be/rc/inheritance[1]

B.3   A look at SeleneseTestCase.java

`SeleneseTestCase.java` was contributed by Nelson Sproul and provides a quick way of accessing JUnit functionality by extending the JUnit `TestCase` class, provides a wrapper for helper methods in the `SeleneseTestBase` class and provides a Selenium object which we can use in our tests.

405

```
1  package com.thoughtworks.selenium;
2
3  import junit.framework.TestCase;
4
5  /**
6   * Provides a JUnit TestCase base class that implements some handy
7   * testing (you are <i>not</i> required to extend this class).
8   *
9   * <p>
10  * This class adds a number of "verify" commands, which are like ".
11  * stop the test when they fail. Instead, verification errors are .
12  * tearDown.
13  * </p>
14  *
15  * @author Nelson Sproul (nsproul@bea.com) Mar 13-06
16  * @deprecated Please consider updating to junit 4 or above
17  */
18 @Deprecated
19 public class SeleneseTestCase extends TestCase {
20
21   private SeleneseTestBase stb = new SeleneseTestBase();
22
23   /** Use this object to run all of your selenium tests */
24   protected Selenium selenium;
25
26   public SeleneseTestCase() {
27     super();
28   }
29
30
31   public SeleneseTestCase(String name) {
32     super(name);
33   }
```

Figure B.1: The first few lines of SeleneseTestCase

In this section we will learn a little about the make up of this class.

From the listing you can see that on line 3 we import the TestCase class from JUnit. And on line 19 the SeleneseTestCase class extends this TestCase.

This is the original way of using JUnit. Version 4 of JUnit uses annotations.

On line 21 the SeleneseTestCase class creates private instance of Type SeleneseTestBase called stb. By making it private, only the methods in the SeleneseTestCase class itself can reference it. The vast bulk of this SeleneseTestCase consists of wrapper methods which call the SeleneseTestBase class.

The SeleneseTestClass is an abstraction layer to hide implementation details from you so that you can get on with the business of writing tests. We are looking at it to learn a bit more about what we are using.

On line 24 there is a definition of a protected variable called selenium which will allow us access to an object of type selenium. The Selenium class is the main class we

---

[1]http://java.sun.com/docs/books/tutorial/java/concepts/inheritance.html

care about. By making the variable `protected` it can be accessed by any method inside `SeleneseTestCase`, and any class in the `com.thoughtworks.selenium package`, and also any class that extends `SeleneseTestCase`. Since our test case extends `SeleneseTestCase`, this explains why we can use the `selenium` variable directly in our tests without declaring it.

There is a good discussion of access level modifiers (`private`, `public`, `protected`) on the main Java documentation site.

http://unow.be/rc/accesscontrol[2]

Line 26 has the constructor for the `SeleneseTestCase` class. The constructor is called automatically when a `new` instance of the class is created by by the JUnit TestRunner. And because our test case class is really a `SeleneseTestCase`, the constructor on `SeleneseTestCase` is called.

`super();` means that the constructor of the superclass (the class we extended) is called, in this case the `TestCase` from JUnit.

B.4   Use the SeleneseTestCase Functionality

In this section we will reinforce our understanding of the `SeleneseTestCase` by using some of the helper functionality by:

- adding some asserts

- adding some verifications

- capturing a screenshot when a test fails

B.4.1   Using the IDE to add asserts and verifies

When we record a test using the Selenium IDE, it adds actions for us, but it does not add any asserts or verifies. These we have to add manually, either during the recording of the test (which is easier), or after recording has finished.

In this section we will look at how to add asserts and verifies when recording.

First record the setup steps

Start recording in the IDE. Record a script where we visit our search engine type Selenium RC, and then press the search button.

- http://www.compendiumdev.co.uk/selenium/search.php

---

[2]http://java.sun.com/docs/books/tutorial/java/javaOO/accesscontrol.html

Now that we have done our basic setup we can add some verify statements.

Since the search term is displayed as part of the title, and in the search box, we can add checks for both of these things.

Add the Verify Statements

To add a check for the title, right click on the html page in Firefox. At the bottom of the contextual menu I can see the Selenium IDE additions. These are populated by some common choices. Both assertTitle and verifyTitle methods, and these are pre-populated with the title of the page, so I don't have to do any work.

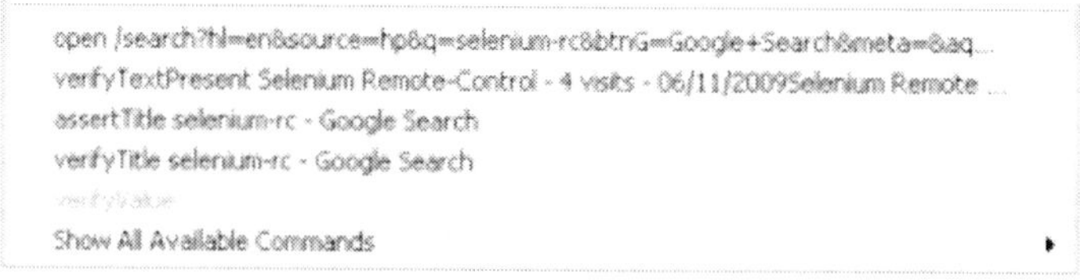

Figure B.2: Context Menu for Selenium IDE

Select the `verifyTitle` entry and a new line appears in the test in the IDE.

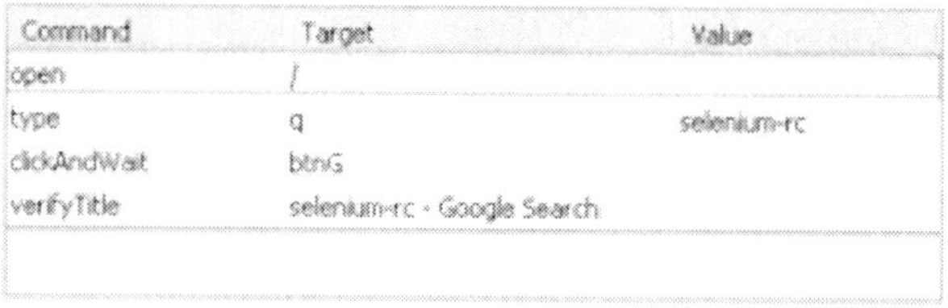

Command	Target	Value
open	/	
type	q	selenium-rc
clickAndWait	btnG	
verifyTitle	selenium-rc - Google Search	

Figure B.3: Selenese Script with verifyTitle

If the option we wanted does not appear, or if you are curious as to what you can contextually add then use the `Show All Available Commands` sub-menu:

This sub-menu shows all the contextual commands available. Clicking any of them will add them to the IDE.

To add a check for the text in the search input field, right click on the search input field and choose `verifyValue q selenium-rc`.

If you run that test in the IDE then both those verifications will pass.

Save that test as `verifys_for_selenium_rc.htm` (PS: I know that is not how you spell verifies, but if there were a plural for verify I'm sure it would be verifys)

Figure B.4: The full contextual list provided by the Selenium IDE

Add the Asserts

To create a similar test which asserts for those two values we could:

- re-record the test from scratch and choose `assertTitle` and `assertValue` instead, and then save the test.

- delete the verify statements, by clicking on the line and choosing `delete` from the context menu (or pressing the `delete` key) and adding asserts from the Selenium right click context menu in Firefox. And then `save as` a different test file.

- amend the values in situ, by clicking on the line in the table and selecting a new command from the drop down, and then `save as` to a different file name.

When I did this, I found it faster to amend the commands in situ and then save the test as a different file name.

B.4.2   What is the difference between an Assert and a Verify?

Selenium IDE supports two types of checks:

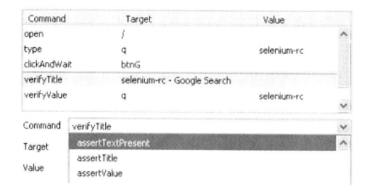

Figure B.5: Command drop-down lists all commands

- assert - which stop the test on the failure of the first assertions

- verify - where the verify statement checks the results and reports an error but the test continues to the end

As an example compare two tests which I created in the IDE. I have changed the search from ''selenium-rc'' to ''wrongvalue'' so that the tests will fail when run.

Figure B.6: Asserts stop test on first failed assertion

Figure B.7: Verify methods allow test to continue after a failure

Both tests run essentially the same script where they type ''wrongvalue'' into the search box, and then check for the title of the page and the value in the search box.

The first test, using the `verifyTitle` and `verifyValue` methods, runs to the end of the test and shows 2 errors in the log and on the script table view. The second test which uses `assertTitle` and `assertValue`, stops on the first error `assertTitle`, and does not check the value in the field.

Verify methods can be useful if you want to create a test that, regardless of the outcome of previous checks, conducts a check so can be useful where you do a lot of setup steps and then perform a whole series of checks.

Asserts are useful if you don't chain checks, and instead need a test to have passed before moving on to the next step.

When these tests are exported to the IDE we get the following JUnit tests.

```
public void testVerifys_for_wrong_value() throws Exception {
  selenium.open("/");
  selenium.type("q", "wrongvalue");
  selenium.click("btnG");
  selenium.waitForPageToLoad("30000");
  verifyEquals("selenium-rc - Selenium Simplified Search Engine", selenium.
      getTitle());
  verifyEquals("selenium-rc", selenium.getValue("q"));
}
```

411

```
public void testAsserts_for_wrong_value() throws Exception {
   selenium.open("/");
   selenium.type("q", "wrongvalue");
   selenium.click("btnG");
   selenium.waitForPageToLoad("30000");
   assertEquals("selenium-rc - Selenium Simplified Search Engine", selenium.
       getTitle());
   assertEquals("selenium-rc", selenium.getValue("q"));
}
```

There are some subtle differences to be aware of when debugging a verify failure compared to an assert failure.

With an assert failure, the Failure trace pane of JUnit will display a single assertion stack trace. And a double click on the test in the JUnit opens the code in the editor at the failed assertion line.

Figure B.8: Failure Trace for an assertion

With a verify failure, the failure trace contains all the assertions that failed.

If you double click on the test you will be taken to the first verify that failed. And to identify the other verify lines you will have to look through the Failure Trace for each of the lines that start

```
java.lang.AssertionError: java.lang.AssertionError: Expected ...
```

You should also look for the line in the assertion that tells you which line the assertion happened on. This is the line that reports an error at the level of the test class you are working with e.g. MyFirstSeleniumTests and then you can see that it happened on line 32. So you look at that line in the code to see the verification statement that failed.

```
At com.eviltester.seleniumtutorials.MyFirstSeleniumTests.
testVerifys_for_wrong_value(MyFirstSeleniumTests.java:32)
```

412

Figure B.9: Failure Trace for a verify

Creating Screenshots on Failure with SeleneseTestCase

Selenium has the ability to create screenshots when running tests with the following methods:

- captureScreenshot

- captureEntirePageScreenshot

The `SeleneseTestCase` class that we are using, has the ability to capture screenshots using the `captureScreenshot` method as part of the default test runner.

Before we can capture a screenshot we have to call the method:

```
setCaptureScreenShotOnFailure(true);
```

It is tempting to think that we would just add this line, inside the test that we wanted to capture the screenshot, or possibly in the `setUp` method so that it applies to all tests.

Unfortunately that isn't the case. We have to call this method in the constructor for the test case class.

A constructor in Java is the method called when an object is instantiated. So in our case, when the JUnit test runner creates an object of type MyFirstSeleniumTests.

But we don't currently have a constructor. Normally you won't need to create a constructor for your test classes, but to use the screenshot functionality, this is what the constructor looks like.

```java
public MySeleniumTestWithScreenshot(){
  setCaptureScreenShotOnFailure(true);
}
```

The constructor goes directly after the class declaration. It is always named the same as the class and has no return value declaration.

Only tests that fail through asserts will actually trigger a screenshot.

Screenshots will be named with the name of the test. And they will be saved in the same directory that you started the selenium server in, because we are calling a command in the selenium server to capture the screen and it doesn't know where our tests are running from.

Try this with your test cases.

- Create the constructor

- Add the setCaptureScreenShotOnFailure method to the constructor

- change one of the tests with asserts so that it will fail the assert

- you should see a message in the console when you run the test e.g.

- Saved screenshot testAsserts_for_wrong_value.png

- after the test has failed, have a look in the directory where you ran the Selenium RC server from and you should see a screenshot of the screen when the test was running. If you have a multi-monitor setup then it will take a screenshot of the windows displayed by the primary monitor.

This default setup which comes with SeleneseTestCase is fun to experiment with but not particularly flexible.

Index

About the Author

Alan Richardson has been involved with testing his entire professional career. Over his career he has created automation frameworks and scripts, using numerous tools and languages. He has also programmed commercially in a variety of languages.

He started using Selenium on his automation projects in 2007.

He writes tests in Java because he generally works on applications that are written in Java. This allows developers to help with the automation. Java is also his current application programming language of choice.

In addition to test automation, Alan has performed test management, test consultancy and hands on testing roles.

He remains committed to improving his hands on skills in: exploratory testing, technical testing and test automation.

He has presented at conferences world wide and maintains a number of websites:

- a general testing blog at http://eviltester.com

- the website for this book at http://seleniumsimplified.com

- his company website at http://compendiumdev.co.uk

CPSIA information can be obtained at www.ICGtesting.com
Printed in the USA
BVOW061334030413

317168BV00004B/42/P